REGULATING BUSINESS

OXFORD SOCIO-LEGAL STUDIES

General Editors: J. MAXWELL ATKINSON, DONALD R. HARRIS, R. M. HARTWELL

Oxford Socio-Legal Studies is a series of books and conference proceedings published by the Centre for Socio-Legal Studies, Wolfson College, Oxford (a research unit of the Social Science Research Council). The series is concerned generally with the relationship between law and society, and is designed to reflect the increasing interest in this field of lawyers, social scientists and historians.

Published simultaneously with this volume
J. Maxwell Atkinson and Paul Drew: ORDER IN COURT: THE ORGANIZATION OF VERBAL INTERACTION IN JUDICIAL SETTINGS
David P. Farrington, Keith Hawkins and Sally M. Lloyd-Bostock (*editors*): PSYCHOLOGY, LAW AND LEGAL PROCESSES

Forthcoming titles
Donald R. Harris, Mavis Maclean and Hazel Genn: COMPENSATION AND SUPPORT FOR ILLNESS AND INJURY
Doreen J. McBarnet: CONVICTION: THE LAW, THE STATE AND THE CONSTRUCTION OF JUSTICE
Mavis Maclean and Hazel Genn: METHODOLOGICAL ISSUES IN SOCIAL SURVEYS
Alan Paterson: THE LAW LORDS

REGULATING BUSINESS

LAW AND CONSUMER AGENCIES

Ross Cranston

First published 1979 by
THE MACMILLAN PRESS LTD
London and Basingstoke
Associated companies in Delhi
Dublin Hong Kong Johannesburg Lagos
Melbourne New York Singapore Tokyo

Printed in Great Britain by
Unwin Brothers Limited
Gresham Press, Old Woking, Surrey

British Library Cataloguing in Publication Data

Cranston, Ross
  Regulating business. – (Oxford socio-legal studies)
  1. Consumer protection – Law and legislation –
  Great Britain   2. Consumer protection – Great
  Britain
  I. Title   II. Series
  343′.41′07   KD2204

  ISBN 0–333–23890–7

For my grandparents
George and Ivy Davies

Contents

List of Tables

DIAGRAM

Acknowledgements

In writing this work, I have incurred many debts, above all to numerous consumer officers who must of necessity remain anonymous. Officials at the Office of Fair Trading, the Department of Prices and Consumer Protection and Consumers' Association also answered many enquiries and made available some invaluable information.

The book is based on a doctoral thesis submitted to the University of Oxford, and my supervisor, Donald R. Harris, Director of the Centre for Socio-Legal Studies, provided strong support during the research and then had the heavy burden of reviewing successive drafts of the study. Clive Grace and Phillip Wilkinson, also at the Centre for Socio-Legal Studies, were a source of intellectual stimulation, and Sally Lloyd-Bostock, Diana Vernon and Philip Whittall assisted me with statistical data. Dr Alan Milner, Dr Max Atkinson and Professor Gordon Borrie, now Director of Fair Trading, have made valuable comments on the manuscript.

November 1977   Ross Cranston

1 Introduction

The growth of private economic power has long been associated with a concern for its undesirable effects on society, which has led to specific measures to subject it to social control. One area of control, the regulation of the conditions of employment, was the outcome of the political power of trade unions. The physical location of enterprises has been restricted by planning legislation and businesses have also been subject to environmental controls. In America, anti-trust laws were designed to keep the giant corporations within bounds and to make them more responsive to competitive forces, while the regulatory agencies were supposed to impose community control over those services of a public nature which remained in private hands, e.g. in matters such as the prices charged to consumers. In Britain, the control of some businesses has taken a more drastic form, with public ownership, and in other cases the government has assumed a significant role in industry through government loans and the ownership of shares. In both the United States and Britain, however, as in other liberal democracies, businesses are still relatively free from controls and most of their activities are untouched by government. The internal affairs of businesses are relatively immune from state interference, and in the main the price and quality of their goods and services are unregulated.

Control of private economic power casts light on a number of important issues in socio-legal studies. What is the nature of legal change in society? For example, do businesses have a veto over legal change so that they can thwart restrictions which are not in their interest?[1] Is the law effective in controlling behaviour? For instance, are the effective controls on economic power legal or non-legal? How can law most effectively act as an instrument of control over businesses? What, for example, are the advantages of different types of legal regulations? How do agencies responsible for enforcing the laws controlling businesses actually operate? Are they, for instance, subverted by the businesses which they are supposed to control? The present book is mainly concerned with the last of these matters. An examination is made of the implementation of consumer protection law in Britain by consumer agencies and of the impact of both this law and its enforcement on businesses.

I BACKGROUND TO THE REGULATORY PROCESS

Little consideration has been given to the operation and impact of the agencies administering legal controls over businesses. How do these agencies adjust to their environment and to the legislatures which create and sustain them; to the businesses over which they exercise control; and to the public in whose interest they supposedly act? A legislature, supported by public opinion, may intend a regulatory agency to pursue a vigorous policy of curbing abuses in an area of commercial activity. The spur to legislative action may be a particular source of abuse or a general cumulation of incidents leading to dissatisfaction with business behaviour. Once established, however, the regulatory agency may develop its own perspective which may diverge markedly from that envisaged by the legislature and the public, but which it is able to pursue because of the discretion it has in enforcing the law. As Hofstadter remarks when discussing the discrepancy between the public sentiment which lay behind the public movement for anti-trust laws in the United States and the growth of anti-trust as a legal and administrative fact:

> The fact of antitrust is an excellent illustration of how a public ideal, vaguely formulated and often hopelessly at odds with stubborn realities, can become embodied in institutions with elaborate self-preserving rules and procedures, a defensible function and an equally stubborn capacity for survival.[2]

The most extensive examination of the operation of regulatory agencies which control businesses concerns the regulatory agencies in the United States. The Interstate Commerce Commission, created in 1887, was the first of these agencies, and in the next half-century it was followed by many others established to oversee important areas of commercial life. A long-standing complaint against these agencies has been that they have become lethargic in approach, bowed by precedent and incapable of exercising administrative initiative.[3] More importantly, the critics say that the agencies identify with the businesses they were designed to control and tacitly accept that commerce and industry ought not to be interfered with to any great extent. A well-known critique of this genre is *The Nader Report on the Federal Trade Commission* (the federal consumer-protection body in the United States) whose conclusions about the officials of the Commission were:

> Lifelong amicable exposure to those they are supposed to regulate has given them a perspective more sympathetic to business interests than to consumers. The Federal Trade Commission, in effect, becomes the very thing it is designed to regulate.[4]

Of course it is often fallacious to assume that a legislature intends an agency regulating business to make any dent on commercial practices. Regulation as conceived by the legislature may not be designed to reduce business power or to redress the balance of social forces in society.[5] Laws which regulatory agencies are supposed to implement may be riddled with ambiguities and gaps. Perhaps they are symbolic from the outset in that the legislature never intended that they should bite into business practices: their purpose is simply to assuage public opinion and divert its attention.[6] The failure of even a model statute may be foreshadowed by the omission on the part of the legislature to establish adequate enforcement machinery. In discussing how responsibility for 100,000 establishments was transferred at the one time from local authorities to the factory inspectorate, Marx notes that 'care was taken at the same time not to add more than eight assistants to their already undermanned staff'.[7]

Furthermore, laws which ostensibly control businesses are not always antithetical to their interests. Many of the American regulatory agencies were established to attract capital and enterprise into an industry and their business orientation is a condition endemic because of their tasks.[8] Indeed, the specific legal controls – as distinct from the general objectives to which they are supposedly addressed – may have been promoted by the regulated industries, either for the purpose of stabilising competition and guaranteeing profit and growth or to immunise the industries from further and more far-reaching controls. Kolko's study of the origins of anti-trust law in the United States demonstrates that it represented a victory for big business in its efforts to attain conditions of stability, predictability and security in a period of rapid technological development, when newly established businesses were entering the market and often competing successfully with established corporations. Moreover, big business was aware of the advantages that anti-trust regulation would have in shielding it from hostile public opinion and any radical alteration in the distribution of wealth.[9] A similar investigation of the origins of the Factory Acts in Britain reveals that the more substantial manufacturers supported limited state interference in the affairs of industry, partly because improving the welfare of workers improved productivity, but also because regulation gave them a competitive advantage over their smaller trade rivals for whom it was relatively more expensive to comply with the new standards.[10]

Whatever the nature of the legislation or its background, there is the separate issue of how it is enforced. Various explanations have been advanced in the United States for the fact that the practices of the regulatory agencies are less effective than might be thought appropriate. One is the underrepresentation of the public: ordinary citizens are neither as powerful nor as organised as commerce and industry and therefore cannot have the same influence over regulatory agencies. Regulatory agencies develop a shared interest with businesses because of their day-to-day contact with them, rather than with those representing the community interest.[11] Further, the business community is viewed favourably by the public. Dependence on the employment it generates, and general satisfaction with the goods and services it produces, lead ordinary citizens to identify with its continued well-being. Those purporting to represent the community interest therefore not only lack the wealth and organisation of commerce and industry but also have to contend with the fact that public opinion offers little support.

Businesses cannot afford regulatory agencies to be hostile, because they are invested with wide powers and consequently businesses attempt to mould them to ensure that they have a favourable outlook.[12] Even if nothing sinister is present, the simple fact is that commerce and industry are immensely powerful and can deploy public relations and legal resources to sway the agencies.[13] A favourite target of critics in the United States is the so-called 'deferred bribe', where staff leave regulatory agencies and accept appointments in the regulated industries. A closely related point is that regulatory agencies operate in a potentially unfavourable environment, which can cause them to relate their objectives to those of the commercial world. At one level regulatory agencies may simply not wish to antagonise those whose influence could cause them a loss of political support,[14] but at another level regulatory agencies may actually absorb the values of the business community. Finally, there is sharp criticism of the quality and training of the staff of regulatory agencies, and in some cases this extends to an attack on their tenuous commitment to the goals originally envisaged for controlling businesses.

II OUTLINE OF THE PRESENT STUDY

The main focus of the present study is on consumer agencies and how they perform their tasks. As background, I look at the nature and perceptions of consumer agencies and of the enforcement and advice officers who staff them. Consumer agencies have developed from the former weights and measures departments, and it is relatively simple to show that this historical development influences certain of their present practices. The local government character of consumer agencies is another factor which can be shown to have an important effect; for example, on how they exercise their discretion. In the past, prosecutions of consumer offences had to be approved by a local authority committee. Since these often comprised a majority of businessmen, they were generally unfavourable to prosecution and so legal proceedings were approved in only the very serious cases. Again, there has been a constant concern with what consumer agencies regard as the leniency and ignorance of the courts. Consequently, there is a reluctance to institute legal proceedings unless it is fairly certain that their outcome will be successful.

As far as the perceptions of consumer agencies are concerned, particular attention is devoted to what they regard as their impartiality; namely, holding the balance between businesses and consumers. Impartiality has particular salience because it leads consumer agencies to eschew an advocacy role on behalf of consumers. In everyday relations with businesses it serves the purpose of minimising hostility and of preventing consumer officers from becoming too personally involved. The impartiality of consumer agencies is compromised, in part, by a conflicting role in which they see themselves – as advisers to industry. In recent times, there have been strong moves in consumer agencies to provide expert assistance to businesses with a view to preventing consumer offences before they arise. The difficulty is that this may lead consumer agencies to accommodate themselves to businesses, so that, in practical terms, they are less than willing to institute prosecutions. An independent reason why consumer agencies accommodate themselves to businesses is the plain fact that there is an imbalance of power; there are about 1250 enforcement officers in England and Wales to police the whole range of businesses relevant to consumers.

Consumer agencies have definite typifications of businesses which, although grounded in experience, can have an independent force. Essentially they believe that most businesses are honest but that a small minority of unscrupulous businesses in identifiable trades commit breaches of the civil and criminal law either intentionally or with a complete disregard for legal requirements. Although the unscrupulous are only a small minority, a number of other businesses, including some well-known national businesses, give rise to a disproportionate number of breaches of consumer law. As compared with the unscrupulous, however, their offences are more the result of adopting undesirable trade practices than of intentional or reckless wrongdoing, and the complaints which consumer agencies receive about them are less intractable to settle. Consumer officers use these typifications to produce hypotheses for their everyday work. For example, the secondhand-car trade is typified as unscrupulous, and therefore a consumer officer approaches a secondhand-car dealer on the basis that he is likely to be in the wrong.

After sketching the background to consumer agencies, I proceed to examine how they obtain their cases. Basically, this divides into two: cases received from complaint, and those which are the outcome of an agency's own initiative. Complaints are particularly important for consumer agencies since the limitation on their resources and the nature of some consumer offences lead them to rely on consumers to bring to their attention certain breaches of civil and criminal law. On the other hand consumers are not aware that some offences have been committed, even though they may be harmed, and therefore there is a disadvantage in agencies relying too much on complaints.

The most striking feature of national surveys is that many consumers who think that they have experienced consumer problems fail to complain, lack a rudimentary knowledge of their legal rights, and are ignorant of official bodies, such as consumer agencies, which may be able to assist them. Interviews conducted with consumers as part of the present study throw further light on the process of complaining. There is an under-representation of those in the lowest income groups, which seems to arise mainly because socio-economic position is associated with social attributes such as confidence. Complaining involves more than knowledge, for even consumers who know that consumer agencies exist must find the local agency and feel that it is worth while approaching it.

The expectations consumers have about what a consumer agency will do form the context within which it handles complaints. Most consumers expect advice – expert advice – rather than more detailed assistance. Whatever their expectations, consumers are not dominated by consumer agencies when they approach them about consumer problems. An important reason is that few consumer problems are crucial to the lives of consumers, in contrast, for example, to the problems usually facing persons applying for social welfare benefits. If persons approach a social welfare agency in a state of despair, the agency has an opportunity to redefine the problem – for example in terms of personal inadequacy rather than of the social reality of poverty. Although consumers may realise that they have consumer problems, very rarely do they perceive them as falling within the civil or the criminal law. A consumer agency therefore has wide discretion as to whether it will institute a prosecution when a consumer offence is revealed by a complaint. Indeed, there is little public comment about the activities of consumer agencies, which means that they are largely insulated from critical evaluation.

Consumer agencies acquire some cases through their own initiative, mainly by the routine inspection of business premises, coupled with sampling at retail outlets to check whether there is adherence to product standards. They can therefore control the official rate of consumer offences by varying the amount of detection work in which they engage. The characteristic feature of inspection and sampling is that these originated in the period when consumer agencies had little concern with what is now regarded as consumer protection. More recently, the greater concern with individual consumers has led some consumer agencies to question whether existing methods of inspection are efficient and whether it would be better to concentrate on known areas of malpractice. However most consumer agencies view any change in inspection practice as likely to undermine their preventive work, and so adhere to the traditional means of detecting offences.

How do consumer agencies deal with the cases which they receive by complaint or discover through their own initiative? The formal procedure of consumer agencies filters out matters not involving a consumer offence and deals with them by advising the consumer of his rights and the course of action he should adopt, or by negotiating on his behalf with the business involved. In many consumer agencies this task is now assigned to specially appointed officers. In deciding whether to handle an enquiry by giving advice, rather than by rendering more positive assistance, the policy of the particular consumer agency is important. Some agencies adopt the approach of educating consumers to deal with their own problems and stress advice, but others believe that they exist as a service and regularly negotiate for consumers. Although the latter resolve the majority of complaints, consumers can remain quite ignorant of their rights and of the practicalities of enforcing them.

Before a consumer officer decides to negotiate with a business on behalf of a consumer, he tries to evaluate whether a complaint is justified. In practice this involves testing the consumer's account against the officer's experience with other complaints and against any independent evidence. The hallmark of negotiation with a business on behalf of a consumer is the low posture which consumer officers assume. They do not regard themselves as consumer advocates, and in any event they lack any legal backing unless a consumer offence is involved. At most, if the complaint is justified, consumer officers can point out to the business that the consumer can commence civil legal proceedings if redress is not obtained. A consequence of the mediatory approach to consumer complaints is that compromise is sometimes the accepted solution to an enquiry: some consumers fail to obtain their full legal entitlement, but others receive satisfaction despite the fact that their legal claim is weak. Where consumer officers fail to obtain satisfaction, they may assist a consumer to institute a civil action, although most are deterred because they are not familiar with the procedure.

Theoretically, criminal matters should not be dealt with by negotiation with businesses. In practice, if the evidence of an offence is weak, or if an advice officer fails to see a criminal aspect to a complaint, consumer offences may be settled by obtaining redress from the business concerned. Even if there is no question of obtaining redress for a consumer, it is not often that a business which commits a consumer offence will be prosecuted. The figures show quite clearly the small percentage of known consumer offences which are prosecuted. Businesses are cautioned for many consumer offences and in some cases no action whatever is taken against them. The use of discretion in this way derives, in part, from the typification of businesses as basically law-abiding. It is assumed in most cases that when informed of its legal obligations a business will correct any defects in its trade practices.

The exercise of discretion implies criteria which enable decisions to be made on how consumer offences will be treated. Law has a limited role and acts mainly to set the boundaries within which decisions are made. For consumer officers, law assumes a simplified form, for they could not cope with, nor do they need, its full complexity for their routine activity. Non-legal factors which inform the exercise of discretion cannot be reduced to an all-embracing concept such as moral fault. An offence may still lead to prosecution, even if a business has not acted dishonestly, with gross negligence, or in some other blameworthy manner. Any particular decision may be the product of a range of factors, including the nature of the offence, its effect on consumers and the character of the business. Personal factors are also relevant such as the temperament, ideology and commitment of enforcement officers. The chief officer sets the tone for the prosecution policy of a consumer agency, but his influence is mediated by institutional factors.

Finally, I consider the impact of consumer law and its enforcement on businesses. There is no clear-cut answer to whether legislative goals in the field of consumer protection are being achieved. The number of pre-judicial trade practices in a community cannot be easily estimated, and, even if it could, it would be difficult to isolate the causes of any changes in these practices following the introduction of consumer law or its enforcement. Certainly, transformations in the external behaviour of businesses are sometimes obvious following the introduction of new legislation or its enforcement. Interviews with businessmen, together with statistical data about the prosecution records of a number of businesses, lead to the general conclusion that consumer legislation can produce changes in business practices when first introduced, although these are rarely fundamental changes in marketing and promotional practices. It appears clear that certain businesses find it acceptable to commit a number of consumer offences instead of changing their trade practices; for instance, some national businesses have incurred an annual average of twenty prosecutions for consumer offences, and there is an absence of any downward trend in their offences over the years.

The less than fundamental adjustment which some businesses make to consumer law and its enforcement reflects the drawbacks to the basic sanctions of present consumer law. Fines can be treated as an acceptable expense and any publicity surrounding the conviction of a business is no incentive for change because it has no effect on sales.

The interviews with businesses suggest that the strongest influence in the number of breaches of consumer law committed by a business is its basic trading policy, rather than any impact which the law may have. The available evidence suggests that although some businesses are frequently prosecuted, others of a comparable nature are responsible for few consumer offences, which is a result of their marketing practices, and the training and conditions which they provide for their employees.

III THE METHOD OF APPROACH

Legal philosophers have noted that when some laws are applied there seems to be a discrepancy between their intention and what actually happens. As Lon Fuller comments: 'By the words of the Code the act is criminal, but judged by the realities of official behaviour the act escapes any effective legal restraint.'[15] The present study is not so much concerned with the divergence between the law in the books and the law in action, but with how legal actors such as common agencies manage legal propositions in their routine activity, and how this affects those to whom the legal propositions are directed. Instead of the usual approach of lawyers of beginning with the rules and mapping out possible patterns of behaviour, I focus on the actual implementation of law in particular situations and only if relevant do I refer to the manner in which this is linked to legal categories. In other words, the concern is with the operation of consumer agencies and the procedures through which law takes meaning in everyday situations both for them and for the businesses over which they exercise legal control. The emphasis of the research is that the law is rarely problematic for consumer agencies or for businesses and that it is generally applied in a routine and unambiguous manner. Moreover, non-legal factors typically entwine with the law in dictating the behaviour of consumer agencies and of businesses in concrete situations.

Research for the present study proceeded along a number of lines. Various disciplines were drawn upon to suggest hypotheses for the research and a number of methods were utilised to elicit information. Information about how consumer agencies obtain their cases relies in part on the results of interviews with some 220 consumers – what I call the *Consumer Surveys* in the text. Chapter 6, on the impact of consumer law and its enforcement on businesses, is based on some forty interviews with businessmen and on various other data. Details of these two studies – the *Consumer Surveys* and of businessmen – are dealt with at further length in the appropriate chapters.

The material on which most of the book is based was acquired during a period of seven months' fieldwork in 1974/75 in three consumer agencies: one based on a large provincial city, one located in a London borough, and the third situated in a semi-rural area of England. The findings thus obtained were supplemented by information gleaned from shorter visits, usually of a day's duration, to some fifteen other consumer agencies; from a perusal of over 250 annual reports from different consumer agencies; and from conversations with consumer officers at several of their conferences. No claim is made that the three areas studied in depth are representative, but the additional research in other areas was useful in showing that what I found in the three areas had a more universal application.

During the seven months – three months in what I call 'Metropolitan County' and two months each in 'London Borough' and 'Blankshire' – I attended the consumer agencies during regular hours, observed the conduct and listened to the conversations of consumer officers, accompanied them in the course of their duties and read agency files, to which I had almost full access. Formal interviews were kept to a minimum, but extensive notes were made of observations and conversations. Well over 1000 prosecution files were perused which dealt with consumer offences detected in the period 1967–75. The reports were prepared mainly for internal use and provided valuable insights into the exercise of discretion by consumer officers. However, in the course of the investigation it became clear that the files were also used by outsiders, mainly prosecuting solicitors, and for this reason factors in the exercise of discretion were sometimes omitted. Efforts were made to discuss with the relevant investigating officers as many files as possible, and in several cases this revealed important elements in discretion which were not mentioned in the reports. Details were extracted from 699 prosecution files involving 791 offences – over 95 per cent of the prosecutions between 1969 and 1975 in the three jurisdictions.[16] Their analysis forms the basis of what I call in the course of the work the *Prosecution Survey*.

The methodological issues associated with participant observation have been canvassed in detail elsewhere.[17] Sociologists favourable to participant observation point out that it is a blending of methods, so that people are interviewed, documents are analysed and events are directly observed. The advantage over simply examining documents or conducting interviews is that people have a good deal to hide from what they regard as prying or unfavourable comment. The continuous presence of a researcher over a substantial period makes it much more difficult for them to conceal opinions or practices. Those engaged in participant observation are also able constantly to test their theories against their empirical observations. There are dangers to participant observation, such as adopting the perception of those being studied. Where the participant observer does not conceal his role, those being studied may alter their behaviour in his presence. Another problem is unrepresentativeness, for participant observation is less concerned with the frequency and distribution of events than with a thorough examination of the particular.

The numerous points of access I obtained to consumer agencies convinced me that consumer officers rarely altered their behaviour because of my presence or deliberately attempted to mislead me. By cross-checking sources, I was able to allow for exaggeration and other inaccuracies. Moreover, I often acted and was treated as an assistant to consumer officers. While seeking to perceive the world through the eyes of consumer officers, I hope to have retained sufficient objectivity to assess critically their beliefs and practices. This particular task has been facilitated by conversations with a number of persons knowledgeable about consumer matters but not employed by consumer agencies, and through the writing-up process, which has enabled me to distance myself from the material.

2 Law Enforcers and Law Enforcement

The present task is to introduce the remainder of the work by focusing on the consumer agencies which enforce the bulk of consumer protection law, and the activities of which are the central theme of the study. On the enforcement side, consumer agencies direct most of their attention to implementing the criminal provisions of the Trade Descriptions Act (1968), which prohibits false descriptions by businesses; the Food and Drugs Act (1955), which bans unacceptable food, regulates food additives, and fixes some food standards; and the Weights and Measures Act (1963) which regulates the quantity side of consumer transactions. Some effort is also directed towards assessing whether hazardous products comply with the standards fixed under the Consumer Protection Act (1961). The passage of the Fair Trading Act (1973) and the Consumer Credit Act (1974), however, means that consumer agencies will become involved increasingly with the control of specific trade practices. When this legislation is fully in operation, consumer agencies will enforce the statutory orders made under the former Act regulating unfair trading practices, and will also bear the main burden of administering controls over the credit industry. In addition, consumer agencies are now devoting attention through consumer advice services or Consumer Advice Centres to advising the community about their individual rights as consumers. This work is mainly concerned with the quality of products and services which consumers purchase. In some cases, it involves consumer agencies actually taking up consumers' complaints with businesses in a mediatory capacity.

I THE BACKGROUND OF CONSUMER AGENCIES

Central to an understanding of consumer protection in Britain are two facts: first, consumer agencies fall within the ambit of local government; and second, consumer agencies are founded on what were weights and measures departments. Both features have influenced the historical development of consumer protection, and are factors in moulding the present attitude of consumer agencies to their tasks.

THE ORGANISATION OF CONSUMER PROTECTION

In general, central government is the source of consumer legislation, while its administration is almost entirely in the hands of local authority consumer agencies. Information received by central government from consumer agencies forms the compilation of trends regarding consumer protection which enable it to assess when action on its part is warranted. In the main, this takes the form of promoting new statutory controls, informing consumers of specific problems in publicity material, and directing the attention of consumer agencies as a whole to particular problems.

At the national level, the Department of Prices and Consumer Protection has the major responsibility for reviewing existing consumer protection programmes and for proposing new initiatives. However, the Ministry of Agriculture, Fisheries and Food has important duties regarding food law, and the control of drugs falls within the auspices of the Department of Health and Social Security. The fact that a Cabinet Minister oversees consumer protection through the Department of Prices and Consumer Protection is a recognition of the importance of the subject in political terms. During the life of the present Labour Government the Department has taken initiatives in a number of areas; for example, it established the National Consumer Council and has encouraged consumer advice services to widen their access to consumers. Established in 1973, the Office of Fair Trading has a dual responsibility: to encourage competition and to protect consumers. The first centres on certain powers regarding monopolies, mergers and restrictive trade practices. Protecting the interests of consumers involves administering the consumer protection parts of the Fair Trading Act (1973) and certain provisions of the Consumer Credit Act (1974). Under the latter, the main duty is the licensing of businesses offering credit to consumers, although the enforcement of a number of other provisions is shared with consumer agencies. Under the Fair Trading Act (1973), the Office proposes regulations for controlling trade practices adverse to the economic interests of consumers; obtains undertakings from, and cease and desist orders against, persistent business offenders; negotiates voluntary codes of practice for sections of commerce and industry; and distributes a certain amount of information to consumers about their rights.

Enforcement of the bulk of consumer protection legislation devolves by law upon the county councils of England and Wales, the regional councils of Scotland and the boroughs of Greater London. These authorities have either established consumer agencies or come to an arrangement with other local authorities about how their obligations are to be performed. In all, there are seventy-four consumer agencies in England and Wales. The pattern for consumer agencies is not uniform, however, since local political influences have determined the details of administrative structure. In many areas, for instance, responsibility for controlling the quality of food is divided between consumer agencies and environmental health departments. Broadly, provisions relating to the composition, labelling and advertising of food are allotted to the former, while the food safety and hygiene aspects of the legislation are entrusted to the latter. As it operates, the division in enforcement causes few difficulties where food is obviously unfit, since that relates to food hygiene, but the overlap is a source of friction where extraneous matter is detected in food, for that could fall within the jurisdiction of either agency.

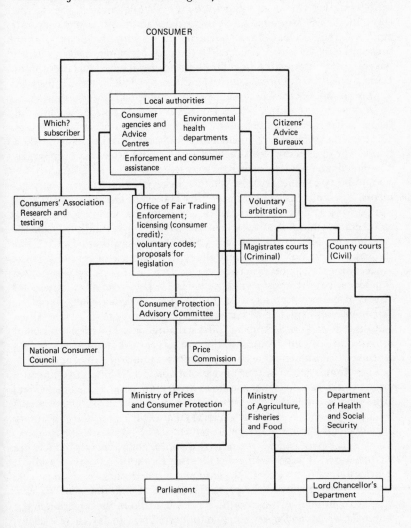

Figure 1. The pattern of consumer protection

SOURCE: Adapted from Tom Hadden, 'Guidance for Consumers', *New Society* (18 September 1975) p. 639.

Being local authority departments, consumer agencies are answerable to
a committee of elected councillors. Senior councillors of a local authority
typically sit on the prestigious committees such as finance, education and
social services, while consumer protection is usually the responsibility of a
junior committee which may be in charge of other public-protection duties
such as the fire service. Consequently, consumer agencies can be denied
adequate resources because the senior committees have a greater influence
in determining the local authority budget. While consumer protection
committees have interfered rarely in the daily administration of consumer
agencies, they have been an element in shaping the policy for the
prosecution of consumer offences. In the past, consumer agencies had to
have the prior approval of the committees before an individual prosecution
could be instituted. Overall, the committees were unfavourably disposed
to prosecution, not least because they often had a majority of businessmen.
In a few cases, this attitude led to grave abuses when offending
businessmen exerted influence on committees not to bring prosecutions.
The careers of some enforcement officers suffered when they refused to bow
to this type of pressure. Now the influence of committees has been largely
eliminated, and in many cases consumer agencies have been delegated full
responsibility for the decision whether to prosecute consumer infringements. The only example of impropriety observed during the field work
was in Metropolitan County, when a prosecution was proposed by an
enforcement officer against a member of the Opposition party on the
consumer protection committee, who was also a local businessman. The
councillor intimated to the chief officer that because of his position the
proceedings should be dropped, but in view of this suggestion, it was
concluded that there was no alternative but to prosecute. Committees still
display considerable interest in the bringing of prosecutions, however,
demanding an explanation if prosecutions are unsuccessful, especially if
costs have been awarded against the local authority. The important point
is that local authority control in the past has contributed to the cautious
attitude of consumer agencies at present to the use of prosecution.

The administration of consumer protection law by local government is
justified on the grounds that consumer matters are best handled at the local
level and that the most readily available unit of local administration is
local government. For example, it is said that it is better to detect statutory
infringements in the many retail outlets scattered across the country,
where consumers can be prejudiced directly, than where products are
manufactured. The government claims that localisation is indispensable if
information and advice about consumer problems are to reach a wide
range of consumers and the greatest number of consumers are to have
access to consumer agencies for their complaints.[1] On the other hand, the
major factor advanced by some consumer officers in favour of central-
isation is the desirability of uniformity in administration. The argument
runs that the existing system is synonymous with a duplication of

enforcement programmes, and that enforcement policy varies between agencies, which is frustrating to some businesses and encourages others to wrongdoing. For example, it is said that after being prosecuted fraudulent businessmen move to other parts of the country and continue their malpractices, while national firms sometimes take advantage of lenient agencies and continue to market their products in those areas, although they might have to withdraw them in others. Another factor mentioned is that recent years have witnessed the replacement of local businesses by national firms with multiple outlets. Local authority consumer agencies are said to be unequal in strength to the larger corporations, and are often unable to match the professional expertise which the latter can employ when objecting to the enforcement of legislation or the claims of particular consumers.[2]

Central government has limited supervisory powers over consumer agencies. Since it adheres to the view that it is preferable to enforce consumer law and dispense consumer advice at the local level, local authorities in the main are left a wide discretion. By law, it is mandatory for local authorities to implement most consumer legislation, and in some circumstances central government can conduct inspections and local hearings to check whether a local authority is performing its obligations adequately. In the period 1967–75, fifty inspections were made of consumer agencies, but it was not felt necessary to publish the results or to institute any local hearings.[3] A degree of uniformity between agencies is achieved because in certain respects central government performs a co-ordinating role. For example, the Department of Prices and Consumer Protection and its predecessors have supervised the enforcement of the weights and measures legislation for almost a century. They have certified enforcement officers as competent to administer the legislation and have approved new patterns for weighing and measuring equipment. Under certain legislation, consumer agencies must notify central government of an intended prosecution, which it can then conduct itself if it considers the matter to be of national significance. But in the actual operation of these, central government has not interfered with the independence of consumer agencies. It has rarely undertaken to investigate or prosecute an infringement, and neither has it adopted the role of approving particular prosecutions. However, the provisions enable it to accumulate data on prosecutions and this is a useful source of information for consumer agencies about businesses which they may intend to prosecute for unlawful action.

Another impetus for a common approach by consumer agencies is the professional association of consumer enforcement officers: The Institute of Trading Standards Administration. Founded in 1893 as the Incorporated Society of Weights and Measures Inspectors, the Institute promotes the interchange of ideas between consumer agencies through its national and regional conferences and through the pages of its journal, the *Monthly*

Review. The Institute issues confidential bulletins to members on a regular basis, containing requests for information about particular businesses, and lists of cautions, intended prosecutions and convictions. Consumer agencies can therefore avoid wasting resources through pursuing enquiries about particular businesses along parallel lines. The executive of the Institute divides itself into a number of committees, which have plenary power between its meetings. The legislative committees are consulted by central government officials about the drafting of legislation and in turn make representations on legislative proposals and other consumer matters. The committees also answer specific queries from members and trade associations about the interpretation of consumer legislation. Since central government refuses to do this, regarding it as a matter for the courts, the views of the committees are of great value and are usually treated as authoritative by consumer agencies.

TRADITION AND CHANGE IN CONSUMER AGENCIES

From being primarily concerned with weights and measures, consumer agencies now have a wide responsibility in relation to protecting the consumer. The approval of weighing and measuring equipment for commercial use still has a high priority because it is a statutory duty and a necessary prerequisite for trading activity. An example is with changes in the price of petrol, where certain types of petrol pumps must be reverified before they can be used. On average, however, weights and measures work comprises a small proportion of the work load of consumer agencies.

The passage of the Trade Descriptions Act (1968) was perhaps the single most important fact in transforming weights and measures departments into consumer agencies. Since 1968, the role of consumer agencies has expanded still further with the enactment of additional legislation such as the Fair Trading Act (1973) and the Consumer Credit Act (1974). A repercussion of local government reorganisation in 1974 was that many older officers took the opportunity to retire early, thus enhancing the prospects of younger officers who have different conceptions of what consumer protection involves. The advent of consumer advice has meant an influx of advice officers lacking a commitment to traditional values, and a different orientation for departments historically rooted in law enforcement. Some indication of the changing nature of the law enforcement work of consumer agencies is reflected in the pattern of prosecutions. Table 2.1, which is drawn from the *Prosecution Survey*, shows the number and proportion of each type of prosecution instituted in the three agencies studied in the years 1967–75. The proportion of weights and measures prosecutions has obviously declined, and this trend will continue as the agencies become familiar with their – in many cases – newly acquired food and drugs responsibilities, and as recent legislation comes into operation.

If consumer agencies have been transformed functionally, the attitude

Table 2.1. The trend in consumer prosecutions, *Prosecution Survey*

Year	Offences (N = 779)							
	Misdes- cribed goods	Mis- pricing	Misdes- cribed services, etc.	Incor- rect quan- tity	Other weights & meas- ures offences	Sub- stand- ard	Others	Total
	%	%	%	%	%	%	%	%
1969/70	21 (17)*	10 (8)	4 (3)	52 (42)	9 (7)	3 (2)	1 (1)	100 (80)
1970/71	38 (35)	20 (18)	4 (4)	30 (28)	3 (3)	5 (5)	–	100 (93)
1971/72	35 (50)	15 (21)	8 (11)	37 (53)	2 (3)	2 (3)	1 (1)	100 (142)
1972/73	32 (62)	28 (52)	6 (12)	28 (54)	4 (8)	1 (2)	2 (4)	100 (194)
1973/74	28 (953)	28 (52)	6 (12)	23 (44)	10 (18)	4 (7)	1 (1)	100 (187)
1974/75**	60 (50)	12 (10)	5 (4)	18 (15)	–	5 (4)	–	100 (83)

* The figures in brackets show the actual number of cases brought.
** The fall in the absolute number of prosecutions in 1974/75 was because of the interruptions caused by local government reorganisation.

of many enforcement officers has changed less rapidly. In many respects this is simply the result of a difficulty in assimilating new legislation and a preference for the familiar. Some enforcement officers have taken enthusiastically to new responsibilities and realise that what consumer agencies would have once regarded as serious is now quite trivial compared with their present duties. However, other officers prefer the relatively simple and traditional tasks associated with the routine inspection of retail premises. Many enforcement officers dislike consumer complaints, and this attitude occasionally affects the way they deal with an enquiry. The problem was acknowledged by several chief officers. One commented that he was reluctant to allocate enforcement officers to handle consumer complaints because they felt the duty to be below them. Another admitted that he had deliberately allocated staff in the agency, promoting the progressive officers, while confining the remainder to traditional duties where new initiatives could not be sabotaged. A third referred to some of his fellow chief officers in these terms:

> Some of my colleagues still think that consumer protection deals only with loaves of bread and sugar – local things and local manufacturers. But now we are dealing with large firms like British Leyland. The only way to combat these large companies is to do things on as grand a scale as they do.

The journal of the professional association of enforcement officers has highlighted the fact that many of its members are slow to recognise their new role and has urged them to abandon their conventional outlook, for the advancement of the profession.[4]

A factor which shackles consumer agencies to the past is the method of qualification for enforcement officers. Although widely recognised as an anachronism, this continues to be the statutory qualification arranged by central government for those enforcing the weights and measures legislation. As suggested by its purpose, the statutory examination focuses on matters relating to weights and measures law, except for a general introduction to the legal system and to legal procedure. It places a premium on rote learning and on memorising the details of the legislation. In some urban areas, the number of students has made part-time courses at technical colleges viable, but otherwise the main form of tutoring is through a correspondence course combined with a very short full-time course for those about to sit the examination. With the inadequate training, the pass rate for the examination has been low – an average of 33 per cent. Trainee officers obtain various degrees of practical experience by working as assistants to qualified officers. Some agencies continue to under-utilise their trainees, but others entrust them with responsible tasks, such as enforcing legislation like the Trade Descriptions Act (1968).

The inadequate training of enforcement officers was one of the reasons that the Crowther Committee on Consumer Credit recommended against entrusting the enforcement of their proposals to consumer agencies: not only were they overburdened with existing tasks, but they did not possess the necessary qualifications to deal with the intricate legal and financial questions raised.[5] The self-interest of enforcement officers who are already qualified, and the strength of their professional association, have meant that only the isolated consumer agency has broken away from adopting the statutory qualification as the prerequisite for appointing enforcement staff. Together with the local government character of consumer agencies, it ensures that the opportunity for lawyers and accountants to take part in implementing consumer law is minimal. Certainly unqualified staff such as ex-policemen have been appointed to enforce some of the legislation, but they are often allocated to the mundane tasks, and their status, remuneration and promotion prospects are inferior to those of other officers.

The majority of enforcement officers acquire their knowledge of the broad sweep of consumer law in the course of their duties. The inadequacies of the statutory examination led the professional association of enforcement officers to institute a Diploma of Consumer Affairs in 1970. The programme includes consumer law other than the Weights and Measures Act (1963), provides an introduction to the structure of trade and commerce, and familiarises students with wider aspects of consumer protection, including the functions of official and voluntary consumer organisations both in the United Kingdom and abroad. Few enforcement officers have taken the diploma, mainly because study for it is in an officer's spare time and through a correspondence course. An attempt to introduce consumer protection as a degree course at tertiary institutions has never been pursued, although there are several universities and polytechnics which offer degrees for environmental health officers. However, steps have now been taken to provide a comprehensive qualification for consumer protection officers by amalgamating the statutory examination and the diploma. All consumer protection legislation will be included in the course, as well as the economic and commercial environment in which it operates and the techniques used to assess consumer products and services. It is anticipated that on a successful completion of the first two years, a trainee officer will be usefully employed by his agency on limited enforcement duties. The Diploma of Trading Standards, as it will be called, is a part-time course of three years, and the first officers will not qualify until 1979.

The system of qualification locks enforcement officers into their job. The statutory examination is not recognised by commerce and industry and without a Diploma in Public or Municipal Administration (which a few senior consumer officers have) carries little weight even in local government circles. The chances for advancement are therefore confined to the consumer protection field; in fact, there is some mobility between consumer agencies as officers transfer for promotion or better remuneration. The highly specialised expertise of enforcement officers, and the fact that it is difficult to transfer outside the service, is a partial explanation for the tendency of some of them to resist new ideas.[6] The Mallaby Committee noted in 1967 that since consumer law enforcement was a profession with limited appeal, peculiar to local government, it had not attracted school-leavers with outstanding qualifications or graduates.[7] The situation had not changed radically since that report was made, and the typical enforcement officer is still recruited straight from school. Consumer agencies attempt to attract university graduates but it seems unlikely that this will ever be an important source of staff. Of the numerous enforcement officers I spoke to in the course of the field work, none joined a consumer agency because of a commitment to protecting the consumer, but rather they drifted into the position after eliminating other employment possibilities. Although consumer protection work appeared to be interesting, the main attractions were the security of local government service, the relative freedom, and the contact with the public entailed in enforcement work.

Apart from new legislation, the other factor transforming consumer agencies has been the establishment of consumer advice services, which are designed to assist consumers with enquiries, particularly those involving the civil as opposed to the criminal law. The Molony Committee, which reported to the government on consumer matters in the early 1960s, recommended that a country-wide advice service should be established, to advise and inform consumers dissatisfied with the quality or cost of the products and services they purchased.[8] As a result of the report, the government encouraged Citizens' Advice Bureaux and local authorities to increase their facilities for consumer advice.[9] Local authorities gradually imposed the task on their consumer agencies on the basis that, with their back-up facilities, they could more effectively handle consumer complaints than could the voluntary and part-time workers of the Citizens' Advice Bureaux. They were knowledgeable about consumer law and, unlike the Bureaux, had funds for investigating complaints, making test purchases and employing independent testing authorities.

Today all consumer agencies provide some type of consumer advice service for members of the public. For many agencies, because finance is limited, pre-shopping advice is not generally available and the service is confined to consumer complaints. In some cases, enforcement officers deal with all consumer enquiries, including those involving the civil law. Many consumer agencies, however, have now recruited special advice officers, although the volume of complaints means that enforcement officers still handle some. Because of the isolated physical location of many consumer agencies, Citizens' Advice Bureaux and libraries are used as contact points for the services. In Blankshire, one of the authorities in which I did field work, prepaid postcards are provided through libraries and parish organisations, and consumers are invited to complete brief particulars of their complaint and forward them to the agency. As a means of access, this places a premium on literacy or on an involvement in local affairs.

Consumer Advice Centres have been established in a number of areas and are normally located in prominent positions in shopping centres, some local authorities supplement their Consumer Advice Centres with mobile caravans. All but a few Consumer Advice Centres are connected with consumer agencies. The exceptions fall within the ambit of local government but are independent of the control of consumer agencies. In almost all cases Consumer Advice Centres are not directly linked with other social services. The concept of Consumer Advice Centres was first introduced into Britain by the Consumers' Association, the private consumer organisation and publisher of *Which?* magazine, to widen access to consumer advice, to make the public conscious of consumer issues, and to educate them about their legal rights.[10] Certainly the establishment of Consumer Advice Centres has had a definite effect on the number of consumer enquiries. When the first Centre was established in Metropolitan County, another authority in which I did field work, simple enquiries increased from an average of 10 a week to about 100 a week, and complaints from nearly 30 a week to over 60 a week. Another argument for Consumer Advice Centres was that existing institutions providing consumer advice were inadequate, because they were biased towards the middle class. Consumer Advice Centres would be available to all sections of the community, but they would perform a particular service in assisting those on less than average incomes who, it was supposed, were particularly vulnerable as consumers. The argument is now widely accepted that Consumer Advice Centres assist the poorer consumer, which is one of the reasons that the government has encouraged their establishment with special grants and hopes that there will be a network of 200 Consumer Advice Centres by 1980.

The assistance provided by consumer advice services mainly concerns the civil law pertaining to the sale of goods and to the provision of consumer credit. Many problems can be resolved by simple advice, but in some cases the consumer agency may actually investigate the matter. Enquiries involving infringements of criminal legislation are referred to enforcement officers, but with civil law matters a consumer officer will often contact the business involved and attempt to negotiate a solution. Pre-shopping advice goes one step further and involves discussion with prospective purchasers of products best suited to their needs. Its rationale is that consumers cannot undertake many purchases with confidence because of their ignorance about technically complex products. Pre-shopping advice enables them to avoid pitfalls in the purchases they make because they are made aware of the products available and of their advantages and limitations. In economic terms, it reduces the transaction costs involved in consumers acquiring information about products. Rather than recommending a specific product, however, pre-shopping advice supplies consumers with information so that they can exercise their own judgement. Another justification for pre-shopping advice is that it prevents post-shopping complaints – but this can not be the case where complaints arise because particular goods are faulty.

The background and approach of many advice officers is quite different from that of enforcement officers. The majority have been recruited externally – in many cases from outside local government – a considerable number are university graduates, and some are committed to the consumer movement and joined consumer agencies for this reason. Advice officers are trained – mostly by the Consumers' Association – for periods ranging from one to ten weeks, depending on their future responsibilities. The courses concentrate on the social aspects of handling enquiries and on pre-shopping advice, with only a small part of the time devoted to the principles of consumer law. Because of the paucity of their training, and because they are expected to deal with the whole range of consumer problems, at least in their initial stages, a number of advice officers express feelings of inadequacy because they are entrusted with tasks which they are not qualified to resolve.[11] Considerable resentment exists because advice officers can never reach senior positions in consumer agencies, but at most can direct a consumer advice service or a Consumer Advice Centre. Their inferior status is confirmed by their exclusion from the professional association of enforcement officers. As a result, advice officers have formed their own group to represent their interests. The relationship between enforcement and advice officers has implications for the everyday operation of consumer agencies which I refer to in Chapter 4.

THREE EXAMPLES: METROPOLITAN COUNTY, LONDON BOROUGH AND
BLANKSHIRE

To sketch further the background of consumer agencies, and to locate the
study in terms of where the bulk of the field work was carried out, it is useful
to describe briefly the consumer agencies in Metropolitan County, London
Borough and Blankshire at the time of the research.

Metropolitan County is one of the six metropolitan county councils in
England and Wales, which serve the larger urban areas outside London. It
has a population in excess of $2\frac{1}{2}$ million. Its largest city has over 1 million
people, and there are two other substantial cities at the extremities of the
county. The county is in fact a conurbation although it varies from heavily
industrial to desirable residential. Redevelopment in the area has meant
the construction of a number of council housing estates. Highly industrial
overall, the county has enjoyed relative prosperity compared with other
areas in Britain. Recently, however, concern has been expressed about a
decline in the rate of investment, the possibility of greater unemployment,
and the unsatisfactory level of industrial efficiency. Within Metropolitan
County there are seven district councils, their main functions being
education, social services and housing. The Metropolitan County Council
covers the whole county and is responsible for matters which require co-
ordination on a larger scale, including planning, traffic, town development
and consumer protection.

Prior to local government reorganisation in April 1974, there were eight
consumer protection departments in the area. Of these, the majority were
backward, as regards both policy and the amount of resources employed in
consumer protection. Few provided a consumer advice service, and even
these were on a limited basis. Because the area is an important centre for
the manufacture of weighing and measuring equipment, this was an
additional reason to their basic outlook for placing heavy emphasis on
weights and measures to the detriment of other aspects of consumer
protection. Except in the Metropolitan City agency, few prosecutions
were instituted, but these originated in complaints from the public and
were undertaken only when a clear offence was manifest. Metropolitan
City had the largest consumer agency, with some enthusiastic enforcement
officers. The satisfactory staffing situation relative to a city of its size was
recent; two years previously the field force had been a third of what it was
on local government reorganisation, partly because the salary structure
compared unfavourably with other areas, and partly because of the
difficulty in attracting enforcement officers to work in a large city. After a
vigorous campaign by the local voluntary consumer group, which pointed
out that Metropolitan City had the same number of staff as some of the
smallest towns in the country, the situation improved. Although the
agency did not advertise itself as providing a consumer advice service, it

was able to deal with a substantial volume of complaints from individual consumers.

The mandate given to the Metropolitan County consumer agency by the local authority is to provide 'comprehensive services for consumers, industry and trade, which will promote, maintain and develop equitable and fair trading and safeguard the consumer in the supply of goods and services'. The staff comprises 250 persons, allocated broadly to three areas of activity: consumer advice, law enforcement and metrology. The metrology division deals with technical problems, mainly weights and measures, but it is anticipated that eventually it will undertake the testing work associated with research programmes and surveys of consumer products and services. Enforcement and consumer advice are administered through nine districts in the county. Consumer advice work is wide-ranging and includes giving advice, resolving complaints, assisting with pre-shopping decisions and local price monitoring. Considerable emphasis has been placed on consumer advice, partly because the local authority at the time of this study was governed by the Labour Party, which favours this social service aspect of consumer protection. Eventually, nine Consumer Advice Centres will be established in the major shopping areas of the county. In addition to the staff in the area offices, who perform traditional duties such as the routine inspection of business premises, the enforcement division comprises a special investigations unit, which investigates complicated frauds and conducts special surveys of aspects of trading which lead to consumers being prejudiced. Surveys have been undertaken on matters including the marketing of detergents, quality control in the baking industry, and the sale of intoxicating liquors and bulk meat for domestic freezers. These fields were chosen either because they have been of traditional concern to consumer agencies or because of consumer complaints and the attention of the press. Primarily directed to transforming business practices and inducing central government to change the law, the surveys have also produced a number of prosections. (In parenthesis it should be noted that because consumer advice takes priority over enforcement, there is some dissatisfaction among enforcement officers. The total establishment for enforcement staff is about thirty for the whole county – comparable to agencies with a third of the population. The opinion of enforcement staff is that consumer advice and survey work are ancillary to the task of enforcing consumer protection legislation.)

Perhaps the most advanced in the country in terms of policy, the Metropolitan County agency is certainly one of the best endowed financially. Consumer protection is the one activity where the Metropolitan County can have an impact on the public, for functions such as education and social services, which bring local government in contact with citizens, are at a district council level. The Metropolitan council regards its consumer agency as an important instrument of public relations, especially the Consumer Advice Centres. The present chief officer of the Metropolitan County agency is one of the few enforcement officers who have thought through an ideology for consumer protection. In his view, the role of a consumer agency is 'more than a safeguard against fraud or a machinery for complaint and dissatisfaction. Equally it is concerned with fair prices, commercial competition, manufacturing, and the trading environment in the widest sense'.[12] As far as it curbs inflation and ensures that consumers receive value for money, he claims that the work of a consumer agency is as valuable as other local authority services such as education and social services. His argument is that, at present ordinary citizens feel helpless when confronting commerce and industry. The traditional laws of supply and demand and the free market economy no longer operate for the common good. A major reason is the lack of competitiveness arising from the concentration of businesses, misleading advertising, and ignorance on the part of consumers. Consumer agencies, however, can counter this trend by persuading business that it exists to provide a service and not to make a profit: 'Trade and business have to realize that they do exist for the people and that one of our aims will be to develop a third force – the consumer.' Consumer agencies also have an important role, he says, in the formulation of national government policy and in informing the public about how it affects their daily life. Specifically, information can be distributed through press releases, pre-shopping advice and price-lists provided at the Consumer Advice Centres, and a programme of consumer education. In this scheme of consumer protection, the chief officer sees prosecution as playing a necessary but secondary role: 'I don't see this job as purely a matter of enforcing statutory law. I would say it is to promote, maintain and develop an equitable trading climate so that we have fair dealing.' Prosecution according to his approach should be used only as a last resort or where there is a malpractice. Other consumer agencies should realise the drawbacks of their preoccupation with prosecution. Offences occur mainly 'where the supplier has no intention of cheating the buyer'. Intentional fraud is relatively rare, and infringements occur because of bad management and a lack of care and competence. The remedy for this is not in prosecution, but in advising businesses about solutions.

London Borough, with a population of over 300,000, is far less of a dormitory area than the other outer London boroughs. As a major administrative and shopping centre, substantial numbers commute to it daily from surrounding areas. The borough is the headquarters for a number of national firms and also sections of government Departments, and these provide employment for 50,000 people. A large-scale shopping development includes department stores, branches of the principal multiple and chain stores, a large shopping precinct and other shops of various sizes and types. The borough ranges from suburbs of terraced houses to desirable residential areas. A council estate is located on its eastern fringes, and there is a small amount of light industry near by.

The London Borough agency has lost the status of an independent department of the local authority and forms a division of a larger department which includes services such as environmental health. Well staffed by the standards of London consumer agencies, it comprises 3 advice officers and 13 enforcement officers, including the chief officer, his deputy and 3 assistant chief officers. A number of trainee officers are also employed and assist when not attending college. Despite the political environment of the agency, the tone of which is set by a business-orientated and financially parsimonious local authority, certain innovations have been realized, notably the establishment of a Consumer Advice Centre. This is located in the shopping precinct within the central shopping area and has received a substantial amount of local publicity. Its existence has been attacked by some councillors as an unnecessary waste of expenditure, although the local newspaper has editorialised that it is a service which 'should be available to those who feel they have been unfairly treated'. Another feat of the agency was when the local Chamber of Commerce was induced to agree to a code of business practice, which imposes obligations on its members additional to those contained in the existing law. The code also established a conciliation panel, which is designed to achieve the settlement of disputes between consumers and members of the Chamber. Under its chief officer, the agency emphasises consumer advice and the negotiated settlement of complaints with businesses at the expense of law enforcement through prosecution. The lack of interest in prosecution is compounded by the negative attitude of the legal department of the local authority to court proceedings for infringements of consumer law. Agency staff consequently realise that the only course of action which they can adopt is to attempt to obtain extra-judicial redress for individual complainants.

With a population of just over $\frac{1}{2}$ million and an area of nearly 800,000 acres, Blankshire typifies the semi-rural counties of England. The major population centres are Southborough and Northbridge, each having 100,000 people. The economic life of Southborough revolves around a university and research-based industry, while Northbridge has light industry. Northbridge is now being transformed by new development and is absorbing part of the overspill of population from London. Four towns in the county have populations of between 15,000 and 20,000; two of these have experienced rapid growth in the last decade. With mechanisation, the relative absence of livestock, and the consolidation of holdings, agriculture has become less important as a source of employment.

The Blankshire consumer agency dates from the amalgamation of four consumer protection Departments in April 1974. As with consumer agencies in other semi-rural counties, Blankshire easily attracts staff because of its pleasant environment. Although it has 20 enforcement officers, including a chief officer, a deputy and 4 assistant chief officers, the field staff is distributed in 5 area offices, 1 each in Northbridge and

Southborough and the remaining 3 in smaller towns. Area offices are substantially autonomous, and since few staff have been transferred within the county, continue in much the same manner as prior to the formation of the agency. A limited consumer advice service is available, but there are only three advice officers for the whole county. The relevant County Council committee is ill-disposed to prosecution, except as a last resort, and this meshes with the attitude of senior members of the agency. Traditional functions are highly valued; there is no special investigations unit, but the routine inspection of business premises is performed competently.

II THE PERCEIVED ROLE OF CONSUMER AGENCIES

Those engaged in legal and other activities use what have been called 'operational philosophies' – conceptions of the nature of their tasks, of how best to undertake them, and of the relationship of what they do to broader issues. These conceptions may not be particularly developed and they may be rather abstruse, but they will have a practical side in which they can provide guidance as to everyday activity.[13] In this section I discuss the notions that consumer officers have of their role, and then the following section focuses on the attitudes of consumer officers towards businesses and consumers.

THE IMPORTANCE OF IMPARTIALITY

The official view of consumer agencies, and the one adhered to by most consumer officers, is that their role is completely impartial: they assist both businesses and consumers but align themselves with neither. Consumer agencies interpret consumer legislation as safeguarding both; it is taken as a direction to protect consumers from unscrupulous businesses, and reputable businesses from unfair competition. To forestall any criticism that they sometimes appear to have the consumer interest as their paramount object, consumer agencies point out that businesses are well organised, aware of their rights and can draw on the support of strong trade associations to protect themselves. On the other hand the consumer interest is poorly represented, and consumer agencies are the only effective sources of assistance. Competition is not enough to ensure that consumers obtain a fair deal, for they are not organised to use their market power and they lack information essential to effective choice. Besides, for many years consumer agencies have spent their time advising businesses about how to comply with the law, and, in advising consumers, they are simply making their experience available to all sections of the public.

In assisting consumers, consumer agencies emphasise that they are not consumer partisans but operate in an unbiased manner. Any action taken or conclusion reached is said to flow from an objective evaluation of the evidence. In investigating complaints consumer officers assume a strict impartiality between the consumers and businesses. How important consumer agencies view impartiality was illustrated in one county where an advice officer was dismissed when she retained links with a local consumer group which was involved in public protests. Moreover, consumer agencies argue that in assisting consumers they assist businesses. Particularly if a consumer adamantly presses an unjustified claim, the intervention of a neutral consumer officer can relieve tension, demonstrate that any accusation against the business is unfair, and prevent the circulation of adverse reports to its disadvantage. Pre-shopping advice also benefits businesses because it removes the difficulties caused when consumers are unsure of their needs. Instead of questioning baffled shop assistants for details, customers can obtain information from Consumer Advice Centres on the nature of the different products available.

The conception that consumer agencies have of their impartial role derives from a number of factors. First, consumer agencies claim that impartiality is related to effectiveness. If they aligned themselves with consumers, business would refuse to co-operate in preventing the re-currence of infringements, and agencies would have to rely on the threat of legal proceedings. Moreover, when consumer officers presented them with complaints from consumers, they would be less willing to resolve them on an amicable basis. Second, there are more formal limitations on consumer agencies favouring consumers to the detriment of business. Consumer agencies point out that they must be neutral because of their status as local authority departments and as official bodies administering the law.

A simple example of how the impartiality of consumer agencies manifests itself is that when consumer agencies discarded the outdated title 'Weights and Measures Department', a number rejected the designation 'Consumer Protection Department' because this would have indicated bias in favour of the consumer. Instead, the more neutral term 'Trading Standards Department' was adopted, which was said to demonstrate that consumer agencies were really concerned with public protection and not consumer protection in the narrow sense. Businesses, it was said, were part of the public and were entitled to protection along with ordinary consumers. Consumer agencies underline their impartiality in differentiating themselves from other bodies which purport to act in the interests of consumers. Referring to the American consumer movement and its most famous advocate, Ralph Nader, an enforcement officer said:

We don't see ourselves as the British version of Nader's Raiders. But we do see ourselves as standard bearers – Trading Standards bearers – committed to the continuing task of ensuring those standards are respected and neither flouted or eroded. Unlike Mr. Nader we don't see ourselves wholly involved in taking sides in a fight. We know from

experience that we are not best employed fighting battles for or with
consumers, although we do this every day. We are best employed in
ensuring that consumers enjoy the benefits of fair trading and so have
nothing to fight about.[14]

The enthusiasm of these other bodies for consumer protection is therefore
not always a matter for congratulation because it indicates a lack of
balance and professionalism. The attitude of many enforcement officers
towards local voluntary consumer groups is indicated by the remark of one
enforcement officer that they are 'amateur do-gooders', and of another
that they comprise 'some very odd people . . . young intellectuals and
housewives with children who can't get a job, or who have so much money
that they don't know what to do'. Their bias is said to be damaging when it
comes to resolving complaints. When they take up a complaint on behalf of
their members they adopt an aggressive approach which complicates
matters. 'We attempt to reestablish some sort of relationship with the
trade. We achieve redress but in a more professional way,' said an
enforcement officer, contrasting the approach of consumer agencies with
that of consumer groups. Also resented are consumer programmes on the
mass media, which are said so to distort consumer law that it causes
consumers to make unreasonable demands on businesses and on consumer
agencies to press their claims.

THE ROLE OF ADVISER TO BUSINESS AND ITS CONSEQUENCES

Consumer agencies have long eschewed the role of industrial policemen in
favour of advising businesses about compliance with their legal obligations. As advisers to commerce and industry, enforcement officers see
themselves not as policemen whose sole duty it is to detect offences, but as
officials who must prevent them before they occur. Compliance with the
law can therefore be assured without the necessity for prosecution. A
former chief officer noted in a textbook that the enforcement officer is no
longer solely identified as the 'policeman' with primitive power at his
command, but rather as an adviser of the trader, and the guide, counsellor,
and friend of the purchaser.[15] What advice to business actually involves is
sketched out in the following extract from a local handbook produced by a
consumer agency under the sub-heading: 'A Service to Commerce and
Industry': 'We can check and advise on labelling, quality and quantity
control, and the steps to be taken to make full use of the statutory defences
contained in the various Acts we are responsible for.' Advice is said to avoid
considerable inconvenience to businesses; for example, they are not
involved in the expense of relabelling products after infringements are
detected. Advice is perceived as indispensable to businesses when the law is
complicated and obedience is not a straightforward matter. Moreover,
consumer agencies claim to be furthering commercial development by the

advice they provide. Not only does it foster the conditions of fair competition, but it encourages the adoption of procedures which involve less wastage and improved standards.

The advisory role draws support from the typification which consumer agencies have of business – which I deal with below – that they are fundamentally law-abiding. In this view, infringements are rarely intentional or grossly negligent, but rather understandable lapses resulting from the pressure of competition or the carelessness of employees. The assumption is that a business is willing to remedy any infringements if advised about the situation. The typification leads to the differentiation of consumer infringements from ordinary crime; the former are mainly accidental while the latter are committed intentionally. If unlawful behaviour is beyond an offender's control there seems less justification for legal proceedings and the argument is also strengthened that deterrence is better effectuated by advice. Legal proceedings instituted by the police are sharply distinguished by consumer agencies from those that they undertake. Whereas the former are an expression of community outrage and a source of deterrence for the community as a whole, the latter are a last resort when counselling a particular business has failed.

The tendency to enforce the law by advising industry is symptomatic of, and a contributing factor to, the accommodation which develops between consumer agencies and business. This consists in part of an identification with the interests of business. An illustration is provided by the remarks of an assistant chief officer about food manufacturers. 'We're not on opposite sides of the fence; we're on the same side. We both want the same thing – the offering of food in a proper state. That's what we want and that's what they want.' The accommodation between consumer agencies and business is characterised by a reciprocity of benefit. Businesses are shielded from the full force of the law since the tendency is for them to receive advice rather than to be prosecuted when wrongdoing occurs. In the absence of this approach, business might find it more difficult to avoid breaches of the law and would certainly incur greater costs from prosecution. Because the hostility of consumer agencies would be at least an irritant and perhaps a serious threat, business uses various ploys to retain their favour. Consumer agencies are praised for the understanding and the tolerance with which they administer consumer legislation and present consumer complaints. An example is the following editorial in a trade magazine:

> Our purpose here is twofold: It is to praise an often maligned body which is working in the consumer's and the trade's interest. These are the people who give a trade true standards – it isn't just competition that does this! Second: to point out that if it were not for the understanding of these thousands of inspectors the Trade Descriptions Act would result in an even bigger mess.[16]

Consumer agencies are invited individually and collectively through the professional association of enforcement officers to confer with business about its problems and to visit manufacturing and retail premises to see at first hand the difficulties of endeavouring to keep within the terms of the law. Guest speakers from business are available for seminars and conferences arranged by consumer officers. Unlike the Association of Environmental Health Inspectors, however, the professional association of consumer enforcement officers has always excluded businessmen from its membership. It was because scale-makers were admitted to the British Association of Inspectors of Weights and Measures in the 1890s that the present professional association was founded.

On the other hand, consumer agencies benefit from and in fact are dependent on the goodwill of business. A policy of advising industry is not as demanding on resources when compared with instituting legal proceedings. The tasks of consumer agencies are more easily performed because the relationship with business is ·co-operative rather than antagonistic. Consumer agencies avoid the resistance which would develop if they prosecuted every infringement. In their daily contacts, consumer officers approach businessmen in a style designed to blunt the edges of conflict. Its general character is respectful and, even in the case of wrongdoing, businessmen are not exposed to harrassment or unnecessarily embarrassed in public.

The self-appointed role of adviser to business is only one factor, however, in the accommodation between consumer agencies and business. Another factor is the imbalance between the consumer's interest and the commercial world. Whereas the consumer interest is fragmented and under-represented, business has the resources, expertise and organisation and thus a greater impact on consumer agencies.[17] The disparity in strength between consumer agencies and business is a third factor which leads the former to adopt a stance which is not overly hostile to the latter. The total expenditure on consumer agencies in England and Wales in 1974/75 was £13·3 million, while consumer protection staff in that period comprised 3400 persons.[18] By contrast, there are some ½ million retail premises – quite apart from manufacturers – whose activities fall within the ambit of the functions of consumer agencies, with an annual volume of sales of about £5000 million, and employing over 2½ million people.

However, accommodation with business has not developed to the same degree as in the regulatory agencies of the United States. A theme of the American literature on administrative law is that the regulatory agencies there were 'captured', and their proper role perverted, by becoming too closely wedded to the business interests they were designed to control.[19] The agencies were vulnerable because they had become inert and complacent over the years. Because of insufficient resources they had had to rely on the co-operation and assistance of business, but in so doing they became dependent on it. Moreover, the regulated industries actually

engaged in subverting the agencies to transform them into bodies devoted
to their interests. Since they could not afford to have the agencies hostile to
them, they deliberately set out to influence them through public relations,
lobbying, and by the appointment of regulatory staff to the regulated
industries.

How the advisory role leads to an accommodation with business is
illustrated by the task that some consumer agencies perform in advising
manufacturers on acceptable quality control systems. Enforcement officers
inspect manufacturing premises and use statistical methods to calculate
whether items being produced comply with consumer legislation. Agencies
never prosecute as a result of these programmes, although statutory
infringements are detected. The very nature of the advisory role explains
why this should be so: prosecution would jeopardise the rapport essential if
businesses are to adopt any recommendations of the surveys. A memorandum by the chief officer of Metropolitan County, regarding its product
surveys, noted: 'It would have been difficult to expect negotiations to be
carried on with business, with a view to raising their quality control levels,
in the event that they were threatened with prosecution.' Advice along
these lines leads to a close identification with the interests of local
manufacturers. In several consumer agencies I visited, there was clear
resentment that another agency had successfully prosecuted a local
manufacturer whose quality control had been approved by the local
agency. The argument was advanced, almost vehemently, that the other
agencies did not appreciate the problems facing the particular manufacturer, since they did not have first-hand experience. In one case, an agency
actually advised a local manufacturer to defend a prosecution, and
suggested the outline of what proved to be a successful defence. In another
case, the agency suggested steps that the manufacturer could take to avoid
future prosecutions of a similar nature. Just how effective such advisory
programmes are is open to question. Publicly, business welcomes them, but
enforcement officers are sometimes sceptical of this response and claim that
business will not introduce reforms unless there are adverse consequences
in not doing so. A chief officer, whose department is deeply involved in
product surveys, conceded that the reaction of many manufacturers was
one of 'amused tolerance' until such time as comparative testing was
involved, with the possibility that a particular product would be publicly
recommended by the agency.

III THE DEPICTIONS OF BUSINESSES AND CONSUMERS

People need perceptual shorthand systems to give meaning to the everyday
world. Life is so complex that it must be simplified if problems are to be
managed in a relatively uneventful way. Situations are frequently
ambiguous, and assistance is needed if judgements are to be reduced to a

number of elementary steps. An aspect of how consumer agencies simplify and stabilise the commercial world is their evolution of typifications.

Sociolgists have noted the use of typifications among numerous occupations. Typifications are of great interest because they assume importance in how people go about their tasks. There is some dispute, however, about how influential typifications are in explaining the response of particular persons on particular occasions. For some sociologists, typifications become overriding in the actions of individuals, while for others they are no more than man-made constructs which change in the light of a person's constant interaction with the real world.

THE TYPIFICATIONS OF BUSINESSES

In the view of consumer agencies, businesses fall into two basic categories, the reputable and the unscrupulous, with the latter a small minority of businesses in identifiable spheres of commercial activity. Businesses assigned to these different categories are endowed with characteristics – which I shall examine shortly – such as the extent to which they comply with the letter and spirit of consumer law. Because the commercial world is simplified in the typifications, a consumer agency can interact with a particular business in an unimportant encounter without a great concern for its individuality. The typification enables the agency to impute stock features to the business.

The typifications are widely shared in consumer agencies. Their formation is not an artifical construct of reasoning or personal prejudice but largely the outcome of pragmatic induction. Experience informs consumer agencies that certain businesses produce more infringements and complaints than others, or that they are recalcitrant and indifferent when it comes to complying with their legal obligations.[20] On this basis they are allocated to the different categories. Although grounded in experience, typifications develop some autonomy. On occasions, there is a tendency to accept them without an extensive effort to investigate whether they really apply. The inclination is to elicit only the information which supports the preconceived typification. Information at variance with it is ignored, and in this way it becomes self-fulfilling.[21] With unscrupulous businesses, the typification tends to retain its validity unless there are exceptional circumstances. In most cases, however, consumer officers use a typification as a preliminary hypothesis and retain or reject it on the basis of further investigation. The majority of businesses are assumed to be reputable but, as we shall see, they can be recast as an agency gains knowledge of their trading practices. The context also determines the precision with which a typification is applied. Where an infringement is dealt with informally, the dimensions of a situation are left largely unexplored. The consumer officer is unable to investigate how well the typification fits the business and it undergoes little variation in being applied.

The typifications that businesses are predominantly honest and that the unscrupulous are the exception, draws sustenance from the publicly expressed views of those in government and from others like academics. Typical of the views held by government officials is that contained in a Ministerial speech on the introduction to Parliament of what became the Fair Trading Act (1973):

> The purpose of Part III is to create a climate in which the overwhelming majority of traders, who deal fairly with the public, can continue to flourish without interference and in which the minority of traders, who maintain an unhelpful attitude to the justified complaints by consumers, will see sense and, in the end, the necessity of mending their ways and improving their standards.[22]

Even some of those in the consumer movement accept this division of the commercial world. This contracts with the view of the American consumer movement, which attacks as a myth cultivated by business the notion that consumer problems only arise because a small number of unscrupulous businesses pollute the general commercial environment. The American consumer movement argues that large, ostensibly reputable, businesses sometimes support unscrupulous firms behind the scenes and that they directly engage in practices which prejudice consumers.[23]

Whatever the intention of government officials – or for that matter of consumer agencies – this portrayal of business facilitates the process of regulation. Since the state has inadequate resources rigidly to discipline business, it antagonises it at the risk of undermining its own capacity to influence business behaviour. If business were publicly labelled as unscrupulous or exploitive, its resistance to regulation would increase. By emphasising that business is mainly law-abiding, the state and its enforcement agencies can reduce the fear of regulation and maximise the potentiality of obtaining compliance with their designs through persuasion. Business may even be induced to conform to the portrayal of itself as law-abiding. A similar process is involved when new legislation is depicted as simply an amplification of existing principles or the implementation of existing practice. However, the assumption that the majority of businesses are honest – in so far as it is incorrect – deflects efforts away from regulating certain prejudicial trade practices. It thus has a protective function for the business community, because it focuses attention on a small number of deviant businesses and not on the system itself.

As stated, a fundamental perception of consumer agencies, and one constantly reiterated in their documentation, is that most businesses are honest and reputable and go to extreme lengths to ensure that they comply with legal requirements. Large manufacturers, packers, wholesalers and retailers accept their obligations and conscientiously attempt to attain the highest standards. Law, it is said, is virtually superfluous for most businesses, for their sense of social responsibility ensures that they pursue fair trading practices. If new legislation is introduced, the majority quickly bring their products and practices into line. The most potent influence in favour of the consumer is the desire of business to preserve its reputation and to retain customers. Infringements, the argument continues, arise not from an intention to deceive, but because of technical error or employee carelessness. With the more esoteric consumer legislation, businesses also fall foul of the law because of ignorance. Incompetence sometimes enters, whether it be a national organisation or a local firm. In Blankshire, a local businessman with several stores needed the constant attention of the consumer agency because of what it regarded as his poor management. An enforcement officer remarked:

> Mr [ ] is not fraudulent, but he is the sort of trader who becomes careless if you don't keep at him. You prosecute and he does well for a time, but then he winds down again; he couldn't care, and becomes careless.

Legislation and its enforcement are claimed to be in the interests of reputable businesses; they provide legal protection against unfair competition and their absence creates opportunities for the unscrupulous. Voluntary trade control is ineffective in this respect for the unscrupulous are not members of trade associations and neither do they subscribe to voluntary codes of practice. Legislation is not irrelevant to the activities of the honest majority either, for it still provides an incentive for them to aim at higher standards. Precisely because reputable firms conscientiously observe high standards, consumer agencies argue that they should welcome legislation as a confirmation of the spirit, if not the letter, of existing practices.

Unscrupulous businesses are clearly identified by consumer agencies, for specific trades are stereotyped in this way. As has already been mentioned, of prime importance are secondhand-car dealers, but also included are coalmen, market traders, one-day salesmen and door-to-door salesmen. Not all members of these trades are branded as unscrupulous, but the burden is on individual members to demonstrate positively that they are not of this nature. The manner in which characteristics are automatically ascribed to members of an unscrupulous trade is illustrated in these typical statements by two enforcement officers about secondhand-car dealers. 'How do I know—is a crook? He's a car dealer, isn't he?.' 'Car dealers accept that [prosecution is a] hazard of the profession; 60 per cent are rogues. I haven't met an honest one yet.' Unscrupulous businesses are not necessarily dishonest although this tends to be the case. They are sometimes said to have a natural propensity to dishonesty. An assistant chief officer commented in this context: 'There are some people – if they could earn £100 honestly and £101 dishonestly they would be bound by their very nature to choose the latter.' Another view is that unscrupulous businesses are so aggressive in their pursuit of profits that they consider it irrelevant whether or not they break the law. Even when their failure to take precautions to prevent offences does not constitute intentional wrongdoing, consumer agencies argue that it arises from their recognition that it is better to know little about the law and the products and services they market. Enforcement officers concede that some businesses in the unscrupulous trades may not commit many offences but add that often their commercial practices cause others to do so. For example, consumer agencies claim that although larger car dealers may not commit many criminal offences they bear a major responsibility for the activities of dishonest secondhand-car dealers, for whom they act as a source of supply of unsound cars.

Labelling the trades I have mentioned as unscrupulous is facilitated by a number of factors. First, their unlawful activity is akin to traditional crime because it often involves dishonesty; indeed, it not infrequently could support an ordinary criminal charge. In such cases, it is not surprising that consumer agencies describe the practices of these businesses in the terms used in the criminal law. For example, the practice of secondhand-car dealers of reducing the reading of car odometers is depicted in conversation by consumer officers as 'fraud' and 'criminal deception'. Another influence on consumer agencies is that those engaged in these trades sometimes have criminal records for activities divorced from their businesses. A standard joke among enforcement officers in some parts of Metropolitan County is that in the past coalmen were recruited at the gates of the local prison because, as a high employment area, this was one of the few sources of labour for coal merchants. At least five of the car dealers prosecuted in Metropolitan County under the Trade Descriptions Act (1968) over the five-year period immediately preceeding the field work had convictions for offences involving fraud, theft or violence. Enforcement officers in Metropolitan County engaged in these prosecutions argue that for these people the secondhand-car trade provides a haven from police harass-ment and an opportunity to accrue quick profits relatively easily. The association of unscrupulous businessmen with traditional crime is highlig-hted in a report prepared by an enforcement officer in Metropolitan County:

> There is a hard core of unscrupulous car dealers operating in [Metropolitan County], many of them with criminal records, whose continuing activities cause untold hardship to those consumers unfor-tunate enough to fall into their clutches, and who bring into disrepute the whole of the used car trade. They hide their identities behind the façades of £100 companies which are changed at intervals, to avoid

paying their creditors, and move about the area from site to site, interchanging their staff regularly. Their salesmen are skilled liars and dissimilators, promising everything to make a sale to a prospective customer, and willing to use violence afterwards to persistent complainants.

A second factor is that businesses in the unscrupulous trades have been heavily prosecuted by consumer agencies. The coal trade has always been a target for enforcement activity, and secondhand-car dealers have been a central concern of consumer agencies from the inception of the Trade Descriptions Act (1968). In the *Prosecution Survey*, secondhand-car dealers ranked second in terms of the absolute number of prosecutions. In focusing on these areas, consumer agencies obviously produce a crime rate justifying their activity. If they turned to other commercial practices they might reveal comparable levels of wrongdoing. At the same time, there is independent support for concentrating on some of these trades because of the number of consumer complaints. For example, the great majority of prosecutions involving secondhand-car dealers arise from complaint. But not all the unscrupulous trades are heavily prosecuted; for example, one-day salesmen and door-to-door salesmen constituted only 5 out of a total of 791 prosecutions in the *Prosecution Survey* and consequently, the way they are typified must be derived from other factors. Another point is that trade practices which are highly prejudicial to consumers are not always clearly illegal under existing law. Objectionable but legal sharp practices obviously escape censure and consumer agencies are confined to prosecuting their perpetrators for incidental, if minor, offences.

Third, unscrupulous businesses are generally of a marginal nature. The experience of consumer agencies is that a number accumulate quick profits and then disappear leaving dissatisfied consumers. Businesses in the unscrupulous trades are usually small in size and frequently occupy shabby premises in the less salubrious areas of cities. For example, a prospective secondhand-car dealer needs only to rent an uncovered allotment and to stock a few relatively inexpensive cars with which to begin trading operations for finance companies to readily provide him with credit facilities. Little technical skill is required, for emphasis is on the appearance of the cars and not on their mechanical reliability. The small size of unscrupulous businesses is significant, because it is possible to personalise wrongdoing and to attribute it directly to the individual businessmen behind small firms. On the other hand, the intentional wrongdoing of individuals is not easily located in the organisational structure of larger businesses, except where it can be linked directly to the activities of the directors. Interestingly, enforcement officers attribute the policies of some national firms with unsavoury reputations – but which are not regarded as unscrupulous – to the persons identified in the public mind as their leading lights. The remark about one national supermarket, repeated in substance on several occasions, was that its founders 'started as barrow boys and still have a barrow-boy mentality'.

The impact of the trade practices of unscrupulous businesses is a final factor leading to the unfavourable typification drawn by consumer agencies. This is simply the fact that the fraud of unscrupulous businesses bears heavily on vulnerable sections of the population. For example, the less affluent are the most likely victims of dubious door-to-door salesmen and as a result become entangled with burdensome credit obligations. Consumer officers are also of the view that the less affluent are attracted by schemes such as one-day sales – in which a hall or hotel is hired for a short period and a sale conducted along the lines of an auction – which are regarded as entertainment and as a source of cheaper items. Consumers who purchase the shoddy goods sold in this manner because they succumb to audience manipulation have no recourse when the operators leave the area. Consumers purchasing secondhand-cars can be considerably prejudiced if the cars prove to be unsound. Particular difficulties arise for less affluent car buyers, who buy the cheaper but more fault-prone secondhand-cars.

As I have mentioned, consumer agencies assume that businesses are basically honest apart from the unscrupulous. But the reputation of businesses falling into the 'honest majority' category is tarnished when they engage in practices which, while not necessarily dishonest, at least display an indifference to their legal and moral obligations. The practices which consumer agencies find relevant in making a judgement about a national business usually revolve around the quality of their goods and services and the nature of their marketing techniques. Many mass-produced products are of an inferior standard, which is said to occur not simply for technical or economic reasons, but also because some firms are too concerned with profit-making or are in a monopoly position. Too frequently when consumers complain about such products, businesses refuse to take any action. Sometimes marketing techniques 'sail close to the wind' – to use a popular phrase of consumer agencies. Advertising often deflects public attention from the real quality of goods and services because it is cleverly phrased or even misleading. The Annual Report of a consumer agency noted:

One has, however, occasionally seen a newspaper advertisement inserted by a substantial firm, which gave the impression that a considerable amount of time and ingenuity had gone towards drafting it in terms which, though in accordance with the letter of the law, paid little regard to its spirit.

Additional factors have a bearing with smaller businesses or with the different branches of national businesses – for the reputation of national businesses is not necessarily the same throughout the country. The attitude of those business personnel with which consumer officers come in contact is important; for example, evasiveness on their part is likely to lead to an unfavourable inference being drawn. This is illustrated in the statement of an advice officer: 'I asked [the retailer] what his honest opinion of the carpet was and he hummed and hawed and finally said: "It's all right", so it sounded dodgy.' The general appearance of business premises is often indicative: untidiness hints at carelessness and a casual attitude to legal requirements. If a number of breaches of law are involved, consumer officers are inclined to conclude that what is involved is intentional wrongdoing rather than a mistake. As an enforcement officer commented with respect to secondhand cars which are discovered with altered odometers: 'One can be an accident, two can be a coincidence, but when there are three, something is wrong.'

The reputation of a business takes specific shape for consumer agencies in its prosecution record and the number of complaints that consumers make about it. The isolated offence will usually be ignored, but the view of an agency will be revised if lapses are more regular. The absolute number of offences is not crucial, however, and allowances are made for both the size of a business and the nature of the offence. A number of minor deficiencies over a period can be cumulated if they are symptomatic of basic wrongdoing. Perpetrators of legal but highly prejudicial trade practices will not retain a 'reputable' image with consumer agencies. Businesses acquitted by the courts can still be branded as undesirable if they remain morally responsible in the eyes of consumer officers. An example is businesses which manage to escape legal liability by using the statutory defences to blame their staff. There is clear resentment against businesses which adopt marketing techniques which must give rise to offences because they are administered by poorly paid and inexperienced junior staff. Several agencies even allege that the marketing practices of some businesses virtually force their staff into committing offences – as this extract from the annual report of a consumer agency indicates:

> Some supermarkets for example, give their managers an allowance for 'shrinkage', i.e. customer or staff pilferage and other losses. In such cases, in order to balance his books and thereby stay in his job, the manager is forced to practice 'price bunching' by indicating a lower price and charging a higher price on goods, the difference helping to balance his accounts. Those companies who give no allowance, and yet use the defences are, in my opinion, those who trade on the very borderline of the written law and might well be considered by some to be over the moral line:

Since becoming involved in consumer advice work, consumer agencies have used complaints as another dimension of reputation. Firms which are the source of a substantial volume of complaints, and which fail to settle them amicably, are adversely typified. Another factor is the ease with which consumer officers can obtain satisfaction for consumers. Because the volume of work prevents consumer agencies from giving detailed attention to the nature of complaints, the image that consumer officers have is often founded on whether they face resistance when they present consumers' complaints to businesses. A typification can therefore be based on a standard which is more onerous than that embodied in consumer law.

CONSUMERS, COMPLAINTS AND THE EFFECT OF AGENCY DEPICTIONS

A London Consumer Advice Centre claims in a public relations brochure that enquiries from consumers bring to light 'instances of desperate need, absolute frustration, idle curiosity, nagging uncertainty and complete ignorance of available assistance'. But if consumer enquiries are so wide-ranging, consumer officers have developed stock depictions of how complaints about businesses arise and of the type of consumers who complain. These interpretations function to reduce the ambiguity inherent in their everyday activity and to guide them as they handle complaints. The depictions are more varied than the typifications of businesses and less compelling for the outcome of particular enquiries. Consumer officers use them flexibly and are prepared to modify their approach when the evidence suggests that they are largely irrelevant.

In the opinion of consumer agencies, a substantial body of complaints arises because consumers fail to take the necessary precautions before entering transactions. Many grievances could be easily avoided if consumers were circumspect in their dealings – all the more so when considerable expense is involved. The annual report of one consumer agency noted:

> On some occasions it becomes obvious, as a caller's story unfolds, that the cause of the complaint is really the purchaser's haste or ill choice in buying the goods in question. Whilst every officer in the department will listen with sympathy to such stories and perhaps suggest a solution, it still behoves the purchasing public to buy wisely – 'caveat emptor' should perhaps head every shopping list.

According to consumer officers, legislation cannot give universal protection and no amount of law can protect consumers from themselves. Many complaints could be avoided if consumers read documents before signature, if they clearly informed businesses about their requirements, if they generally ignored advertising, and if they examined articles before purchase. Consumer officers suppose that the failure of consumers to take elementary precautions and their completion of hasty and ill-considered bargains stem from ignorance and the deficiencies in consumer education: many consumers are unsophisticated and gullible and cannot be expected to protect themselves in all circumstances. But it is conceded that even the most prudent of consumers may be deceived by unscrupulous businesses and that the increasing complexity of consumer products means that few consumers have the knowledge to assess their suitability and quality. Several consumer officers, such as the one now quoted, thought that consumers were also caught in prejudicial transactions because of basic human failings like greed.

> You get this chap with an old banger. It's done him for six or seven years. He takes it into a reputable dealer and they only offer him a few quid. So he takes it to a back-street dealer who says: 'You've got a nice little car there. We'll give you £150 on another one.' The fellow is so pleased that he spends more time on the car that he's selling than on the one he's buying.

A second source of complaints, say consumer agencies, is because ill-feeling which is irrelevant to the matters in dispute develops between consumers and businesses. Consumers adopt an unreasonable approach in bringing problems to the attention of businesses, which are frequently prepared to offer recompense to complainants. Instead of accepting a reasonable solution, consumers will argue the point when they have no legal basis for doing so. Conversely, complaints are also said to arise where a consumer has a justified grievance, which a business fails to resolve after being approached in a reasonable manner. The consumer may take a matter further not so much because he is adamant that an injustice has been perpetrated but simply because of the negative attitude of the business when the matter was broached. The situation is exacerbated in either case, and the parties are so antagonistic that only the intervention of a neutral third party – a consumer officer – will settle the matter. The self-conceived mediatory role for consumer agencies in this type of situation is exemplified in this extract from an annual report:

> 'On occasions, it is found that customer relations have been somewhat strained between seller and buyer as a result of the complaint, and the impartial and tactful approach adopted by the investigating officer enables the matter to be adequately resolved to the ultimate satisfaction of both parties.'

Third, consumer agencies recognise that large numbers of consumers complain in circumstances where they have at least a partial justification. Bad workmanship and faulty goods are the cause of many complaints, which are exacerbated when businesses are in some cases openly indifferent or tardy in rectifying such genuine grievances. Frustration is an additional reason behind complaints, and consumers often contact consumer agencies after despairing of achieving a solution themselves. Many consumers have genuine reasons for believing that they have been prejudiced or misled, but because of the state of the law there is no available remedy.

Little thought is given by consumer agencies to the type of consumers who complain to them. When the question is posed, the stock answer is that the agencies deal with a broad spectrum of citizens. The view that consumers are predominantly from the articulate middle class is firmly rejected, but it is conceded by some that there is this tendency with pre-shopping advice. A sociology graduate, employed as an advice officer in Metropolitan County, summed up the prevailing view:

> I was quite surprised when I first came in. I got snide comments from my friends about helping the articulate middle class to complain. But my eyes have been opened. You get the people on the shop floor, the inarticulate, the working class – although we don't really know who the working class are – those who really need help.

The actual socio-economic background of those contacting consumer agencies is examined in the following chapter.

Although complainants are assumed to be generally representative of the population, they are seen as placing varying demands on consumer agencies. Because of their inadequacies certain consumers, such as the aged or inarticulate, are given additional attention with their problems.[24] Working-class complainants are regarded as quite demanding, but their evaluation hinges on the outcome, and not on the style or apparent expertise of a consumer officer. The articulate professional classes are said to turn to consumer agencies either as a supplement for a claim which they can competently advance or because all avenues have been explored and proved unfruitful. Accordingly, their complaints fall at the extremes: either they are simple or they are intractable. Professional people are also seen as expecting a high standard of competence from consumer agencies. All depictions distort reality, and consumer officers modify their depictions of complainants when a particular individual deviates from what is expected. They realise that the type of consumer is sometimes a misleading indication of the origin and nature of a complaint.

The pressure of work means that consumer officers perceive some of the demands placed on them by complainants as unreasonable. What complainants treat as crucial is regarded as routine by consumer officers. For example, complainants often demand individual attention without realising that an officer has other matters of greater importance: 'You have a bloke there with a complaint. A complainant will think that he is the only man in your life,' said one consumer officer sarcastically. Consumers, it is said, do not appreciate that strong moral grounds are inadequate to base a legal claim, and their frustration rubs off on the agency. They also fail to realise the broader implications of their complaints: their underlying motive is having their own difficulty resolved and not to assist in a basic

cure. Self-interest means that they lose interest if early investigation fails to
produce results or if court proceedings are involved. Like other professionals, consumer officers distance themselves from consumers and
sometimes speak of them disparagingly. Backstage argot has evolved to a
limited extent, and particular types of complaints are labelled as 'sillies'
and particular complainants as 'thickies' or 'nutters'. Cynicism of this
nature functions to prevent consumer officers becoming too involved
personally with consumer problems and from discriminating between
consumers.[25]

The depictions which consumer agencies have of consumers have little
relevance, however, to the mundane contact between the two groups.
Consumer officers distance themselves from complainants but still treat
them civilly and handle their enquiries with diligence.[26] Complainants are
never openly criticised and even the most difficult are treated with tact and
courtesy. Complainants who 'fall to pieces when they get a problem' are
acknowledged to need assistance precisely because of that trait. Professional complainants are rare, but if they approach an agency the
standard practice is to treat them tactfully, both for public relations
reasons and because they may have a genuine complaint. A consumer may
not have taken elementary precautions or may have unreasonable
expectations about a product or service considering the price paid, but if
the complaint is justified it will be handled as any other. In a later chapter,
I shall show in greater depth that whether a complaint is *justified* is crucial
to its processing, but that the *type* of complainant is unimportant when
consumer agencies seek a solution. The one exception is that articulate
consumers – or at least those who continually contact a consumer agency
to enquire as to how their complaint is progressing – are likely to get
priority if there is a backlog, because consumer officers will want to get rid
of a source of annoyance.

Consumer officers are assessed both by their superiors and the public
according to their ability to resolve complaints, and therein lies the
incentive to achieve a satisfactory conclusion regardless, in the main, of the
peculiarities of the complainant. Furthermore, consumer officers can
develop a sense of obligation to consumers while at the same time having a
poor opinion of their competence, as illustrated by what an advice officer
told me:

> It's a peculiar trait of the British, wanting something for nothing instead
> of paying the right amount in the first place. They pay £40 for a car and
> expect a Rolls-Royce. But they come to you in good faith and you feel
> that you have let them down if you do nothing.

In this way, consumer officers see themselves as playing a supportive role
for consumers, and a common remark is that they provide 'a shoulder to
cry on' for those with consumer problems. A complaint may appear trivial

in monetary terms, but a small amount to a consumer officer may be substantial to a complainant. 'You have the little old ladies who are conned – £25 is a lot of money to old people,' said one advice officer. Sympathetic treatment of consumers for whom nothing can be done is recognised as performing a valuable function in winning the good will of the community. Consumers, it is said, go away happier than when they arrived, and the fact that someone has been prepared to listen to a problem and carefully to explain the position removes the sense of helplessness and frustration which is often an integral part of a complaint.

Where the depictions of consumers and their complaints have important repercussions is, first, in the overall direction of agency activity. The assumption that in many cases consumers are to blame means that if they could be educated about consumer matters, problems would be largely eliminated, except that no amount of awareness will protect them from certain malpractices of unscrupulous businesses. A memorandum in Metropolitan County, advocating an extensive programme of consumer education, argued:

> An analysis of consumer complaints received by this department shows that ignorance, carelessness and uncertainty on the part of both trader and shopper is the prime cause of most of the complaints and disputes which arise. The implications of this may seem to be obvious but nonetheless have considerable significance: if traders and the general public could be made more aware of their rights and obligations under civil and criminal law when buying and selling goods or contracting for services then there would be a significant reduction in the number of complaints. It would permit the department's resources to be concentrated on more serious cases, concerning deliberate fraud and deception.

Second, because consumer officers are immersed in the problems of particular consumers, complaints are viewed largely from the level of individual difficulty and not as a deficiency of the system. Consumer officers tend to be unconcerned with whether matters are linked with wider issues and a broader approach to solving consumer complaints has been slow to emerge.[27] The Office of Fair Trading is the first indication of a change in outlook: its rationale is that the satisfaction of individual complainants will not always attack the root of a problem, and steps may have to be taken to improve commercial practices. Businesses which are the cause of numerous complaints have been encouraged to improve the standard of their services, mainly through the introduction of voluntary codes. In addition, the Office of Fair Trading has initiated the process for the issuance of statutory orders and has invoked its cease-and-desist power where the pattern of criminal offences and consumer complaints have indicated that businesses are acting against the interests of consumers.

A third point is that, because consumer agencies assume that they cover a wide section of the population, they do not give close attention to those who, for various reasons, do not complain. Passivity is the outstanding feature of consumer agencies in relation to consumers. Consumer enquiries are handled once they reach consumer agencies, but little effort is made to extend the service to segments of the population who may not obtain access. As an example, few consumer officers recognise a need for special efforts to reach poorer consumers. The idea of Consumer Advice Centres, to widen the base of consumer advice to the less affluent, originated from outside consumer agencies. When consumer agencies concede that there are gaps in their coverage, this is not necessarily regarded as a matter of concern. Relatively few consumers in rural areas complain, but consumer officers do not interpret this as their ignorance of consumer agencies or their difficulty in obtaining access, but assume that rural people are more independent, can resolve complaints on their own initiative, and find it unnecessary to invoke the assistance of consumer agencies. Another argument is that even if certain consumers do not complain they are being protected by the enforcement work engaged in by consumer agencies on their own initiative. For example, food-sampling programmes cover a wide selection of basic foods consumed by average members of the public. Indeed, some consumer officers attack the excessive preoccupation with assisting consumers as going too far and creating an unhealthy dependency on the part of the public. They warn against the dangers of creating a consumer neurosis, in which every transaction is regarded with mutual suspicion, and that the more that official bodies do for consumers, the less careful they become. Clearly such attitudes are not conducive to special efforts being made to extend the ambit of consumer agencies.

IV THE RELATION OF CONSUMER AGENCIES TO OTHER LEGAL INSTITUTIONS

Links which consumer agencies have with other legal institutions obviously influence the tenor of their operation. Parliament and the courts are the two organisations which have particular salience for the activities of consumer agencies. Consumer agencies, Parliament, and the courts interact in a reciprocal manner, and the discretionary decisions of each affect those of the other two. By enacting consumer legislation in certain ways, Parliament can narrow the discretion of consumer agencies. It can also amend laws which in its view are wrongly interpreted by the courts. Depending on the form of a law, consumer agencies may have discretion to interpret and apply it in the light of their perceptions and policies. Consumer agencies may modify the original aims of the law through enforcement. When consumer agencies institute proceedings for what they consider to be a breach of legislation, the courts are in a position to rule on the validity of that action and can also restrict the operation of the original law as passed by Parliament. But the operation of consumer agencies in detecting and disposing of wrongdoing regulates the input of consumer matters to the courts. To the extent that consumer agencies caution businesses for offences, instead of prosecuting them, the courts are deprived of an opportunity of assessing business behaviour. Not only are the courts unable to evaluate its legality, but they cannot pass judgement on any moral fault involved, either by judicial comment or by the extent of the punishment imposed. When consumer agencies exercise their discretion and matters are not pressed to prosecution, the courts are powerless. In the absence of any organisational control over the discretion of consumer agencies, courts cannot exercise direct control until cases enter the judicial process. They have no formal organisation to enforce their views and can only hope that consumer agencies will heed what they have expressed on other occasions.

THE CRITIQUE OF PARLIAMENTARY EFFORTS

In framing consumer legislation, Parliament obviously regards certain behaviour as prejudicial to consumers. To the extent that consumer agencies evolve a different view of prejudicial behaviour, and act on it, the goals of Parliament are undermined. Generally speaking, consumer officers do not dispute the value for the community of the legislation which they administer. They agree that existing legislation covers a wide area of undesirable business behaviour and provides considerable protection for both the public and reputable businesses. The mere enactment of legislation, they concede, has a deterrent effect on many businesses. With legislation that proves to be inadequate, consumer officers point out that they can easily make representations to the government about its amendment. The channels of communication are well-established and there is no need for a vigorous public relations campaign to draw attention to any defects.

Despite a general satisfaction with consumer law and the attention which the policy-makers give to their opinions about its amendment, consumer officers make specific recommendations for changes along a number of lines. Their motivation for doing this is threefold: first, certain legislative changes would facilitate the performance of their tasks; second, their prestige would increase if they were given additional responsibilities; and third, reforming the law in certain ways would further the goal of protecting consumers. Penalties in criminal legislation are one source of dissatisfaction, for it is said that they are too small to discourage unscrupulous businesses from committing offences. Legislation is some-times criticised for being ineffective and for complicating enforcement. Attention is drawn to the sections of the Trade Descriptions Act (1968) which regulate prices and services as being unduly weak and exempting important areas of undesirable trading activity. The defence provisions in consumer legislation are subject to attack for limiting the prospects of successful legal action in cases where punishment is justified. Consumer officers also suggest that the general coverage of consumer legislation should be extended to some consumer transactions which are unregulated. For example, prices could be more strongly controlled, since they are a basic cause of consumer dissatisfaction, and fuller and more relevant information could be made available to consumers to enable them to assess value and to make meaningful comparisons between rival products. The feeling of some consumer officers is especially intense because they perceive deliberate and unnecessary shackles on their powers. A particular source of dissatisfaction is the low penalty for obstructing consumer officers in the course of their duty, which is said to hamper investigations because unscrupulous businesses find it worthwhile to give false information in an effort to avoid prosecution. The paltriness of that penalty is contrasted with the harsh penalties for consumer officers who disclose information acquired in the course of their duty, even to other law-enforcement agencies in an effort to eliminate business malpractice. Among consumer officers, such deficiencies in consumer legislation are not simply attributed to drafting errors or to the ignorance of the draftsmen about the practical implications of their work. In addition, consumer officers contend that inadequate legislation can be intentional. Powerful lobbies secure the ear of government Departments, and Parliament is influenced by business interests. By contrast, consumers are not strongly represented when legislation is drafted and consequently their interests are less well protected.

THE ATTITUDE TO THE COURTS

It should not be surprising that there is a degree of friction between consumer agencies and the courts. The courts sometimes construe consumer legislation so that businesses escape sanction. Occasionally this is because the courts use the doctrine of *caveat emptor* as a guiding principle, but in the main it arises when they interpret consumer law according to the same strict principles as used with the ordinary criminal law. The courts adopt this approach without being concerned with whether it is appropriate to treat business crime as equivalent to ordinary crime. By contrast, consumer agencies have little truck with broad-ranging principles and concentrate on punishing businesses which they think are guilty of behaviour prejudicial to consumers. A decision by a court not to convict a business which is prosecuted is not only personally frustrating for consumer officers but in their view also undermines their capacity to control unlawful behaviour. The attitude of the courts can lead to the apparent paradox where consumer officers may strongly favour punishment of a business which they think is guilty of wrongdoing, but be less than willing to institute a prosecution. Although the courts alone are capable of imposing an enforceable sanction, consumer officers may prefer to rely on other means of enforcement such as cautions because consumer officers perceive the courts as being hostile. Apart from the punishment that they can institute in the criminal courts, however, consumer agencies lack strong sanctions to control businesses.

The prejudices which consumer officers have against the judicial system are buttressed by the belief that their own skill and knowledge is superior to that of the courts.[28] Long usage and previous practice convince them that their interpretation of consumer law is correct and that they can better divine Parliamentary intention. Some judicial decisions are said to deprive consumers of the protection intended by Parliament or the result of action by consumer agencies. Business is seen as only too ready to exploit a favourable decision to its advantage, which causes the spread of practices prejudicial to consumers. Consumer officers therefore juxtapose them-selves – practical people enforcing the law and assisting the public – to the judiciary, which is portrayed as being remote from the real world of business malpractice. Associated with this point are allegations that the courts are unconcerned with the practical difficulties of enforcing the law and do not interpret it to facilitate its implementation. The courts are accused of operating on the basis of inadequate knowledge and abstract principles so that they cannot evaluate the seriousness of infringements. Consumer officers emphasise that they would never assume the arduous burden of a prosecution if they did not know that a business was guilty of wrongdoing. Commenting on a Crown Court hearing, in which a conviction was quashed, an enforcement officer expressed resentment at the manner in which his motives were misinterpreted and his word doubted: 'The learned judge chose not to believe me rather than that rat. I don't go to court to lie. If I don't get the evidence I don't go to court. It makes me sick to think about it.' Further, consumer officers argue that they take mitigating factors into account in their decisions to prosecute. The record of a firm is closely scrutinised and other relevant matters examined such as whether a firm is genuinely ignorant of the law. For this reason it would be a mistake to characterise consumer agencies as punitive and the courts as lenient, since consumer agencies decide – albeit at an earlier stage – whether leniency is deserved.[29]

The criticism of magistrates courts takes various forms. At its strongest, allegations of bias have been levelled against magistrates; either they are subject to local influences or are recruited from the trading community. Comments of this nature are unusual today, however, and as put by enforcement officers refer only to occasional lapses in rural areas. More common is the accusation that magistrates, if not incompetent, are at least deficient in the knowledge essential for the proper discharge of their duties. Magistrates are said to impose fines without knowing the maximum that can be imposed and generally to display an ignorance of the rudimentary principles of consumer law. No doubt such a view is strengthened by incidents similiar to one I observed in Metropolitan County where, following a hearing in a magistrates court, the clerk to the court admitted in private discussion with enforcement officers that the justices had been quite incorrect in dismissing one of the charges. It is also said that magistrates can be intimidated by defence counsel, but this cuts both ways. The chief officer of a consumer agency in a rural area characterised the attitude of country magistrates when a business employs a barrister to defend a prosecution: 'The magistrates might be frightened out of their wits. "We can't convict in case they might appeal." But the more prevalent attitude is: "Ay, they must be bloody guilty to bring someone down like this."'

A constant complaint of consumer agencies has been that the level of fines imposed by magistrates is too low to provide an adequate deterrent. A view of a number of enforcement officers, including several ex-policemen, is that they are not accepted by the courts to the same extent as the police. Magistrates still perceive them as weights and measures departments, and the level of fines imposed are appropriate to weights and measures offences and not to the serious nature of modern consumer offences. Consumer agencies appreciate that to some extent Parliament is at fault in fixing maximum penalties which are inadequate. Magistrates cannot be blamed for imposing small fines or for thinking that the offences are trivial if the statutory penalties are low. Granted this, it is still argued that magistrates have a certain responsibility because the fines they impose are often a small fraction of the maximum permitted. Condemnation of the fines imposed is not universal, however. Sometimes enforcement officers explain their satisfaction because of the rapport which has been established with the local magistrates court: the magistrates realise that the agencies prosecute only in serious cases and they impose penalties commensurate with the circumstances. Significantly, such expressions of satisfaction do not relate to specific cases and are usually the opinion of senior officers. The variation between different benches of magistrates is another reason for the frustration of enforcement officers. While some are 'fair' in the penalties they impose, others are said to have no inkling of the seriousness of consumer offences.

With higher courts, the cleavage between the judiciary and consumer agencies widens. Magistrates courts have limited control over consumer agencies because the decisions of one court are not binding on another; but the decisions of higher courts have a wider effect because of their precedent value. Over the years, enforcement officers have responded irately to a number of High Court decisions. The main cause of complaint is that decisions do not accord with the realities of the commercial world. Sometimes the criticism goes beyond individual cases to include the method of judicial decision-making.[30] The accretion of case law is objected to because it complicates matters unnecessarily; makes it difficult for hard-pressed and under-financed consumer agencies to determine the solution to particular problems; and enables the clever lawyers employed by business to find loopholes for their clients. The wide criticism of judicial review has even led to suggestions that the courts should be excluded from the interpretation of consumer legislation, and that an alternative but less expensive forum be established for resolving conflicts. Consumer agencies are not invariably hostile to the judiciary or to their decisions, however, and individual decisions have been welcomed as an aid to consumer agencies in their work. Difficulties which are initially thought to be associated with a case do not materialise. On balance, consumer agencies concede that the totality of judicial decisions may be neither favourable nor unfavourable to the consumer. However, unfavourable decisions provoke lengthier comment and therefore the attitude of consumer agencies to the higher courts appears to be characterised by hostility.

3 Consumer Complaints, Agency Initiative and the Enforcement Process

The enforcement of the law is problematic. If an infringement of a legal rule occurs, it does not follow that the violator will be penalised automatically – someone must take the initiative and activate the legal process.[1] Basically, a legal system acquires its cases in two ways, through complaint, or through its own initiative.[2] Although the entrepreneurial role of citizens is most obvious in the civil law, where they must initiate legal proceedings, it is of inestimable importance for agencies enforcing the criminal law. Studies of the police have demonstrated that except for a few areas, such as the work of vice squads or traffic patrols, the criminal law is largely activated by complaint. Enforcement agencies initiate action against wrongdoers but also rely on citizens who assist in enforcing the law by either complaining or by being witnesses to criminal offences. In addition, citizens are involved in the law-enforcement process when they complain about the quality and quantity of enforcement.

The present chapter focuses on how consumer agencies obtain their cases. The major concern is not so much with the actual nature of such matters as investigative techniques, but with the conceptual problems of how consumer agencies acquire knowledge about violations of consumer law. In the course of the discussion, attention is also directed to those who complain to consumer agencies about consumer problems. To what extent are complainants representative of the population at large, and how do they actually come to bring their problems to consumer agencies? A point to be made is that the outsider may have difficulty in distinguishing between consumer complaint and agency initiative in the actual operation of consumer agencies. Complaints may have to be verified, and to do this consumer officers may solicit their repetition by posing as ordinary consumers. From the inside, however, there are no difficulties in categorizing matters because consumer agencies quite clearly define them as complaints if they originate from members of the public, whatever the nature of the succeeding investigation.

I COMPLAINTS AND ENFORCEMENT

Consumer agencies rely heavily on complaints in enforcing the criminal law. From a total of 791 cases in the *Prosecution Survey* just over 500, or some 64 per cent of the proceedings, were from complaints. A major factor is that limited finance and a shortage of manpower limit the ability of consumer agencies to detect violations. As an illustration, resources were being quite heavily allocated to consumer advice by the Metropolitan County consumer agency when the field work was conducted, and consequently only 9 per cent of the prosecutions brought by it were the result of its own initiative. Even in normal circumstances consumer agencies are limited in the initiative they can take and for this reason depend on complaints from consumers. One example is the enforcement of legislation controlling claims about reduced prices. Unless a contrary indication is given, a statutory presumption operates under Section 11 of the Trade Descriptions Act, and a claim regarding reduced prices is unlawful if an article has not been offered at a higher price for a continuous period of twenty-eight days in the previous six months. Since consumer agencies lack the resources to monitor prices, infringements come to light only when citizens complain and a subsequent examination of business records by consumer officers shows that the requisite higher price has not been charged.[3]

Offences are revealed by complaint which would otherwise be difficult or even impossible for consumer agencies to discover. Without complaints, certain infringements would continue undetected because consumer agencies are unable to survey all pertinent areas of commercial activity.[4] Certain offences, such as the presence of foreign bodies in packaged food, are not obvious in shops, and consumer agencies depend on consumers who find them at home to bring them to their notice. Other offences are easily discovered by consumer agencies because they are enduring and predictable. The frequency with which certain types of supermarket mispricing are uncovered by detection work is partially explained because once committed they usually remain in existence for some time. The high discovery-rate for some offences depends not on their relative prevalence, but on the fact that they are readily detectable once they occur. An unlawful misdescription in a newspaper advertisement is blatant, for example, and little supporting evidence need be assembled to institute a prosecution.

The extent of dependence on complaint varies with the type of offence. Table 3.1 sets out the origin of the main offences examined in the *Prosecution Survey*. Whereas the overwhelming majority of misdescription and substandard food offences arose out of complaints, agency initiative played an important part in detecting pricing and quantity infringements.[5] The variation derives from how consumer agencies use their initiative, as well as from the differences in the nature of the offences. Consumer agencies devote considerable effort to inspecting retail premises, which enables

Table 3.1. Origin of the main offences, *Prosecution Survey*

Origin	Type of offence					
	Mis-described goods	*Mis-pricing*	*Mis-described services, etc.*	*Incorrect quantity*	*Other weights and measures offences*	*Sub-standard food*
	%	%	%	%	%	%
Inspection	10 (28)*	48 (77)	27 (1)	59 (140)	74 (28)	10 (2)
Complaint	90 (244)	52 (81)	98 (46)	41 (98)	26 (10)	90 (19)

* The figures in brackets show the actual number of cases brought.

them to examine pricing and quantity matters. On the other hand substandard food involves mainly foreign bodies or mould, and these are more likely to be found by members of the public, since most foods are wrapped or prepacked and therefore their contents are concealed from casual inspection.

Complaints give life to the enforcement process by identifying patterns of wrongdoing. An inordinate number of complaints about one firm, taking into account its size and the nature of its business, sets in bold relief the need for a thorough investigation of its trading methods. Indeed, a series of complaints may strongly indicate to a consumer agency that legal proceedings are desirable. The recurrence of similar breaches of consumer law suggests that the firm will fail to reform its practices in the absence of prosecution. The manner in which complaints inform the exercise of discretion was underlined in a passage in a prosecution report in Metropolitan City, where the enforcement officer supported his recommendation for a prosecution by recalling the history of complaints about the delinquent firm and its apparent disregard of warnings to prevent them.

In the 18 months trading in Metropolitan City, 18 complaints have been received from members of the public, more than for any other car dealer in the city. In addition, Mr R—the principal of the business has been interviewed and warned by me and other members of the Department from time to time.

The utilisation of complaints for the enforcement of consumer law requires their collation, and recognition of the affinity between similar complaints. This is largely a matter of organisational record-keeping and the classification of the information in ways meaningful for what consumer agencies do. Because of the requirements of the Office of Fair Trading the records of consumer agencies now reveal patterns in the types of trading practices and the classes of goods and services about which complaints are received, but the accumulation of data about particular firms is less systematic and more dependent on the enthusiasm of individual officers and agencies. Investigations of the compliance of firms with criminal legislation, after a series of complaints have been received about their breaches of civil law, are still unusual. The link between law enforcement and complaints is most evident in the efforts of the Office of Fair Trading. The Office places heavy reliance on complaints to choose those prejudicial trade practices which it recommends that the government should regulate by statutory order, and to identify businesses against which cease- and-desist orders should be obtained for consistent breaches of the civil or criminal law. If sensitively handled by consumer agencies, isolated complaints may also lay bare widespread wrongdoing. A valuable example, in which serious consumer fraud was discovered, followed the receipt of three complaints by the Metropolitan County consumer agency about a secondhand-car firm. Because one of its principals was known to the investigating officer from a previous matter, a thorough review was undertaken, in which customers of the previous months were painstakingly traced and interviewed. By the time the firm and its principals were indicted in the Crown Court for breaches of the Trade Descriptions Act (1968), systematic deception had been disclosed, involving at least twenty consumers.

Complaints have a democratic force, for they concentrate the attention of consumer agencies on areas of trading practice of concern to consumers. Consumer agencies which frequently prosecute mispricing in super-markets, even though the discrepancies are individually small, justify their action partly on the grounds that, particularly with inflation, consumers regard prices as a first priority. The role of complaints for the priorities of consumer agencies was affirmed in an incident I observed in the course of the field work. An enforcement officer, who had been investigating complaints arising from the sale of secondhand cars, was informed that he would be transferred to enquire into fraud in the supply of items in bulk quantities to institutions such as schools and hospitals. The officer strenuously resisted the move, arguing that such fraud was not a matter of public concern, for no complaints had been received, whereas the purchasers of secondhand cars, who were mainly from the lower socio-economic groups often needed assistance in obtaining redress from unscrupulous car dealers. As this example suggests, the views of consumers are not always taken into account in setting enforcement policy. Some evidence for this comes from examining the outcome of offences that arose from complaint over a six-month period in a district of the Metropolitan County consumer agency (Table 3.2). Whereas the bulk of complaints which the agency decided were justified involved breaches of the criminal law concerning mispricing, relatively few of these were the subject of legal proceedings.

In addition to indicating the concerns of members of the public,

Table 3.2. Cautions and prosecutions from justified complaints involving criminal offences, Metropolitan County, Area A, six-month period

	Voluntary redress	*Cautions*	*Prosecutions*
Misdescribed Goods	5	5	4
Mispricing	2	25	2
Misdescribed services, etc.	3	2	–
Incorrect quantity	1	3	1
Other weights and measures offences	–	3	–
Substandard food	–	9	1
Total	11	47	8

complaints have a vindicatory character, both for the existence of an agency and in particular investigations. To stifle any institution with a supporting constituency is a formidable task, and consumer agencies constantly exhibit complaints to their political masters to justify their activities, as well as to support the case for the allocation of additional resources. In the context of particular investigations, complaints become a prop used by consumer officers engaged in potentially unpleasant interaction. They can give the impression to businessmen that since a complaint has been registered with their agency, they have no choice but to make enquiries. In other words, consumer officers can divorce themselves from the origin of their activity and portray themselves as neutral functionaries performing an unenviable but inevitable task. A common ploy of an enforcement officer I accompanied was to emphasise in his dealings with businessmen that the matters he was investigating were the upshot of complaint. The use of this technique as a defence-mechanism was particularly appropriate, since he was working within the hostile environment of the secondhand-car trade.

Despite their importance for consumer agencies, distinct disadvantages attach to too great a reliance on complaints from members of the public. Consumers have a limited perspective which prevents them from complaining about certain types of infringements.[6] In these cases, agency initiative is a more effective basis for detecting wrongdoing. A major problem is that consumers may not recognise that they have been adversely affected by an unlawful trade practice. A characteristic of certain consumer offences is that they are complex, diffused over time, and unpublicised. Consumers lack information about their importance or sufficient incentive to complain. The adverse effects of some food additives and medicines are cases in point, for these are not manifest until after use over a period. Where large numbers of the public are mildly affected by an activity, no one may suffer sufficient deprivation to complain because the benefits of doing so are so small as to be disproportionate to the effort involved. In this way, unlawful trade practices can be shielded from the scrutiny of consumer agencies. A specific example is that consumers overcharged a small amount may think it trivial, but viewed from another perspective – the illegal profits accruing to firms – the effect is more serious.

Another reason that consumer offences go unnoticed is the nature of some prejudicial trade practices. Consumer fraud, for instance, is characterised by stealth and an attempt to conceal its effects from the public. The consumer may not realise that he has been sold a car with an altered odometer; the victim of switch-selling may assume that he has freely chosen what is really an unintended purchase; the visitor to a one-day sale may be convinced that he has received a bargain; and the client of the fraudulent mortgage broker, who is insured for a lesser amount than agreed, may not discover that the difference has been embezzled if the need never arises to claim the full amount. As one enforcement officer succinctly expressed it: 'The most successful frauds are where the mug doesn't realize he had been conned.' But the problem also occurs in the absence of fraud. The average consumer is not always able to protect himself against supermarket mispricing because he is not in a position to check the actual prices charged against those advertised or marked on the goods. For example, consumers are unable to assess whether retailers have made the appropriate reduction with 'flash offers', where prices are claimed to be less than those recommended by the manufacturers, since they are not conversant with those recommended prices.

A second disadvantage of consumer agencies relying too greatly on complaints is that complaints can distort priorities by diverting resources from enforcement. A consumer agency may be so overwhelmed with a number of time-consuming, trivial complaints that staff have to be transferred from enforcement work of a preventive nature to assist in their resolution. A constant theme of the recent annual reports of consumer agencies has been that the routine inspection of retail premises has suffered because of the deluge of complaints. Despite this, the total enforcement effort of some consumer agencies has not decreased. Prosecutions have remained constant in number and have concerned significant malpractices, although a greater proportion may have been based on complaint. The reason is that, although routine inspection has been reduced, it has been replaced by investigations which are concentrated in known areas of wrongdoing. Other agencies, however, rely on complaints to determine their priorities, instead of evaluating their goals in the light of the total spectrum of consumer problems.[7] The commitment is to resolving complaints received, without any consideration of their seriousness, the vulnerability of the victims, or the failure of certain sectors of the population to complain. As we shall see, consumers who complain are not completely representative of the population and it may be that these agencies are directing effort to areas which are not of pressing importance to the lives of ordinary people. In other words, they are subordinating preventive work, which involves removing the sources of consumer complaint, in order to resolve the individual complaints they receive. The preoccupation with projects of marginal significance is especially clear in the context of actual agency work, where the goal of individual consumer officers is often to close cases in the quickest possible time. In the resulting allocation of resources, relatively trivial complaints rank equally with potentially serious deceptions.

The difference in the orientation of consumer agencies to complaints is best exemplified by specific discussion. Two area offices in Blankshire, Northbridge and Southborough, have similar resources and serve populations of roughly the same size. Table 3·3 presents data, derived from agency records, on investigations under the Trade Descriptions Act (1968) conducted at the initiative of these offices in the two years preceding the field work for this study. The statistics portray accurately a real difference in the routine ways in which the offices operate. These derive from opposing rationales of what consumer protection involves, as well as from other factors – the enthusiasm and orientation of individual officers, and the fact that Southborough has always received about three times as many consumer complaints as Northbridge, partly because it receives more publicity and perhaps partly because Southborough consumers are more sophisticated because the area is more middle-class. Southborough takes as its mandate the resolution of consumer complaints, and this has priority once the minimum of enforcement work required by law and by its head office has been performed. The justification is that the public finances the agency, and that the primacy which it attaches to complaints should be incorporated into the working of the agency. Since the overwhelming majority of consumer complaints concerns the civil law, such as that relating to the quality of goods, the result is that this aspect of consumer protection is emphasised. The relegation of criminal consumer law to a minor role is underpinned by the assumption that businessmen are

Table 3.3. Agency-initiated investigations, Trade Descriptions Act (1968), Blankshire, two-year period

Types of offence	Northbridge	Southborough
Misdescribed goods	13	6
Mispricing – Supermarkets	73	2
– other	11	2
Misdescribed services, etc.	3	2
Other	1	2
Total	101	14

basically law-abiding and comply with its terms. The minor role for law enforcement is evident from the fact that there were only 11 prosecutions over the six-year period preceding the field work, of which 9 originated from complaint. As the officer in charge of Southborough expressed it:

> This is a 'no prosecution' department. We attempt to resolve a matter if this is possible and get redress for the consumer. We have a good relationship with the trade in Southborough – it is mostly static. We have always considered that if a trader puts things right, then we won't prosecute. It's worked, and they have reciprocated. We have always considered that to prosecute where there was no intention would affect our good relations with the trade.

Contrast this with the Northbridge area office which instituted 51 prosecutions over the same period, of which 29 resulted from the initiative of consumer officers. With the arrival of three young enforcement officers about four years before the field work, Northbridge has interested itself in law enforcement. To some extent this has been possible because consumer complaints involving the civil law have been handled in the main by a specially appointed consumer advice officer – an innovation which the Southborough area office resisted until its amalgamation into Blankshire. Largely relieved of the burden of civil complaints, enforcement officers in Northbridge have concentrated on enforcing the criminal law. As the statistics indicate, this has involved their taking the initiative, as well as relying on complaint. Particular attention has been given to mispricing, but other potential abuses have been diligently pursued. The Northbridge approach supposes that in the long-run consumers are more effectively protected by law enforcement than by the resolution of individual complaints. Although adhering to the opinion that the business community is generally law-abiding, Northbridge officers are convinced that this does not prevent the honest businessman from indulging in the occasional dubious or careless trade practice. In their view, these can only be prevented by the detection and prosecution of criminal infringements.

II CONSUMER PROBLEMS AND CONSUMER COMPLAINTS

The extent to which consumer problems reach consumer agencies must be looked at as a social process. Analytically, the social process has a number of dimensions. At the outset, the consumer must define a state of affairs as a problem, for otherwise there is no reason to take action or to seek assistance.[8] Then the consumer has to recognise his problem as a consumer problem, although this is not essential if others inform or assist him to recognise this. There is no automatic congruence between problems defined by consumers and those defined by consumer agencies. But the research indicates that consumers contacting consumer agencies have a relatively unambiguous notion of what a consumer problem involves – although this finding is not conclusive as far as the perceptions of the general population are concerned. Almost all enquiries received by consumer agencies fall within their rubric, and few need to be referred to other bodies. For example, statistics kept by the London Borough agency indicate that under 2 per cent of the enquiries have to be referred elsewhere. To some extent this is because consumer matters have a very wide ambit, but it also derives from the media publicity given to consumer affairs.

Problem-definition is only the first element in the social process. It is a necessary but not a sufficient condition for further action. Knowledge is a crucial determinant, knitting together problem-definition and action. Consumers must be cognisant of their legal rights and the remedies by means of which their grievances can be redressed.[9] Consumers must connect their problems with an obligation on the part of businesses to provide a solution. Table 3.4 indicates the findings from a recent national survey of consumers' knowledge about the legal obligation for faulty goods. Most consumers appear to realise that they need not bear the loss with faulty products. A striking feature, however, is the widespread attribution of responsibility to manufacturers, particularly with consumer durables. National advertising, brand promotions, and manufacturers' guarantees are all responsible for making consumers think manufacturers are liable. Retailers also foster the misapprehension by identifying the manufacturers as those to whom complaints should be directed.

Table 3.4. Consumer knowledge of responsibility for faulty goods: A national survey

Body considered responsible	Product							
	Domestic machines %	Cars %	Furniture %	Shoes %	Clothes %	Food: sweets %	Packaged food %	Fresh food %
Retailers	27	27	31	37	38	45	47	64
Manufacturer	69	68	66	60	59	49	48	27
Other	4	5	3	3	3	6	5	9
Total	100	100	100	100	100	100	100	100

Source: 'Product Liability', *Which?* (January 1975) p. 5. See also 'Consumer Survey', *Focus*, vol. 5 (March 1970) p. 14.

Knowledge of legal remedies is not always translated into action, and it cannot be assumed that consumers are sufficiently motivated to press their legal claims. A consumer may have a low sense of civic competence;

specifically, he may feel powerless when faced with a large business.[10] Most consumers who, in their own view, have cause to complain do not do so. There is a widespread toleration of faulty goods. A survey of 600 women in one locality revealed that only 68 per cent of those who recalled a faulty purchase in the recent past complained, while the comparable figure in a later sample of 503 consumers in another area was 69 per cent.[11] Consumers who did not complain said that they could not be bothered, that they had repaired the defect themselves, or that they disliked complaining.

Certainly many consumers with problems involving breaches of the civil or criminal law cope with them without resorting to third parties. In the case of a faulty product or service, the defect may be tolerable or easily repaired. Complaining may be an unpleasant or troublesome experience, and a consumer may feel that the time and effort involved are not worth while when compared with the anticipated outcome. The value of the purchase or the extent of the defect may be too inconsequential to justify complaining. The advantages of continuing to use the purchase, even with its defect, may exceed the benefits of returning it for replacement or repair. Previous experience or the experience of others may inform a potential complainant that he is unlikely to be successful. Personality factors are also relevant; the consumer may be introverted or for some other reason diffident about complaining.

The relationship which consumers have with social organisations and their cultural background are other factors in the extent to which they complain. Complaints may be stifled because consumers are powerless in comparison with a business. Aged, invalid or poor consumers, dependent on a local store, may moderate their complaints because of the barriers to transferring custom elsewhere. In some communities, it may be that complaints are resolved to the satisfaction of consumers through informal procedures.[12] Formal action may be avoided because of cultural pressures to obviate conflict. In another way, the normative system may place a premium on self-help. Norms about 'minding one's own business', 'not getting involved with the law', and 'sorting out problems oneself', inhibit the reporting of consumer complaints.[13] A thorough investigation of the influence of these factors would focus on the extent to which they enter the social consciousness of consumers. At the anecdotal level, however, a consumer officer recalls that a consumer who complained about a foreign body in food, which led to criminal proceedings, was rebuked by several of her neighbours for reporting a petty matter and causing trouble.[14] During the field work of this study, it became obvious that consumers in some communities were less prone to complain to consumer agencies. In Blankshire, there was a relative dearth of complaints from rural areas. Members of the consumer agency interpreted this as reflecting the independent character of rural people, and their preference to settle disputes without reference to official bodies. In fact, community norms may be only a minor factor in comparison with the lack of knowledge about and the difficulties of access to the agency.

Rarely will dissatisfied consumers complain to consumer agencies. The majority make contact with the business which supplied the product or service for the redress of any grievance. Recourse to official assistance is unnecessary for in the main complaints are resolved at this point. For example Lever Brothers operates a consumer service which deals with up to 25,000 enquiries a year. Table 3.5 details the results of a study which examined the course of action adopted by a national sample of 1000 housewives who had received a faulty product or service in the previous year. Disputes reaching consumer agencies were clearly a small proportion of the total body of consumer complaints.

Table 3.5. Action when purchasing a faulty product or service in the previous year: A national survey

	Products N = 570 %	Services N = 350 %
Talked to family	73	58
Complained to shop	60	67
Made a point of not buying again	56	27
Talked to friend	36	44
Complained to manufacturer	28	34
Complained to local authority	2	4
Complained to consumer association	1	4
Complained to MP/newspaper	1	1
None of these	9	6

Source: J. Walter Thompson Ltd, 'Housewives' Attitudes to Marketing' (July 1974).

That businesses mollify dissatisfied customers does not provide a complete account of the relative infrequency with which consumer agencies are approached. Consumers' knowledge of consumer agencies, and the problems of access to them must also be considered. The evidence indicates that consumers are ignorant of the existence of consumer agencies. A National Opinion Polls survey found that nearly half the population (48 per cent) could not spontaneously name any consumer movement or group. Amongst the manual working class this percentage was 65 per cent.[15]

The public's ignorance of consumer agencies stems, in part, from the ambivalent position that many of them adopt. While some have enthusiastically embraced the role of advising and assisting consumers, others adhere more closely to their traditional terms of reference. Many consumer agencies deliberately refrain from publicising their services, on the basis that the increased demand would strain their inadequate resources. Any publicity surrounding these agencies depends on the unsolicited coverage in the mass media and that propagated informally by opinion leaders in the community who know about their services. Consumers must often be sufficiently resourceful to find the telephone number, sometimes classified inappropriately in telephone directories, or an agency's offices, which are commonly removed from the commercial and population centres of the areas they serve. Of course, these hurdles are not universal, and the situation is radically changing with the establishment of Consumer Advice Centres. Moreover, consumer agencies such as the one in Metropolitan County consciously engage in public relations, by issuing press releases, and by having departmental officials appear on radio or television. Consumer agencies which do this can point to noticeable increases in the volume of complaints received.

III CONSUMERS AND CONSUMER AGENCIES – TWO STUDIES

To explore the pattern of contacts between consumers and consumer agencies, I conducted a number of interviews with consumers contacting the Consumer Advice Centre of the London Borough consumer agency. Over a two-week period, 142 consumers were interviewed – every third person approaching the agency who was resident in the area. At the time of the interviews, I was working as an honorary consumer advice officer in the London Borough agency. As far as consumers were concerned, I was the member of the agency who was dealing with their enquiries, which enabled me to obtain a sound appreciation of their nature. In a small number of cases, difficulties in scheduling every third consumer meant that the initial interview was handled by one of the other officers. After the appropriate advice was given, or after details of a complaint were recorded, a number of more formal questions were asked about the consumer's relationship with the agency and about his or her own social characteristics. The exercise was repeated in a Consumer Advice Centre in Metropolitan County, where the interviews were conducted by a member of the agency under my direction. The seventy-eight consumers, who were resident in the area, were chosen randomly from those approaching the Advice Centre over a period of a fortnight.[16]

As I have mentioned, the aim of Consumer Advice Centres is to enable consumer agencies to reach the lower socio-economic groups who, it is feared, are not in a position to obtain consumer advice and assistance, although they are precisely those in greatest need. Table 3.6 presents data on the socio-economic positions of respondents in the surveys, and compares it with that of the population of the two areas. (The population data is the closest available data and comes from the 10 per cent sample for

Table 3.6. Socio-economic grouping of respondents and of the populations of the
areas, *Consumer Surveys*

Socio-economic grouping	London Borough		Metropolitan County	
	Respondents %	Local population %	Respondents %	Local population %
Professional	13 (18)	8	5 (4)	3
Employer/Managerial	14 (20)	18	19 (15)	10
Intermediate & junior non-manual	31 (44)	23	24 (19)	12
Skilled manual	28 (40)	27	31 (24)	42
Semi-skilled manual	2 (3)	10	8 (6)	15
Unskilled manual	2 (2)	4	1 (1)	7
Armed Forces/ unclassified	4 (6)	6	4 (3)	5
Economically inactive	6 (9)	4	8 (6)	6
Total	100 (142)	100	100 (78)	100

* Figures in brackets show the number of persons.

local areas in the 1971 Census). Socio-economic status is some indication of
the likelihood of contact with the agencies, in that there is an under-
representation of the lowest socio-economic groups. The patterns of access
may reflect variations in the problems different consumers experience. For
instance, those in the lowest socio-economic groups may not have the
resources to engage in the type of consumer behaviour which leads to
consumer problems. Family Expenditure Surveys show that the ownership
of consumer durables *per capita* varies somewhat within the population, and
this could give rise to a different incidence of faulty products between
different socio-economic groups. However, any tendency in this direction
may be counteracted by a variation in the nature of the faults different
consumers experience in the products they purchase. The rather inadequate American evidence available suggests that the products which
low-income consumers purchase are defective to a greater extent that those
purchased by others.[17] A stronger argument is that socio-economic status is
associated with social attributes such as knowledge and confidence, and
that the differential access can be related to differences in these factors.[18]
Low-income consumers do not know that problems exist or that consumer
agencies can handle them, and, if they do, are not confident enough to seek
assistance. In the Metropolitan County Survey, the education qualifications of sixty-nine persons were ascertained but there were no significant
variations from the national average. Interestingly, few of those
contacting either agency expressed difficulties in obtaining access, even
when they were faced with irritating, if minor, obstacles, in terms of staff

not being immediately available, or the agency being closed when they first visited. Further, a considerable number of respondents – about three-fifths – claimed to have solved consumer problems in the past by themselves, but approached the agencies because they had failed in this particular instance.

Consumers approaching the consumer agencies professed to know about their existence prior to their present enquiry. Indeed, between a quarter and one-third had contacted the agencies previously about another matter. Knowledge of the agencies' existence was first obtained in a variety of ways, as indicated in Table 3.7. The knowledge of many respondents was less firmly grounded than suggested by the figures. Very few knew about the full range of services offered by the agencies, particularly the pre-shopping advice. Many of those who claimed to know about the agencies through the media knew simply that consumer agencies existed, but not specifically of the two agencies. The television programmes seen were broadly based consumer shows, while the newspaper articles sighted were as frequently general features in the national press as specific references to the two agencies in the local newspapers. Manifestly, consumers who acquired knowledge through television or the press had to engage in additional activity to locate the two agencies, as well as to evaluate their relevance to their problems. The experiences of two consumers are illustrative: 'I've walked all around the town trying to find it. The shop-front display is not noticeable enough. I nearly gave up.' And: 'Advertise more. I had to ask three people just down the road – they didn't know where it was.'

Pertinent to explaining how consumers reach consumer agencies is the

Table 3.7. Source of knowledge of the consumer agencies, *Consumer Surveys*

Source	London Borough	Metropolitan County
Media*	45	21
Saw Consumer Advice Centre	36	22
Relative, friend, neighbour	25	18
Citizens' Advice Bureau	11	2
Through occupation†	9	6
Referred by retailer	3	4
School college, etc.	3	–
Police	2	2
Miscellaneous, and cannot remember	8	3
Total	142	78

* Newspapers: 31 (LB), 17 (MC): Television 13 (LB) 4 (MC): Radio: 1 (LB).
† Employees of local authority, businessmen seeking advice, etc.

function of formal and informal networks. Citizens' Advice Bureaux refer a number of consumers to consumer agencies and assist others to locate them. The police occasionally perform a similar referral task, as do other official and voluntary bodies. No referrals from solicitors were noted in the surveys, although several instances were uncovered in the course of the field work. In one case, for instance, solicitors referred their client to a consumer agency for an independent technical report, and in another a solicitor enquired whether a matter could be pursued informally, for in his view the small sum involved, £12.50, did not justify court action. The surveys reveal that the informal network of family, friends and neighbours is more important than these official bodies in communicating knowledge of consumer agencies to consumers (see Table 3.7). Moreover, the rather simplistic data in Table 3.8 suggest that the informal network has greater relevance for those within the boundaries of certain social groups. Proportionately more respondents in the lower social classes knew of the agencies through informal networks. That a greater proportion of respondents from the upper social classes knew of the agencies through seeing the Consumer Advice Centres is partially accounted for by their respective positions. They are centrally located in major shopping areas, and perhaps the less affluent do not regularly shop there. In London Borough, for example, the large council estate is some miles on the outskirts of the Borough and has its own shopping centre.

Table 3.8. Source of knowledge of the agencies and social class, *Consumer Surveys*

Source of knowledge of agency	London Borough		Metropolitan Borough	
	Upper Classes	Lower Classes	Upper Classes	Lower Classes
Media	26	15	10	10
Seen Advice Centre	27	8	13	5
Relative, friend or neighbour	11	13	4	10
Citizen's Advice Bureau	4	6	1	1
Other	11	6	6	9
Total	79	48	34	35

The impression gained from the interviews was that consumers approached consumer agencies not because they failed to obtain satisfaction from the assistance given by the formal bodies or by the informal network of family, friends and neighbours.[19] Consultation with these was minimal because, instead of attempting to assist, they immediately referred consumer enquiries to consumer agencies as the bodies most competent to deal with them. The general approach of the Citizens' Advice Bureau in the areas was to transfer all but the most elementary consumer enquiries to the consumer agencies. Generally speaking, the police have little interest in consumer matters. Occasionally they prosecute cases of a consumer protection nature, but only where theft, fraud or other criminal offences, such as the sale of unroadworthy vehicles, are blatant. Consumer complaints are regarded as 'civil matters', to be transferred to consumer agencies. If consumers consult members of their family, friends or neighbours about consumer problems, it appears that they act simply as a source of knowledge about the existence and location of consumer agencies and do not attempt to assist with the resolution.

Consumers' expectations form the context for consumer agencies, and are a form of social control determining their success in the eyes of consumers and the structure of their activity. At one level, expectations have a democratic quality and consequently a policy implication for the services offered by bodies like consumer agencies.[20] Articulated expectations, which are reasonable in the light of the resources of an agency, are a factor in assessing its effectiveness. Conversely, an agency defining a claim within the acceptable boundaries of realisation creates an expectation which it must fulfil by performance. In this sense, expectations and the activity of an agency are linked reciprocally. Of course the policy of an agency need not always be in line with consumers' expectations. An agency may reasonably conclude that consumers are unable or unwilling to articulate their expectations, and in any event may take the view that they are neither feasible nor desirable.

Expectations are also relevant to the relationship of power between an agency and its clientèle, for they are a factor in determining whether an agency can impose its definition of a situation on the consumer.[21] The extent to which an agency can redefine any problem depends on the particular situation involved. One element is the nature of the expectation, and a distinction may be drawn between a consumer expecting specific assistance and one with a more general enquiry. In the case of the latter, the scope for redefinition may be greater, and the agency may be able to invoke a scheme of action suggested by its professional expertise. Another factor is the type of decision involved. Decisions tend to be routine when they are based upon objectively defined criteria for which there are concrete indicators. Non-routine decisions entail more complex judgements on the nature of evidence to be collected and on the subsequent application of the available criteria.[22] Then there is the clarity and accuracy of the expectation. If a consumer comes with his problem poorly specified and his needs vague, an agency has greater scope for interpreting the enquiry in the light of its predispositions and official policies.[23] Obfuscation is possible, and the agency may avoid the consumer's enquiry. The consumer with a strongly articulated expectation, and an accurate knowledge that a solution is plausible, is a greater source of pressure on the agency. Either the agency satisfies his expectation, or it will be evaluated in a negative way. This type of consumer may acquiesce in the line taken by the agency, however, if he regards the agency as the repository of expert knowledge, or if he believes a deferential attitude towards it will produce a more favourable outcome.

Those contacting consumer agencies have definite expectations of the manner in which their enquiries will be handled. This can be attributed largely to the publicity which consumer matters receive. In the consumer surveys in London Borough and Metropolitan County, fewer than 10 per cent of consumers interviewed did not know what to expect or were unable to articulate any notion which they may have had. For this minority of consumers ignorance was a major factor, although for some of them uncertainty originated in the difficulties of categorising their problem. For example: 'I wasn't sure. I didn't know whether you could deal with the matter or whether to contact a solicitor.'

The majority of respondents in the surveys viewed the two consumer agencies as sources of advice, but a minority saw them as the providers of more positive assistance.[24] This division of expectations did not depend significantly on how consumers knew of the agencies, nor did it vary importantly with their social characteristics, although there was a slight tendency for respondents in the higher social classes to expect advice rather than positive assistance. Perhaps the dominant image of the agencies as providing advice stems partly from the fact that consumers downgrade their expectations to avoid disappointment. The ways the agencies are publicised and operate may also be important. While nearly 80 per cent of the consumers in the London Borough survey expected advice, the figure in Metropolitan County was just over 50 per cent. The London Borough consumer agency is oriented to consumer advice, but Metropolitan County emphasises a wider service to deal with consumer problems. As one consumer observed in Metropolitan County: 'I've discussed this Consumer Advice Centre with several people – they are under the impression that you could only come for complaints.' Indeed those who knew about the consumer agency because they had seen the Consumer Advice Centre in London Borough were more inclined to expect advice than other forms of assistance. Another aspect may be the culturally derived notions that consumers have of what consumer problems involve. Consumers certainly do not have a sophisticated appreciation of the distinction between the criminal and civil law, but experience informs them that consumer problems are individual problems and that official agencies have an ancillary role in solving them. In other words if consumers find their house burgled their experience tells them that the police will help, but if they buy a faulty product they will think in most cases that it is their responsibility to seek a remedy. Programmes in the mass media stress that it is up to them to return to the retailer with faulty goods to demand a refund or exchange, and only if this fails should they pursue the matter further.

Some of the consumers in the surveys who expected advice recognised the legal element in their enquiries and perceived the agencies as repositories of legal knowledge. The following comments are illustrative: 'I wanted to get some advice, but I didn't want to go as far as a solicitor.' 'I expected you to advise us. You know the law on these matters.' A greater number were less specific and saw the role of the agencies as being that of vetting their enquiries, informing them whether or not they had a case, and guiding them as to the appropriate course of action in pursuing their claims. Of those who perceived a legal element in their enquiries few, if any, comprehended the distinction between the civil and criminal law. Criminal infringements were revealed where, for example, consumers had been overcharged, or had obtained inferior goods or services which had also been misdescribed, and were either interested in receiving advice about possible courses of action which they could take, or in having the agencies obtain redress on their behalf. In other words, it was only when the problems were redefined by the agencies that they assumed a criminal character.

The consumers seeking advice were seeking knowledge, which they realised that they did not have, and its application to their particular situation. Consumers believed that there was a correct position – that there were rights, sometimes of a legal character – and that by approaching the agencies they would learn of it and its implications for their problems. In other words, consumers were largely passive and expected the agencies to redefine the issues. Because of the uncertainties and what they perceived as the technical nature of the problems, they looked to the agencies for an authoritative evaluation.[25] In anticipating redefinition of their enquiries by the agencies, however, consumers were not forfeiting complete control of the situation. In one sense this was because they were free to refuse the advice if they found it unacceptable: for example, they could abandon their claim or obtain access to other forms of assistance. More importantly, their continued independence of the agencies was a function both of the nature of their enquiries and of the operation of the agencies. Consumer problems are not generally of the same crucial significance for citizens' lives as, say, the provision of welfare is for the clientèle of social service agencies.[26] If a consumer problem remains unsolved, the matter can be relegated to experience, for only very occasionally is the material loss crippling. Further, consumers do not approach consumer agencies at a time when they are socially or economically vulnerable. Frustration may characterise complainants to consumer agencies but not desperation. There is some statistical support for this in that only half the consumers in the surveys contacted the agencies within a fortnight of their enquiries arising. Of course, to some extent this may not have been because consumers considered their enquiries unimportant, but because the businesses involved had undertaken to remedy the problems and consumers were waiting to see if satisfaction was forthcoming.

I discuss the operation of consumer agencies in greater detail in the chapter that follows, but at this stage it is sufficient to say that their operating techniques are such that they exercise limited control over consumers. Their interest in consumers is highly focused; it extends over a short span of time and is concerned with a limited aspect of their lives. This contrasts with other organisations, which have an extended interest in their clientèle and devise strategies to retain control over them.[27] Consumer agencies accept need as self-evident, and there is no attempt, as with some social work agencies, to undertake complex assessments of 'real' need. The occasions where consumer problems are reinterpreted as social problems, either of personal inadequacy or social deprivation, are few and far between. Ideally, consumer agencies are designed to produce a more knowledgeable and competent citizen by dispensing knowledge of the consumer law relevant to the situation in hand. Consumers should acquire the ability to deal with their given problems – consumer agencies provide them with information which they can apply to any consumer problems they face.[28]

A minority of consumers in the surveys envisaged the agencies as doing more than simply giving advice. Some simply expected to unburden their frustrations to a sympathetic official. Any further expectation that the agencies would take positive and successful action was either unexpressed or, if formulated, quite incidental. One consumer said:

> We've had the bike six months. They fix it each time, but it's a dud bike. It was only today that I was so angry that I decided to do something about it. I feel better after this. I don't think anything will come of it, but I feel better after coming here.

Others postulated an investigative role for the agencies – they would enquire into the problem and achieve a solution. The manner in which this would be done was generally left unstated by London Borough respondents, although a considerable number in Metropolitan County wanted the agency to bring pressure to bear on the relevant business. They supposed that the recalcitrant business would be galvanised into settling the dispute if visited by an official of the agency. Of course, once other consumers were aware that the agencies would investigate their complaints they frequently appreciated that its intervention was a form of pressure on the business to settle. Those complaining about price increases were the most vehement in expecting the agencies to engage in positive action. When it was explained that price control was less vigorous and wide-ranging than publicity in the mass media suggested, these consumers appeared to be overcome more with surprise than resignation.

Any disparity between consumers' expectations and the knowledge which they acquired about what the agencies actually did seldom seemed to engender dissatisfaction. Of course, the statement is somewhat qualified, since in both cases the interviews were conducted by persons identified with the agencies. But the consumers who expected assistance and did not receive it were small in number although they accepted the agency's approach rather reluctantly. Their attitude contained a distinction between legal and moral issues, and implicit was the belief that if a claim was groundless, although morally justified, the law should be reformed. Because many who expected advice obtained assistance, the more pervasive tendence was for consumers to evaluate the agencies in a positive way, and clearly this was instrumental for a number of those returning with a new enquiry. Previous contact with the agencies was some indication of the accuracy of consumer expectations. Whereas over half of those contacting the agencies for the first time had incorrect expectations, only a quarter of those who had previous experience were in this position.

Although the surveys did not directly attempt to tap what consumers thought of businesses, the general criticisms which emerged were concerned as much with the attitude of businesses as with their refusal to resolve complaints satisfactorily. Frustration in actually getting in contact with someone in a business who was prepared to consider a matter was one aspect of this. The indifference which consumers met was also galling – from the indifference of sales assistants to the behaviour of those in managerial positions. A consumer had this to say of her experience with the manager of a medium-sized business: 'When I went back he sat behind his desk and tapped his pencil. His attitude was to get rid of me.' The interviews also revealed that consumers distinguish between the policies of different businesses, and recognise that some are more liberal in dealing with complaints than others. But complaints about the less generous businesses were muted and very rarely took the form of suggesting that a breach of some criminal consumer law was involved.

IV BUSINESS COMPLAINTS AND CONSUMER AGENCIES

The law-enforcement responsibilities of consumer agencies produce a variety of requests for advice from the commercial world. To avoid becoming involved in legal proceedings, businesses often solicit interpretations on uncertain points in consumer law from consumer agencies or attempt to vet dubious trade practices with them. In this regard, the relationship between businesses and consumer agencies is well developed. Committees of the professional association of consumer protection officers (The Institute of Trading Standards Administration) receive enquiries from trade associations, and through them from individual businesses, on the nature and application of consumer legislation. Advice is given subject to the proviso that it cannot bind the courts, although the discretionary power of consumer agencies means that it has a similar effect in practice, because they will not prosecute in contravention of what they have told businesses.

Recent years have seen some increase in business enquiries to consumer agencies as the latter have expanded their consumer advice services. Businessmen now approach consumer agencies for advice on resolving particular consumer complaints which fall within the ambit of the civil and not the criminal law. Typical enquiries stem from an ignorance of the civil law regarding the return of deposits on orders which consumers have cancelled, or whether the repair or replacement of faulty goods is an adequate alternative to refunding their price. Businesses are also beginning to refer customers to consumer agencies to obtain pre-shopping advice. It would be wrong to give the impression, however, that enquiries originating from businesses are anything other than a small part of the work of consumer agencies. An approximate figure from the records of consumer agencies is that business enquiries constitute no more than 1 or 2 per cent of the matters handled. Business enquiries to consumer agencies are inhibited because large companies have customer relations departments and legal advisers to whom branch management turn for advice. Although small businesses are unable to enlist the same back-up, assistance is available from trade associations and solicitors. Moreover, the interviews with businesses discussed at length in Chapter 6 indicate that many perceive consumer agencies as oriented against their interests. This should not be surprising since the publicity associated with their functioning emphasises assistance to the ordinary consumer and not to commerce and industry, and in specific contacts with businesses consumer agencies are cast either in a law-enforcement role or as the advocates for particular claims by consumers.

Complaints from businesses that their competitors are in breach of consumer law could divert consumer agencies from handling matters of serious public significance. Practices which benefit rather than disadvantage consumers, such as the marketing of new and cheaper substitutes for existing products, could be curbed as consumer agencies diverted their energies to inter-business disputes.[29] In fact consumer agencies in Britain are rarely used at the behest of one industry against another as an inexpensive means of harassing trade rivals. The number of business complaints to consumer agencies is very small. The data in Table 3.9 is extracted from the records of two areas in the Metropolitan County consumer agency where it was possible to identify accurately complaints originating in the business community over a six-month period. They characteristically fall into two categories: complaints against suppliers and disputes with rival businessmen. The following table, Table 3.10, summarises the details of the prosecutions in the *Prosecution Survey* resulting from complaints by businesses. The thirty-two prosecutions represent 4 per cent of the total number examined in the survey, a percentage which is comparable to the sketchy national figures available. The preponderance

Complaints, Initiative and the Enforcement Process

71

Table 3.9. Business complaints in two district offices, Metropolitan County, six-month period

	District A	District B
Complaints against suppliers	6	9
Complaints against other retailers	1	2
Not classifiable	1	1

Table 3.10. Prosecutions from business complaints, *Prosecution Survey*

Short weight/measure	17
Misdescribed goods	12
Incorrect pricing	2
Other weights and measures offences	1

of prosecutions for incorrect quantity suggests that until recently businesses had an image of consumer agencies as weights and measures authorities.

The paucity of business complaints seems independent of the attitude of consumer agencies. Although some consumer agencies are careful that their involvement is not exploited, and are reluctant to undertake proceedings following a trade complaint on the basis that civil action is more appropriate, their general attitude is not unreceptive to such complaints in principle. Contacts with businessmen are a welcome relief for consumer officers from the mundane world of consumers and are an opportunity to deal with other professionals. Consumer agencies also relish business enquiries as a manifestation of their neutrality. Business enquiries are disproportionately publicised in the literature of consumer agencies as testimony to the fact that they are not solely concerned with ordinary consumers. This tendency was particularly manifest in the Metropolitan County consumer agency: to counteract publicity in the media which associated consumer protection with ordinary consumers, the agency placed extra weight on business enquiries and their outcome in their press releases and reports.

More importantly, the context of the commercial world limits the flow of business complaints to consumer agencies. Disputes between parties to a business relationship are commonly resolved by informal means, without recourse to outside agencies or the legal process. Formal devices are eschewed by businessmen intent on continuing a beneficial relationship and on maintaining their reputation in business circles.[30] Businesses withhold complaints against the commercial practices of trade rivals for reasons of their reputation and because vindictiveness would be an incentive for any victim to diligently seek out the infringements of the reporter. Few business complaints examined during the field work represented the irreparable deterioration of what had been a stable business relationship. The complaints against suppliers involved either serious malpractice by unknown firms, such as the provision of unsolicited goods or services; dishonesty by the suppliers' servants; or the unlawful activities of third parties, such as manufacturers. The remainder arose from isolated transactions, and where this was the case the businesses complaining always had alternative sources of supply, and in most cases had unsuccessfully tried to settle the matter privately. An interesting feature of complaints involving suppliers was that they were made almost always by small businessmen. Their reputation in the business community was unlikely to suffer from a complaint against a supplier, particularly a national firm. Furthermore, action by a consumer agency was obviously more convenient and less expensive than private civil proceedings.

V LAW ENFORCEMENT THROUGH AGENCY INITIATIVE

Consumer complaints are of paramount importance in the life of consumer agencies and they permeate the enforcement process. However, consumer agencies expose a considerable amount of unlawful activity through their own intiative. Some idea of this can be obtained from an examination of legal proceedings, and Table 3.1 earlier in this chapter contained details of the origin of the major offences in the *Prosecution Survey*. The main ways in which consumer agencies take the initiative are the inspection of business premises and the purchase of consumer items at the retail level. In addition some consumer agencies scrutinise newspapers to check for infringements of criminal law, although most monitor advertising claims only occasionally, for example during sale periods, and rely on consumer complaints, or on chance discovery by consumer officers in their private reading, to uncover offences.

The inspection of business premises has a long tradition and dates from when the main responsibility of consumer agencies was the administration of the weights and measures legislation. Routine inspection ensured that a trader's weighing and measuring equipment had not deteriorated and enabled an officer to check a selection of items sold for their quantity. An element of surprise was necessary to assess normal operations and to trap the dishonest. The decline of many small shops, the advent of prepacking, and the passage of additional consumer protection legislation has modified, but not fundamentally transformed, the nature of inspection. Visits have been extended to a wider range of premises and are concentrated where turnover is large, such as in supermarkets. An interest has been displayed in the premises of manufacturers of mass-produced goods, particularly of food, on the grounds that it is more efficient to prevent infringements of consumer law at their source than to discover them at retail outlets. A few consumer agencies have inspection programmes for packers and manufacturers in their areas, although these focus mainly on quantity control and on checking labels for errors.

By purchasing consumer items at retail outlets, when posing as ordinary customers, enforcement officers are able to check on a number of trading practices. For example, test purchases at supermarkets permit a conventional examination of the descriptions and quantities of products and also facilitate verification of pricing and check-out procedures. Test purchases are often an essential prerequisite to discovering any offences when items are not weighed, measured, or priced until the point of sale. Sampling for compliance with the food and drugs legislation is a major aspect of retail purchasing. Items are acquired by consumer officers and then despatched to public analysts, who test their deficiencies in composition, quality and labelling. As well as stating the results of these scientific tests, public analysts also express their opinions as experts on the minimum standards to which articles should conform, and on whether a label, advertisement or other description is incorrect or misleading. The annual numbers of samples taken in the three areas in which field work was carried out are set out in Table 3.11.

Table 3.11. Food sampling: Three consumer agencies (annual figure)

	Number of samples	*Percentage deficient* %	*Prosecutions resulting*
Metropolitan County	1003	5	3
London Borough	210	18	–
Blankshire	1152	1	–

Inspection and test purchases are designed not only to reveal infringements of consumer law but also to play an educative and deterrent role. Their educative nature is most prominent following the introduction of new consumer legislation, when consumer agencies attempt to visit all relevant business premises, either in the course of routine inspection or by special call, to ensure that businessmen are aware of the requirements. However, enforcement officers dispense advice to businessmen in the course of ordinary inspection, or as a result of test purchases, and this regular contact is said to make businesses more knowledgeable about their legal obligations. A long-standing assumption of consumer agencies is that inspection and test purchases have an overriding preventive role. Food sampling, for example, is said to make manufacturers aware that infringements they may commit will be detected and thus provides a strong

incentive to maintain standards. A similar relationship between inspection
and the prevention of offences is suggested. The unannounced inspection
visit is said to deter potential offenders and to remind those lacking in
diligence and care of their responsibilities. If a minor infringement is
detected, this will supposedly have a reformative effect without the agency
having to resort to legal proceedings, because most businesses attempt to
comply with legal requirements. The symbolic significance of inspection,
and its analogy with police patrolling, was made explicit to me on several
occasions. For example, an enforcement officer remarked: 'It's a bit like
the bobby on the beat. You've only got to walk up the street and the
managers see you. It's a question of being seen and being known.' So
strongly held is the belief in the preventive character of inspection and test
purchases that consumer officer hypothesise an inverse relationship
between these on the one hand, and complaints and prosecutions on the
other. The more inspections and test purchases there are, the fewer the
complaints and the less need to resort to court proceedings. On this basis,
many consumer agencies justify their paucity of prosecutions by arguing
that their high rate of patrolling deters unlawful activity. However, the
consumer agencies noted for their vigorous prosecution policy dispute any
claim that they have failed in their preventive work. They argue that they
detect a greater proportion of illegal practices in their area than low-
prosecution agencies, and that their exercise of discretion is less favourable
to businessmen.

The conventional wisdom of enforcement offices is that consumer
complaints are symptomatic of the trading policy of businesses. They claim
that slackening in inspection and law enforcement because resources have
been allocated to consumer advice is self-defeating, for it only encourages
malpractices and produces an increase in complaints. The argument must
be treated with some reserve. If inspection has a deterrent quality, it does
not follow that it has any effect on the volume of complaints. Situations
giving rise to complaints may not overlap with those giving rise to criminal
infringements. In any event, the traditional concerns of inspection –
quantity and description – are somewhat removed from the present
sources of consumer complaint; namely, poor quality products and
services. Moreover, it is likely that recent publicity surrounding consumer
agencies, and the reforms to facilitate greater access to their services,
transcend in importance the effect of the decrease in inspection in
explaining the growth in the number of complaints.

Priority of enforcement work is the creature of various forces. Recent
governments have modified the work of consumer agencies by stressing the
desirability of consumer advice by the enactment of additional consumer
legislation. The first has subtracted from the resources available for
inspection, while the second has increased the area it should cover.
However, those effects have been indirect, and the time has long passed
when central government imposed a statutory obligation on consumer

agencies to visit all business premises annually. There is criticism
occasionally of the enforcement of consumer law, and pressure from
consumer groups has produced the occasional burst of enforcement
activity by consumer agencies. But, in the main, unlike other bodies such as
the police, consumer agencies are relatively immune from public opinion
about their enforcement goals.[31] The public-spirited individual, who sees
it as his duty to protect community values through having a prosecution
launched, holds an esteemed position in legal folklore. Yet most consumers
have a low sense of civic responsibility, and in contacting consumer
agencies are more concerned about a solution for their individual
complaints than with whether criminal consumer legislation is enforced.
In the two surveys in London Borough and Metropolitan County, few
consumers complained for altruistic reasons – that the agencies should take
action to protect others – but rather because they were personally
involved. They either resented the business's brusque or non-co-operative
attitude; or felt personally prejudiced by a trade practice; or had a
monetary stake in any action taken.

Manpower, financial resources and the state of technology obviously
pattern enforcement activity.[32] The re-allocation of manpower to consumer advice and the consequent relegation of inspection to a low priority,
has already been mentioned. Costs are a direct limitation on enforcement.
Test purchases require finance, and at the present level of funding of
consumer agencies the more expensive items are frequently ignored. Some
agencies justify this on the grounds that the main aim should be to monitor
the more basic and cheaper products used by the average consumer.
However, an instructive example is the enforcement, or rather non-
enforcement, of the limited regulations pertaining to the safety of
consumer goods. It is optional whether consumer agencies enforce this
legislation. In practice, few have products tested for compliance with the
requirements, and then the selection is made in haphazard and arbitrary
manner, because the costs associated with purchasing them and sub-
sequently testing them in a laboratory are prohibitive. As regards
technology, unless an enforcement agency has access to suitable monitoring devices, offenders may well avoid detection.[33] Further, the technology
of a regulated industry is relevant and determines the burden involved in
detecting legal transgressions. In the consumer field, prepacking means
that misdescriptions and the sources of contamination can be readily
identified. Another example is the trend for coal to be delivered in vehicles
containing bulk fuel, part of which is discharged on each delivery. This
variation from the previous arrangement, when sacks of coal were already
made up for sale, means that there are fewer opportunities for consumer
officers to check deliveries.

The attitude of individual consumer officers, which I discuss more fully
in Chapter 5, bears on the extent to which infringements are detected. The
statement of one senior officer, that 'We don't look for trouble in this area',

represents a frame of mind which is firmly rooted in many consumer agencies. Enforcement officers realise that much depends on their willingness to seek out infringements, conceding that businesses do infringe the laws and it is simply a matter of finding the offences. 'Even the most fair-minded inspector must find an offence sometime,' were the words of one officer. The importance of consumer agencies taking the initiative to detect offences partly explains why some agencies prosecute more than others. It is not simply that they prosecute cases where other agencies would think cautioning sufficient, but that they detect a greater number of infringements in the first place. The deputy chief officer of a consumer agency made this point about criticism of its prosecution rate: 'If they saw the facts on which we prosecuted, they couldn't do otherwise themselves. We have a highly trained inspectorate who get out and find infringements.'

Specialisation within a consumer agency is a particular factor in the number of infringements discovered through its own initiative. Consumer agencies with enforcement divisions specialising in one area produce higher levels of infringements not only because of their expertise, but also because the major criterion for assessing their work is their performance of that particular task. Even without any sense of mission or ideological commitment, bureaucratic structuring ensures that the specialist unit will produce work to demonstrate its activity.[34] The fact that resources are concentrated in a particular area means that a greater proportion of infringements will be found than would otherwise be the case – which, in turn, justifies the original allocation. An example of specialisation in consumer agencies is the fairly recent creation of special investigation units within some agencies to combat consumer fraud. The rationale of these units is that consumer fraud is normally poorly handled because of the concentration on individual cases resulting from consumer complaint. In consequence, the lack of time and the pressure to obtain redress for the complainant mean that patterns of wrongdoing are overlooked. Even if a prosecution is undertaken, the summons will be based on the one incident and there will be no investigation of whether there are similar offences. In contrast, special investigation units are interested in systematic deception and characteristically are not especially concerned with individual consumers. Complaints are important, but to identify areas warranting investigation. The creation of the units has overcome the problem of expertise by drawing together those officers with experience of fraud, such as in the secondhand-car trade or in bulk deliveries, and by concentrating and promoting skills acquired with experience. Contacts have been established with other law-enforcement agencies, particularly the police; with taxation authorities; and with security officers in large industrial concerns. Reciprocal arrangements between these and consumer agencies are founded on the exchange of information, often unofficial, and for this reason special investigation officers have developed interests in unlawful activity beyond the bounds of consumer protection. The police inform them of the conviction records of fraudulent businessmen, and in return they notify the police when they detect non-consumer offences in the course of their duties. Newspapers disclose details of advertisers who are engaged in fraudulent practices, and, in exchange, learn of bad credit risks among their advertisers.

An important influence in the pattern of enforcement is tradition. The notion of the regular inspection of business premises, dating from when consumer agencies were primarily weights and measures authorities, is still firmly embedded in their practice. In the main, inspection for infringements under additional consumer legislation has been incorporated into routine weights and measures work. Thus a supermarket visited for weights and measures purposes is also checked for any mispricing. Simultaneous enforcement is impossible, of course, when the nature of a business is such that infringements would arise under only one statute, or where inspections are performed by consumer officers who are only authorised to administer a limited range of legislation. The weights and measures orientation of inspections means that business premises, unimportant from the point of view of weights and measures, but of concern because of other consumer legislation, are subject to only irregular inspection. Table 3.12, which sets out the number and purposes of inspection visits in London Borough in the year preceding the field work,

Table 3.12. Inspection visits in London Borough one-year period

	Inspection visits*	Premises found to be incorrect
Trade Description Acts (1968) and (1972)	1767	199
Weights and Measures Act (1963)	1250	not available
Food and Drugs Act (1955)	334	15
Prices Act (1974)	220	136
Trading Stamps Act (1964)	164	7
Consumer Protection Acts (1961) and (1971)	69	17
Fair Trading Act (1973)	29	4
Trading Representatives (Disabled Persons) Acts (1958) and (1972)	17	–
European Communities Act (1972) (food quality and grading of fresh horticultural produce)	14	10
Heating Appliances (Fireguards) Regulations (1953)	12	2
Advertisements (Hire Purchase) Act (1967)	5	–
Consumer Credit Act (1974)	3	1

* Any particular premises may have involved more than one piece of legislation and hence more than one type of 'inspection' visit.

demonstrates that weights and measures visits outrank those for other important legislation.

The adherence to traditional methods is also illustrated by reference to the sampling of food and drugs. Sampling programmes have undergone little variation over the years, and the sampling rate adopted by most consumer agencies is that used at the turn of the century. There has been no reappraisal of the pattern of sampling, yet it involves an expenditure of over £1 million a year. A specific example is that some consumer agencies sample milk disproportionately, considering household expenditure on it in relation to the total expenditure on food. In the past, frequent sampling of milk was necessary because of its importance as a food, and because it was adulterated easily by the addition of water. But now the chances of deliberate adulteration are remote with the disappearance of smaller dairies, and the regular inspection of, and the advent of laboratory control in, the remainder. Sampling programmes for drugs have also been relatively stable and confined to proprietary medicines.

Several consumer agencies are abandoning routine inspection as an investigative and preventive tool. The argument used is that inspection does not attack those practices of greatest harm to the consumer. Furthermore, experience casts doubts on its preventive role – businesses regularly visited continue to commit infringements. Instead, resources are being allocated where experience and the texture of complaints suggest that prejudicial trade practices are likely to be found. The formation of special investigation units has already been discussed. Another example of focused enforcement is the product survey, where particular products are tested to assess whether they comply with legislative or other standards such as those of the British Standards Institution. Legal proceedings may be instituted if serious offences are found, but otherwise the surveys lead to recommendations to businesses on the need to remedy their trade practices, or to submissions to central government recommending amendments to the law. A few consumer agencies have even rejected the idea of regularly checking weighing and measuring equipment, hitherto a basic feature of their work. The justification is that little is found to be incorrect, and that in any event it is much more important to assess its actual use by test purchases to determine whether correct quantity is being supplied. The majority of consumer agencies regard this change as heresy, however, and still use the number of weights and measures visits and the amount of weighing and measuring equipment tested as the major yardsticks for evaluating their performance.

The preconceptions of consumer agencies determine how they detect infringements. Their importance was expressed forcibly by the chief officer of a consumer agency notable for its investigative work: 'Perhaps I have a gut feeling. But as a law enforcement officer you feel it [unlawful activity]. When I go to some parts of the country I can feel it. You know it.' The typifications of businesses orient the efforts of consumer agencies – for instance, they play an important part in the targets chosen by the special investigation units. In addition, they pattern particular investigations and affect the diligence with which consumer offences are canvassed. Officers visiting the premises of a reputable firm on inspection assume that they will unearth few, if any, infractions, and that in the unlikely event that they do extenuating circumstances will be forthcoming. Accompanying enforcement officers on supermarket inspection, I quickly became aware of those where 'trouble' was expected, and observed the application with which the search for infractions, particularly mispricing, was conducted there. Admittedly the influence of preconceptions is not substantial in certain cases. Either experience has not produced a coherent interpretation of business activity, or enforcement officers are unable to apply it to particular situations. For example, enforcement officers often have some discretion under food-sampling programmes, but their choice is largely random and unrelated to any larger view of enforcement priorities. A partial explanation is that liaison between public analysts and consumer agencies is limited, with the result that there is little feedback from the latter about nation-wide patterns in undesirable practices.

The perceptions of consumer agencies, discussed in the previous chapter, assist enforcement officers in their investigation work. The essence of investigation is the diligent search for violations which may result in legal proceedings. A degree of conflict is thus endemic in the relations between consumer agencies and businesses. Not only is this conflict distasteful to enforcement officers at a personal level, but it is also a limitation on their efficacy. Since only a fraction of infringements are prosecuted, cordiality is essential if compliance is to be secured in the remaining cases. Rapport between consumer agencies and businesses is also required for the successful resolution of many consumer complaints, for in the absence of a breach of criminal law it is necessary to persuade businessmen to make voluntary settlements. Conflict is inhibited to some extent because investigations which do not lead to cautioning or prosecution are largely concealed. Test purchases are made by enforcement officers posing as ordinary customers, and even inspection is sometimes done without the knowledge of the business involved. Where investigation is public, however, means must exist to minimise hostility. The role in which consumer agencies cast themselves is of assistance in doing this, for an enforcement officer can present himself as the representative of a body which sees itself as helping businesses and which regards the majority of infringements as an unfortunate accident. Despite this, the inherent conflict can never be completely eliminated. The tension is evident in the following passage from an annual report:

Almost all inspection visits are 'surprise' visits, in that the trader does not know when an inspector might visit his premises, and thus a true picture of the standard of trading in these premises can be gained. This system is not intended to 'catch anyone out', but it is obvious that if it is known that an inspector 'always calls in the first week of March' everything of concern to the department in those premises will be perfect during that week, but the danger is that it won't be during all other weeks.

Enforcement officers utilise additional ploys to minimise hostility between themselves and businessmen. A polite detachment is combined with an amiable persuasion in an attempt to avoid antagonism and accomplish the task. The dramaturgical quality of their behaviour is particularly evident in the strategy of presenting themselves as neutral agents of legislative and departmental masters. Even if their performance is entirely innovative and unsanctioned, consumer officers purport to be merely discharging their rather unpleasant obligations. In personal conversation one officer summarised the approach: 'If they get funny with me, my particular attitude to them is: "I don't like doing the job, but I've got to pay the mortgage".'

The way enforcement agencies obtain their cases is related to discretion for it determines the opportunity to monitor the behaviour of enforcement officers.[35] The exercise of discretion by an enforcement officer may never be known to a consumer agency, depending on whether he himself observes the commission of the offence or the agency is alerted by a consumer. In the case of a complaint, an officer's superiors have independent knowledge of the matter and can assess his performance.[36] With offences which he unearths, however, the enforcement officer exercises a considerable, sometimes a total, power over their outcome. A positive decision on his part to report a matter commits the agency to further action – even if this is only a decision not to proceed. An exceptional case which occurred in Blankshire is instructive. Enforcement officers in Northbridge were discontented with what they considered to be the timid and lethargic policy of their head office regarding law enforcement. Prosecution reports were submitted, but excuses were found for not proceeding. In protest, and in order to commit the agency to action in one particular case, a Northbridge enforcement officer seized goods relevant to a false description offence, without referring the matter to his superiors in head office. Under the relevant legislation, the position of the agency was compromised, because not to proceed would have made it liable for any loss of profits incurred by the business as a result of the seizure.

Conversely, infractions detected by enforcement officers may never acquire the official status of a crime.[37] Offences unobserved by other officers or by consumers may not become known to a consumer agency if the investigating officer or his assistant choose not to inform it. Consumer officers recognise the wide discretion that this gives them in the field. As one commented to me: 'It depends on what's in the man. When something out of the ordinary arises, it depends on the individual entirely. There's

nobody to prod him. His boss never knows unless he reports.' Since the
decision to ignore an offence is usually made immediately, reconsideration
is impossible even if an officer has second thoughts and desires to take it
further. The chief officers of consumer agencies are also aware of the
discretion of their enforcement officers and of their ability to preclude
further action. In larger consumer agencies, where close supervision is
impossible, attempts have been made to develop objective means by which
the performance of individual officers can be assessed. Enforcement officers
are required to submit reports of their enforcement work and in particular
of all violations discovered. An officer recalled the manner in which this
control operated, both directly and indirectly, in a consumer agency where
he had been employed previously:

> We had infringement sheets which had to be filled out and sent through
> to HQ. If they thought we didn't take a correct course of action they
> would ring up and the vibrations would come down. They wouldn't say
> "Why didn't you prosecute", but "Why didn't you do this", for
> example, check all the items on the shelf.

Despite such attempts, enforcement officers can readily dispose of minor
contraventions encountered in the course of inspection. Violations may be
ignored, or verbal cautions given, without any entry being made into
official records. Factors affecting this are additional to the general
elements in the exercise of discretion discussed in Chapter 5. The personal
convenience of officers is obviously relevant. The infringement may have
been discovered near the end of the day, or when an officer was without an
assistant. Further proceedings always involve additional work and
consumer protection is, after all, work. An enforcement officer observed,
after issuing an oral caution for a price infringement and not a written
caution: 'When I come back to the office, if I am going to give a written
caution, I have to sit down and write a report. Consequently, there are
more verbal cautions.'

4 Assisting the Public: Advice and Negotiation with Businesses

Traditionally, consumers have been treated as responsible for taking the initiative to enforce their rights under the civil law. The state was not directly involved, except in major cases where it may have provided the services of a lawyer through legal aid. Consumer advice services have now been established within consumer agencies and actually intervene in disputes on behalf of consumers where it appears that there has been a breach of the civil law. Representations are made to businesses on behalf of aggrieved consumers, in the hope that redress will be forthcoming without the need to take court action.

An enquiry from a member of the public to a consumer agency is consequently dealt with in one of two ways. First, consumers can receive advice, either pre-shopping advice if they are contemplating a consumer transaction, or much more commonly advice about their legal rights after they have purchased products or contracted for services. An advice officer may actually assist consumers who appear to have a justified complaint, but who are not in a strong position to obtain a remedy, by contacting the business involved and attempting to negotiate a solution on their behalf. Second, a complaint involving a criminal offence can be referred to enforcement officers for investigation. The matter is looked at from the point of view of possible prosecution, although enforcement officers often withhold action if a business suggests a satisfactory solution.

The division between assisting consumers and enforcing the criminal law is reflected in the structure of those consumer agencies which have a separate advice service for dealing with consumers' problems and an enforcement side concerned with the criminal law. Consumer agencies like Metropolitan County are quite strict in maintaining the administrative division between advice and enforcement functions. On the other hand, London Borough and Blankshire blur the two, and, while advice officers are permitted to perform only civil law tasks, enforcement officers handle both civil and criminal law complaints even if the sole aim is to secure redress for consumers. Nevertheless advice services in these agencies still tend to be the point of contact for citizens with enquiries even if these are treated as enforcement matters.

I CATEGORISING AN ENQUIRY – ADVICE OR MEDIATION?

When consumer officers are faced with an enquiry which does not involve the criminal law, they must decide whether to deal with it by simply dispensing advice on the spot or by treating the matter as a complaint and approaching the business involved. The nature of an enquiry bears on the way it is handled and trivial enquiries or complaints which are patently unjustified are clearly matters for advice. The resources of a consumer agency are relevant: pressure of work tempts hard-pressed consumer officers to dispense legal advice because it is simpler than investigating a matter. A related factor is the attitude of consumer officers to consumer enquiries, for unenthusiastic officers tend to give advice rather than accept matters for investigation. Another example of the relevance of attitude observed in the course of field work was that advice officers in London Borough were reluctant to transfer enquiries to enforcement officers, most of whom they regarded as unsympathetic to consumers. Complaints which they had transferred on other occasions had not been attended to for considerable periods and were finally dealt with in a cursory manner. Therefore advice officers gave consumers advice about the initiatives that they could take on their own behalf or they attempted to deal with the complaints themselves even where a criminal element was involved. Where enquiries could not be handled in this way, advice officers sought to influence the destination of matters so that they reached one of the more sympathetic enforcement officers. The expectations of consumers are also important, so that if a consumer opens an enquiry with the familiar phrase 'I just wanted some advice', an officer is oriented to give advice rather than to take the matter up with the the business. Expectations are not determinative, however. The consumer surveys discussed previously demonstrated that enquiries were redefined by consumer officers and that many consumers who expected only advice in fact received additional assistance. A procedural rule adopted by all consumer agencies is that they cannot take up matters on behalf of a consumer but only advise him, unless he has already contacted the business. The assumption is that reputable businesses are willing to satisfy legitimate complaints and must be given this opportunity before consumer agencies intervene. The rule is waived if a criminal offence or a dangerous or fraudulent practice is involved; if experience suggests that it is fruitless for a consumer to approach the business against which he has the complaint; or if the consumer is incapable of presenting his or her own case.

Superimposed on these factors is the policy of individual consumer agencies, for this can greatly circumscribe the discretion of individual officers. Metropolitan County for example adopts a policy of treating enquiries as matters for investigation unless they are completely trivial or the consumer states distinctly that he or she wants only advice. Any hesitation a consumer has dissipates in the light of assurances – such as the following – by receptionists or advice officers: 'If you want us to plead your case for you, then we will.' To a large extent the policy is founded on self-interest: the agency wants to create support for itself by providing definite assistance to consumers. Arguments used publicly to support the policy of providing assistance rather than simply advice are that, because of the recalcitrance of business, many complaints will remain unsolved until a consumer agency intervenes; that normally the complexity of enquiries makes it impossible for consumers to cope without assistance; and that members of the public expect consumer agencies to assist them because they are a branch of local government.

Organisational features in the Metropolitan County consumer agency are relevant to the way this policy is implemented. While telephone enquiries are routed directly to advice officers, receptionists are employed to interview consumers who make personal visits and to record their enquiries, which are then transferred to advice officers. The receptionists could possibly screen enquiries and dispose of some matters by dispensing advice, but this rarely happens because there is no incentive to do so.[1] The personal satisfaction that they could achieve by exercising responsibility is more than counterbalanced by the desire to avoid the unpleasantness and perhaps hostility associated with telling consumers that there is no basis to their enquiry. If receptionists wrongly treated an enquiry as being unjustified, there is always the possibility that an insistent consumer would register an official complaint against them. Besides, receptionists are unsure about what constitutes a justified complaint, except when they are instructed by advice officers or overhear advice officers give the same response to a particular type of enquiry on a number of occasions.

A policy of treating all enquiries as worthy of investigation means that many matters are accepted by an agency like Metropolitan County which could be resolved immediately by simple advice.[2] The work-load is increased unnecessarily and extra demands are placed on advice officers because acceptance of an enquiry raises a consumer's expectation that something positive will be done about his or her problem. If a complaint is without foundation, an advice officer is in the invidious position of having to inform the consumer of this. One advice officer in Metropolitan County expressed these sentiments: 'They [the receptionists] accept complaints which should never be accepted in the first place. The complainants expect us to do something. The attitude is: "Well, you've had my shoes for three weeks, what are you doing about it?"' Another result of the policy is that although a problem may be resolved satisfactorily, the consumer need never know how this has been done or why.

Consumer agencies like London Borough adopt the procedure of routing all enquires to a trained advice officer who can decide on the spot whether it is enough to advise consumers. Unless consumers can achieve nothing more by themselves, the theory is that it is sufficient to dispel their ignorance about their legal rights and the procedures to enforce them. The approach is said to enhance the personal efficacy of consumers instead of making them dependent on consumer agencies. An official of the Consumers' Association, which pioneered Consumer Advice Centres in Britain, provided the rationale for such an approach:

> Consumer Advice is not spoonfeeding. It's making the laws of this country work and work because the people themselves know their rights. If people come back with a broken pair of shoes and they are told what to do this week, then they shouldn't have to come back next week with the same problem.

Advice officers in London Borough respond to some three-quarters of the enquiries they receive with informal advice. Since they exercise considerable discretion, factors such as their attitude or the expectations of consumers can play a more important part in determining how an enquiry is handled than in an agency like Metropolitan County.

II THE INVESTIGATIVE STANCE

Where a public agency with limited resources provides a service to citizens on an individual basis, it must necessarily chose between those seeking its assistance.[3] To determine whether an applicant has a justified claim according to the criteria used by an agency, the agency must regard each applicant's claim sceptically. What has been designated the investigative stance of a social welfare agency consists in treating an applicant's story as no more than a loosely organised collection of claims requiring evidential support.[4] The investigative stance of consumer agencies is less forceful than with social welfare agencies because of the difference in the services provided; an obvious point here is that the consumer advice is far less costly than social welfare. Another factor may be that consumer agencies regard most of the complaints they receive as justified; the trivial and unsubstantiated are outweighed by those where consumers have genuine reasons for believing that they have been unfairly treated. Over a three-month period in a Metropolitan County area office, consumer officers classified 91 per cent of the complaints as justified. The breakdown of these complaints in Table 4.1 shows that fewer price complaints were justified than average, but further analysis reveals that this was because consumers failed to appreciate that many price rises were legitimate.

As well as the need to ration services, the investigative stance of consumer agencies also derives from the impartial role that they claim for themselves. Unlike other bodies, such as the Citizens' Advice Bureaux, which consumer agencies criticise for having a non-professional advocacy approach to complaints, consumer agencies reject the role of consumer partisanship and believe that the consumer's side cannot be accepted at

Table 4.1. Justified complaints according to consumer officers, Metropolitan County, Area A, three-month period

Nature of Complaint	Justified	Unjustified
Inadequate redress (e.g. replacement rather than refund)	1	2
Restrictive contractual conditions	52	1
Prices – failure to indicate, alleged price saving, unfair increase, etc.	30	10
Non-availability of goods and services	18	–
Inferior quality of goods and services	134	9
Lack of information	8	1
Involving criminal law	72	11
Miscellaneous	7	1
Total	322	35

face-value. Complainants are said to be naturally biased and a version of an incident must be sought with equal care from the business involved before any conclusion can be drawn. The course notes for the Diploma in Consumer Affairs stresses the need for consumer officers to treat complaints with an open mind:

> It is very easy to be swayed by a complainant who appears to have a just complaint and approach the trader with a prejudicial attitude. This must not happen. There are two sides to every story and the situation may appear very different when the other side is heard.

A consumer officer soon discovers that wholehearted commitment to consumers is unwise. Newly appointed consumer officers find that it is disapproved by higher officials, and if a consumer's view is adopted automatically the difficulties increase in approaching a business in an atmosphere conducive to mediation. Embarrassment can also result with the business if an officer has not seen the subject-matter of a dispute and personally evaluated the complaint. As a consumer officer told me:

> I did drop a few clangers when I didn't go to see the item. In one case the retailer asked: 'Have you seen the suite? How do you know the complaint is justified?' Luckily I could say that a person in the shop had admitted sending the wrong suite. But I had learnt my lesson and I always insist on seeing the item.

Consumer officers relate how they have poorly acquitted themselves when they have been too trusting with consumers. They discover that a consumer's account, which appears perfectly reasonable at the outset, is later found to be incorrect, exaggerated or not as clear-cut as originally portrayed. It may be that an enquiry reveals that a product is defective because of misuse by the consumer; that the product was sold as a 'second', so that the consumer expects an unreasonably high quality; or that the consumer wants to renege on a bargain because he has decided on reflection that the product or service is really not what he or she wants. A consumer officer gave these illustrations of how a consumer agency could be misled if it relied solely on a consumer's version of the facts:

> You get a lady who buys a dress. She takes it home and someone makes a remark, 'It doesn't go with the colour of your eyes'. So she takes it back and says it's too tight, and she's like this [pretending it is too tight]. You get a lad who says his car went 'bang'. But he only paid a few pounds for it, put on an extra carburettor, and went down the Ml at 110 mph, then hit the brakes. A woman comes in with little Tommy and says that he has only had the shoes three months, and they are falling apart. But, if you knew, little Tommy has been kicking stones around with his shoes.

At an elementary level, the investigative stance involves consumer agencies in assessing complainants rather than their complaints. Determining whether a complainant is honest and accurate is particularly crucial where the circumstances are ambiguous and independent evidence of a transaction is lacking. A product may have been orally described with only the consumer present; a consumer who claims that a product was purchased recently from a store may have lost the receipt evidencing sale; a consumer may have destroyed evidence of a fault in a product by repairing it himself. Situations like these require a consumer officer to evaluate a complainant – as one said to me, 'determining what sort of person she is' – and for this reason consumer officers prefer to meet consumers in person to judge better the veracity of their claims. 'If a complainant is face-to-face to you they are more likely to tell the truth. On the telephone they can fictionalise and you can't tell whether they are telling the truth.' Consumer officers vary in the extent to which they give consumers the benefit of the doubt.[5] Very few are as searching as the one in the following interview, who deliberately feigned ignorance to test a consumer's recollection of what might have been a false trade description given orally in relation to the sale of a secondhand motor-bike:

CONSUMER: Why did they say it was a *trustworthy* bike? Why did they tell us lies? [Slight Pause.]
OFFICER: What did you say?
CONSUMER [genuinely puzzled]: What do you mean?
OFFICER: You said something.
CONSUMER: I don't know what you mean.

OFFICER: About the bike.
CONSUMER: Mr—said it was a *reliable* bike and it would do the job.
                [My emphasis]

The consumer officer later commented to me on the inconsistency in the use of the descriptions 'reliable' and 'trustworthy':

> I wouldn't believe a word she says. You think: ' "Trustworthy", there's a trade description there.' If I had immediately taken her up on it, she would have agreed with me and in half an hour she would have firmly believed that the fellow said 'trustworthy'.

Independent evidence is valued because it can either support or contradict a consumer's account. A consumer who has not complained within a reasonable period of a fault developing is usually regarded as having an unjustified claim. A complaint about a faulty product or about services which have not been performed to a reasonable standard may be verified by the actual quality of the goods or workmanship involved. A useful illustration of how products are examined to test a consumer's account is provided by complaints about faulty furniture. Consumer officers in a number of agencies described to me quite spontaneously how they visited complainants' homes to determine whether a fault was inherent in the material or caused by extraneous factors such as the activities of animals or children. One comment suffices: 'If there are kids running around and the house is a bit tatty then that tells us an awful lot about the suite.'

III NEGOTIATING WITH BUSINESSES

When negotiating with businesses about consumer complaints, consumer officers vary their tactics according to the strength of the consumer's case and the nature of the business. However strong the consumer's position, an overall limitation is that consumer officers lack effective power to enforce a settlement in the case of civil law matters. Consumer officers are acutely aware that businesses which know that it is ultimately the responsibility of consumers to enforce their rights under civil law need not be intimidated when they are presented with a complaint.[6] Problems within the rubric of the criminal law are clearly distinguishable, and consumer officers know that these place them in a position of strength because of the court proceedings that they can institute.

Matters are straightforward if a business is reputable. Consumer officers can simply refer a complaint to the appropriate official, whom they may know on first-name terms. The assumption is that a reputable organisation will contact the consumer and resolve the problem as a matter of course.

Tactics are quite different for a 'problem store' or an unscrupulous business, and consumer officers may not accept a civil law matter for investigation if experience informs them the business involved ignores complaints even when they are totally justified. Consumer officers are aware that several national firms oppose all but the most clear-cut complaints and take this as far as requesting a full trial if a consumer initiates a small claims action. If, however, consumer officers perceive that the resistance of a business to complaints is localised – for example, an obstreperous manager or one without authority to settle complaints – they will approach the head office of the business on the basis that head offices generally take a lenient attitude towards complaints to retain goodwill.

Having relatively little power and inculcated with the impartial ideology of consumer agencies, consumer officers adopt a low-keyed posture in making representations to business about civil law complaints. The course notes for the Diploma in Consumer Affairs are again instructive. When a complaint seems genuine, they say, a consumer officer should make 'a diplomatic approach to the trader, stating the consumer's complaint, the legal position and quoting the relevant Act, making observations and requesting the trader's comments'. As this extract suggests, consumer officers do not adopt the approach of consumer advocates but briefly outline the facts obtained from the consumer and enquire about the viewpoint of the business.[7] The burden of continuing the conversation rests very much on the latter. To elicit the maximum response from a businessman, a consumer officer will range widely in the discussion, introduce matters which are not especially relevant, and may even feign ignorance.[8] In the process of being presented by a consumer officer, a complaint therefore loses much of its thrust. Personal contact with a businessman is preferred to dealing with a matter by telephone or letter, because officers can establish better rapport and demonstrate that their position is entirely impartial. Details can also be fully canvassed and there is a greater personal satisfaction than in handling problems at a distance.

After contacting a business, as officer may conclude that the consumer's position is quite implausible and that the complaint should be regarded as without foundation. Alternatively, the business may agree that the complaint is justified and suggest a solution which the officer considers satisfactory. When the intervention of an officer quickly produces a favourable outcome, the conversation can remain at the unspecific level and an officer need not identify with the complainant's position. Occasionally a businessman will enquire how the officer recommends the matter be resolved. Some officers readily reply, but others do so reluctantly and will perhaps add that the businessman should not feel that he is being forced into a course of action against his will. When a businessman takes a negative attitude from the outset, officers avoid suggesting definite courses of action to spare themselves the embarrassment of a direct conflict of views.

A business is rarely approached with overt hostility or any hint of threat.[9] Not only is this wasted in many cases because the official contacted in an organisation will not be familiar with a matter, but it infringes the principle of impartiality and creates a climate which is not conducive to successful negotiation.[10] Despite the absence of overt pressures, consumer officers use various ploys to obtain redress for consumers with genuine grievances. Advice officers mention to businessmen that if no solution is reached the consumer may sue in the County Court. Hints are dropped so that a business is well aware that although a consumer advice service lacks statutory backing, it is associated with a law-enforcement agency. Correspondence, for example, is written under the letter-head of the consumer agency or over the signature of its chief officer. Advantage may be taken of the nuisance value involved in a consumer officer constantly contacting a business about complaints. Emphasis is laid on the fact that a consumer is an elderly person or an invalid, and past associations with businessmen are drawn upon to allay fears about the present complaint.

The overriding goal of negotiation is to obtain enough redress to satisfy consumers without appearing to favour them unduly in the eyes of a businessman. Within consumer agencies redress is an all-important consideration in evaluating the performance of consumer officers. This is taken to extremes in Metropolitan County, where regular lists of the amount of redress obtained by each consumer officer are distributed in the form of an internal memorandum.

Although some consumer officers describe their position in negotiation as that of a referee or an arbitrator, others are more accurate in preferring the term 'mediator'.[11] Arbitration is exceptional in the sense of consumer officers deciding on a solution to a dispute, and, instead, consumer officers achieve what the annual reports of consumer agencies call 'a negotiated settlement' or 'a satisfactory and fair solution to all parties'. In acting in a mediatory capacity, however, consumer agencies are often satisfied with compromise. Businesses agree to modify their original position but consumers may not obtain their full legal entitlement. An advice officer remarked that success in terms of an agreed settlement was achieved in 75 per cent of the cases, but that the figure was only 50 per cent in relation to what he thought complainants were entitled to at law. Consumers are largely by-passed in the negotiation process. Matters are settled without reference to them and they are treated simply as the source of problems which must be resolved as quickly as possible.[12] Negotiation leads to duplicity on the part of consumer officers as they seek settlement of complaints. An advice officer described negotiation as 'soapsudding' and another as 'hypocritical – you say one thing and mean another'.[13] Several consumer officers thought that they were being 'two-faced': both consumers and businesses were assured that their approach was reasonable but were informed that it would be useful if they compromised a little to satisfy the other side. A simple example of what they mean is based on my field notes from Metropolitan County:

A consumer officer received a complaint about a product which the complainant alleged was faulty and for which payment had not been made. The consumer said that the retailer agreed to return it to the manufacturer for either replacement or repair but that an inordinate length of time had elapsed. The advice officer told the consumer that the complaint seemed justified and that action would be taken by the agency on her behalf. 'If you aren't satisfied then don't pay, although they may keep it [the product] until you do.' The retailer was then contacted and he explained that the delay was the fault of the manufacturer. The officer did not mention that by law the retailer was the responsible party and not the manufacturer. The retailer was told that if he contacted the manufacturer to urge it to hurry the position could be explained satisfactorily to the consumer. 'It sounds reasonable to me,' the retailer was assured, 'I think she will accept what we say.' The consumer was contacted again and assured that the manufacturer was the cause of the delay but that the product should soon be returned.

So far a paradigm has been offered derived from the negotiating tactics of most consumer officers in resolving complaints. There are a few consumer officers, however, who adopt an advocacy role on behalf of consumers and who are not averse to using threats against a business to achieve what they believe is a satisfactory outcome. I observed one in Metropolitan County and another in London Borough; both were enforcement officers. One of these saw his role as 'meting out rough justice'; if firms settled a complaint – if they 'show good faith to me' – he would 'consider justice done', but if not, he would threaten to pursue them diligently until he discovered an offence for which they could be prosecuted. Speaking of a justified complaint about a secondhand-car dealer where no criminal offence was committed, he set out the alternatives:

We have a choice. We can say that there is no [criminal] offence. It is an advisory job. Or we can go down and see what they say. If we do that we shall find out what they are like. They can either repay the money or tell me to get stuffed. If they make out a cheque for £30 I shall consider justice is done. But if they tell me to get stuffed they shall go on the list. Or this is another alternative. I can write a letter. 'Dear Sir, I am sorry that that there is no substance to your complaint. I return your documents'.

Despite the accepted view that consumer officers must retain their impartial role, both Metropolitan County and London Borough consumer agencies give tacit support to these 'hatchet men' among consumer officers who 'heavy' businessmen on behalf of consumers. Their tactics are thought justified – although they are not publicly approved – against businesses whose trade practices are prejudicial to consumers but who do not commit clear-cut criminal offences.

IV THE LAW AND CONSUMER COMPLAINTS

The pressure of complaints and the rudimentary nature of their knowledge impels most consumer officers to simplify the civil law. Simplification is also necessary if consumers are to be informed of their basic rights in a way which is readily understood or if a consumer officer suspects that a businessman is not familiar with his obligations under civil law. The legal position will be omitted, however, if it would hinder settlement of a dispute. The complexities of civil law are thus reduced to stock phrases which can be readily dispensed as legal advice or applied to resolve problems: 'If the goods are faulty, then you're entitled to your money back.' 'If you can repair it as good as new, then that's fair enough.' 'If you can't get it [a faulty product] back to them, then they [retailers] should come and get it.' Such simplified depictions conceal the fact that some experienced consumer officers acquire a detailed knowledge of consumer law, but the complexities of civil law are generally absent from the everyday concern of most consumer officers, who operate with condensed versions of legal rules. As an example, when considering a complaint about a defective product, few officers consider if the consumer examined it before purchase and whether the defect could have been discovered – points which are very relevant in civil law for the liability of a business – but instead concentrate on whether the defect is a manufacturing fault or the result of consumer misuse.

A number of consumer officers are uneasy at their limited knowledge of civil law. Their concern is not simply that they want to appear competent before complainants and the businessmen with whom they negotiate. Rarely can their opinion be proved 'wrong', for that needs a judicial decision and very few consumer cases get to court. An exceptional case in London Borough was when a consumer failed in a small claims action in the County Court after being advised by the consumer agency that she had a sound case. Besides, the legal element of disputes is usually minimal and they revolve mainly around factual issues. The more important element in consumer officers' feeling inadequate is the belief, however illusory, that a firmer grasp of the law would enable them to come to grips with borderline complaints. The law is regarded as a fount of knowledge which will ease the burden of deciding whether complaints are justified. A particular concern is the open texture of the civil law: whether a product is 'merchantable' or 'fit for the purpose' or a service performed reasonably, cannot be decided by reference to legal standards, for the statutory definitions are vague and the case law is based on commercial situations largely unrelated to consumer transactions. Nevertheless, some consumer officers welcome the relative freedom that the civil law gives them, for the broadly stated provisions regarding faulty products and inadequate services permit them wide discretion. In this view no one can say with certainty whether most complainants have a sound legal case, so that officers can make moral judgements and seek to have them adopted by businesses.

Instances occur where consumer officers deliberately ignore the provisions of the civil law to settle complaints. The obvious case is where a consumer has a strong moral claim which cannot be supported legally. Thus consumer officers sometimes inform businesses that while there is no legal obligation to refund a deposit where a consumer has cancelled an order, this course is advisable as a gesture of good will. Similarly, officers may point out that, while a consumer's acceptance of a credit-note closes a matter legally, the business should realise that there was an entitlement originally to a cash refund. When an aged or invalid person is involved, a business may be informed that it would be good customer relations to alleviate a source of complaint even though it is without legal foundation. To advance successfully such moral claims, consumer officers are conscious that they must accumulate a store of good will with businesses which can be drawn upon on such occasions. Further support thus exists for consumer agencies to adopt an impartial position rather than to identify with consumers.

Another occasion on which the legal position is underplayed is when it would interfere with the successful resolution of a justified complaint. At law a retailer is to blame for the faulty products which it sells, but consumer officers will not object if he points to its supplier as the party to which a consumer should look for redress, provided the latter undertakes the responsibility. Legally, a finance company bears the burden for faulty products supplied on hire purchase, but consumer officers almost always negotiate with the dealer. Circumvention of the law makes sense and does not complicate matters unduly, for a finance company will generally require its dealers to resolve complaints about their merchandise as a condition of providing credit facilities.

Alternative avenues to those suggested by legal requirements are tried where a business refuses to settle a dispute. A recalcitrant retailer may be by-passed and a manufacturer contacted directly to determine whether it will repair or replace a faulty product. Manufacturers are not legally liable in the absence of negligence, but consumer officers recognise that many are prepared to stand by their products and use this fact to the advantage of consumers. Consumer officers also know that some publications carrying advertisements which can be shown to have misled or occasioned consumer loss will offer compensation as a gesture of good will. Matters are occasionally referred to trade associations when other avenues have been exhausted, for they will sometimes apply pressure to their members to settle consumer complaints.

Theoretically, consumer agencies vet enquiries to check whether they involve statutory infringements. If so, they are transferred to enforcement officers for investigation. Metropolitan County requires senior advice officers to be qualified in enforcement duties, in part so that they will recognise criminal infringements. In practice, enquiries involving criminal law are sometimes dealt with by the advice staff of consumer agencies. This is the only plausible course where there is a shortage of enforcement officers, but with trivial matters the attitude is often that it is hardly worth while informing the enforcement staff. When evidence of an offence is weak or the complainant would be a poor witness, the only practical course is to deal with a complaint on the advice side. Sometimes receptionists and advice officers fail to recognise that a criminal infringement is involved. Their knowledge of criminal statutes is minimal since their training courses concentrate on methods of handling civil law complaints, and senior advice officers are so involved in their own case-load that they do not have the opportunity to supervise subordinates in every matter. The whole tenor of consumer advice services is biased against enforcement of the criminal law. The satisfaction of consumers rates more highly than the prosecution of businesses. An advice officer, as I have mentioned, is judged on the number of complaints resolved and the amount of redress obtained, which obviously encourages negotiated settlements, even for complaints containing a criminal infringement. Unless a criminal infringement is quite blatant, complaints are usually settled by negotiation with the business involved.

V THE OUTCOME OF NEGOTIATION

Consumer agencies which keep records claim success in about 70 to 80 per cent of the complaints they receive. If only justified complaints were considered, the success rate could be even higher. A detailed analysis of some seventy-six complaints, selected randomly over a three-month period in London Borough, yields further information on the degree and nature of success as seen by consumer agencies (Table 4.2). The view of consumers as to whether negotiation is successful may be quite different.

Agencies account for their success in part in ways which accord with their depictions of businesses and consumers. First, businesses are said to be ignorant of their legal obligations and when enlightened stand ready to offer suitable redress. Next, many disputes are believed to be founded on a genuine misunderstanding which the intervention of a consumer officer unravels. Mediation reveals mistaken intentions and effects a reconciliation between the parties. Then, consumer officers point out that,

Table 4.2. Achievement with consumer complaints, London Borough, three-
month period

Successful, i.e. agency achieved something	49
Unsuccessful:	
Justified 5	
Unjustified 15	20
Consumer satisfied by time agency investigated	7
	76

Outcome of the successful complaints:

Goods		Services	
Refund	21	Work completed	1
Credit note	2	Firm agreed to	
Exchange	15	investigate	4
Repair	3		
Expedited matter	3		

unlike the consumer, they may know the appropriate person to contact
within a business and the correct procedure to adopt. Another explanation
of consumer agencies is that the improvement in the position of the
consumer in recent years – to which they have contributed – has made the
commercial world more conscious of its legal obligations. Consumer
agencies occasionally concede that they also obtain redress for consumers
because of the powers they have as enforcement bodies over other aspects
of businesses. An Annual Report comments on the suggestive influence
that consumer agencies have because of this: 'There is no doubt that official
backing has a remarkable effect on the quick settlement of complaints.
This is partly due to the fact that it is known that the Department is
prepared to prosecute in suitable cases.' The more perceptive consumer
officers also recognise their nuisance value and that it is rational for
businesses to settle complaints involving small amounts.

Explaining that complaints are not justified or that the offer of a business
is reasonable involves consumer officers in forestalling any dissatisfaction
on the part of consumers. In addition, there is the function of convincing
consumers that someone is interested in their problems, however groundless. Particularly with aged or invalid consumers, consumer officers go to
considerable lengths even though they cannot really assist. Not only is
action like this good public relations, but it serves an educational purpose.
An advice officer spelt out how she dealt with unsuccessful complaints
about cars: 'You poke around, pull a few things here and there, use a few
big words. You can't do anything except to tell them to check the car next
time. They have paid £25 for an old banger. But at least they know
someone cares.' Sentiments such as these underlie the view that every

complaint is important, however trivial or unjustified, if the matter can be explained to a consumer in its true light. According to consumer officers, a few consumers find an adverse opinion unacceptable but the bulk behave reasonably if the position is properly explained. To some extent, consumer officers are supported by their position when they inform consumers that nothing can be done. Advice is imbued with a persuasiveness because it comes from the member of an official and ostensibly knowledgeable body. Obviously, techniques in managing unsuccessful complaints vary with the personality and ability of individual officers.[14] A few officers inform a consumer frankly that his complaint is unjustified and that the position of the business is acceptable in the circumstances, but many officers believe that consumers must be told 'gently' that they have no case. Speaking of his technique on such occasions, a consumer officer told me: 'You tactfully lie to them. You tell them you sympathise with them. You can't say "No" outright. You have to chat them around: "Don't you think, Madam", and so on.'

Delay can also be used to give the impression to consumers that their complaint is being given careful consideration. Several consumer officers explained that they did not inform consumers immediately if their complaint was unjustified because the delay would give them the satisfaction of knowing that thought had been given to it. Where consumers are advised in person that there is nothing to their complaints, a consumer officer may call over a colleague to confirm the unfavourable opinion. Not only are consumers thereby assured that they are receiving close attention, but they are confronted with the perhaps unpalatable fact that members of the agency are uniformly of the view that the claim is unfounded. Emphasis in other cases is placed on the evidential hurdles facing a consumer in establishing a claim. One piece of advice that I often heard was: 'We don't think there is sufficient evidence to justify a County Court action. You can't prove that you're in the right.' In other cases it was pointed out more specifically that the consumer's position was prejudiced because there was no receipt evidencing purchase, or because the business could quite plausibly say that the fault was because of misuse of the product, or because there was no written estimate before the work began.

The official policy of impartiality that consumer officers adopt restrains them from informing consumers directly that their dispute is with a 'problem' or unscrupulous business, but consumer officers impart this knowledge circuitously. Consumers will be told that in the majority of cases the agency is successful with complaints but that businesses have different trading practices and some are more 'difficult' than others. Eventually the consumer is expected to see through the euphemisms that the problem is a recalcitrant business. The law is useful in situations like this and its inadequacies can be used to explain why an officer has been unsuccessful. Consumer officers can draw the distinction between criminal and civil law and point out to consumers that, while the former can be enforced by consumer agencies, they are limited to informing a business about its duties under the latter and that it is up to the consumer to take action.

Consumer agencies can do little in the short-term about justified complaints where attempts at negotiation are unsuccessful. Mention has already been made that where a business is a source of considerable complaints a consumer agency will try to discover whether it is committing criminal offences. Consumers are sometimes advised to institute a small claims action if a business is still in existence and has sufficient assets, in the hope that if several consumers are successful this will have a salutory effect on its trade practices. Consumer officers are reluctant to advise court action where a consumer appears incapable of presenting a case. A few actually assist consumers contemplating a small claims action by drafting the court documents or appearing with them at the relevant hearings. Consumer officers admit that the small claims procedure is not fully exploited: they lack confidence in their ability to assist consumers and the pressure of work gives them little time to acquire the skills. Moreover, for reasons discussed in the previous chapter, few consumers are prepared to press their claims to the courts.

Apart from court action, other techniques, such as the use of publicity, are rarely exploited by consumer agencies. Only one instance was observed during the field work where a consumer officer referred a case to a consumer column in a local newspaper in the hope that the publicity might induce the business involved to give redress to the consumer. Informal warnings are given by advice officers to consumers, who are also alerted to the fact that certain types of businesses, like discount houses, have a poor reputation for after-sales service and that they should consider this when purchasing products. Nevertheless, formal warnings, such as black lists of businesses, are resisted – in the words of a memorandum in London Borough – 'as presenting a partisan approach which could arouse the hostility of local traders alarmed that it may become subject to abuse'. Display lists of comparative prices are being encouraged by the government for Consumer Advice Centres but they are limited in their coverage of both products and retailers.

In the long-term, the solution is thought to rest with the Office of Fair Trading and its power to obtain undertakings and cease-and-desist orders against firms in persistent breach of their legal obligations. However, consumer agencies are not entirely satisfied with the Office of Fair Trading, which appears remote from the everyday problems of consumer protection and which appears to administer this provision very much on its own initiative. For example, several requests by the Metropolitan County agency that action be taken against particular businesses were gently rebuffed. The reply of the Office of Fair Trading to such criticism was that it has a considerable backlog of businesses for such action and that it was processing them methodically. Depending on the size of an enterprise, an adequate volume of complaints or prosecutions must be registered against a business before an undertaking can be sought. Additionally, the present policy of the Office of Fair Trading is to acquire experience by proceeding against marginal firms before moving against larger organisations which will understandably offer resistance. At present, then, consumer officers can only threaten recalcitrant businesses with ultimate action by the Office of Fair Trading and continue to forward information to it on the trading practices of particular businesses.

5 Enforcing the Criminal Law

At the one extreme, the discretion of consumer agencies comprises the unmonitored and largely irrevocable decisions of individual enforcement officers to overlook offences of which they become aware. At the other extreme is the institution of legal proceedings, with the possibility that this may involve a matter progressing through a hierarchy of courts. Consumer agencies exercise a wide ameliorative discretion within these outer boundaries. Routine decisions are made not to proceed where unlawful behaviour has obviously occurred. If a consumer complains about a matter which involves a criminal offence, there is no guarantee that a prosecution of the offending business will be brought.

The assumption of consumer agencies is that normally advice or a warning is sufficient when dealing with the majority of businesses. Prosecution is regarded as superfluous if businesses will voluntarily introduce genuine safeguards to avoid future wrongdoing. The exercise of discretion is utilitarian and the crucial question is whether a course of action ensures future obedience to law. Court proceedings are seen as a backstop to be used where advice and persuasion have failed, or for unscrupulous businesses which are immune to other reformative action. Discretion does not detract from the role of the courts but instead ensures that they are not overloaded by trivial consumer cases. Nor does it constitute the non-enforcement of legislation but rather its enforcement by different and more effective means. The argument is that law enforcement involves the prevention of crime, and advice or a caution can achieve this in most cases. In this view, the number of prosecutions is not the primary standard for evaluating an agency, and its success is better judged by their absence. Prosecution is an admission of defeat, for other means must have failed in preventing malpractices. On occasions, enforcement officers say that a surfeit of prosecutions indicates that a consumer agency is prosecuting trivial cases to give a false impression of effectiveness. Another argument is that a policy of prosecution actually hinders the implementation of legislation by alienating businesses and thus undercutting efforts to achieve compliance through co-operation:

> The 'detect and prosecute' philosophy in consumer protection enforcement may be called 'negative enforcement'. It is negative because it overlooks the basic fact that successful enforcement in today's complex trading structure depends upon goodwill and co-operation between

manufacturers, distributors, and enforcement officers. Unless trades people and officers can discuss problems freely, uninhibited by fear of prosecution, the quality of the service must suffer.[1]

If this is the general setting for the prosecution policy of most consumer agencies, there is a divergent view which is more favourable to prosecution. In practice, prosecution-minded consumer agencies – which are in a definite minority – may conduct some five times as many prosecutions a year as other comparable agencies. Prosecution-minded enforcement officers maintain that offences should be more regularly detected and prosecuted. They attack the view that prosecution is an indication of failure and refer to the prevailing policy as one of avoiding responsibility. A number of other arguments are adduced to support their position. They point out that they decline to trespass on the judicial domain and perceive their principal duty as prosecuting offences to enable the courts to decide the matter. Resentment may result amongst businesses if some offenders escape prosecution through the exercise of discretion. Prosecution demonstrates to the public that they are being protected by the enforcement of consumer law. It benefits all the consumers affected by an offence, not just those who are articulate or knowledgeable enough to complain. Legal proceedings stimulate Parliamentary action by publicising weaknesses in existing law, and they assist in identifying unscrupulous businesses against whom the Office of Fair Trading can take action. Furthermore, prosecution is a reminder to businesses that they must exercise constant diligence to avoid committing infringements. An enforcement officer summarised these sentiments to me as follows:

> The view is that you only prosecute as a last resort. This is fine in theory but it doesn't work out in practice. If you don't take some action that reminds them of the law, they become reckless and careless. If you have a kid who writes on the wall, you can tell him time and again and he will do nothing, so you give him a smack. It's the same as the factory line. If you don't have a supervisor on the line, then they become slack and careless. We are like foremen on the line. There's nothing that brings home an infringement more than a prosecution. You can issue cautions until you're blue in the face. If you don't enforce the law, then you get a fall in the trading environment, and you get more complaints. So it's a false economy.

As with the majority of consumer agencies, however, prosecution-minded consumer agencies settle numerous matters informally. There can be no suggestion that they prosecute all, or even a substantial proportion of, the offences which they detect. Irrespective of other factors, the constraints of manpower and resources limit the number of prosecutions which can be undertaken.

I BACKGROUND TO DISCRETION

In numerical terms, the exercise of discretion overall by consumer agencies is obvious in the attrition of matters between the point where offences occur and the point where they are prosecuted. For example, in one year the 48,300 weights and measures offences which were detected in the Greater London area produced only 204 prosecutions. Of 21,430 infringements discovered under the Trade Descriptions Act over a six-month period, 1003 were prosecuted, 5885 were cautioned, and 14,542 were resolved by giving advice to the businesses involved. These national statistics, collected by the Institute of Trading Standards Administration, confirm the finding made in the course of the field work. Table 5.1 contains figures on how misdescription offences were disposed of in two areas of Blankshire over a two-year period. (The variation between the areas was discussed in Chapter 2). Table 5.2 then follows with the outcome of offences arising from complaint in one area of Metropolitan County in one year.

Table 5.1. Outcome of misdescription offences in Blankshire, two year period

	Northbridge	*Southborough*
Prosecution	24	3
Caution	165	71
Advice/No further action	203	286
Total infringements	392	360

Table 5.2. Outcome of offences arising from complaint, Metropolitan County, Area A, annual figure

Prosecution	10
Caution	78
Advice/No further action	149
Pending	61
Total infringements:	298

ADVICE AND CAUTIONING

Consumer agencies which detect a consumer offence have four courses of action open to them – to overlook the matter, to advise the business how to avoid its recurrence, to warn it by issuing a caution, or to institute a prosecution. In many cases the distinction between advice and a caution is glossed over in practice, for a communication with a business will contain elements of both. The four possibilities do not constitute a hierarchy of responses, and businesses are not always dealt with progressively by advice, cautioning, and then finally legal proceedings. An offence is often sufficiently serious to justify a prosecution although a business has not been previously advised or cautioned about similar incidents. Although an argument of enforcement officers is that advice or a caution is usually a prerequisite to prosecution because a business may be ignorant of its legal obligations, this is overcome in the case of a serious offence by imputing knowledge of consumer law to a business simply because it engages in trade.

As a matter of policy, some consumer agencies refrain from cautioning. One argument is that cautions are of doubtful effectiveness and it is better to ignore offences which do not warrant prosecution. Another concern is that cautioning fetters the discretion of consumer agencies because it obliges them to prosecute a similar offence committed by the same business in the future, otherwise the impact of its threats – as contained in its cautions – is blunted. Another argument against cautioning, although used relatively infrequently, is that it is wrong to accuse a business of committing an offence via a caution when it has not been convicted by a court. However this objection is overcome in practice because cautions are phrased in such a way that a direct imputation of illegality is avoided. A business is simply informed of the circumstances of the alleged offence and advised that a more serious view may be taken if they recur. A closely related belief is that a business should not be cautioned if it would not be convicted in the circumstances. While many consumer agencies caution precisely because a prosecution is impossible – for example, because the evidence is insufficient – a few scrupulously avoid doing so unless the chance of a prosecution succeeding would be high if it were instituted. An element in this approach is the fear that on receiving the caution the business may challenge the agency to implement its threat which, of course, it would be unable to do. Consumer agencies of this persuasion distinguish between cautions and letters of advice. The latter merely present the circumstances, add that no further action is contemplated and conclude, if appropriate, that the trade practice is undesirable in that it has given rise to a complaint by a consumer.

In addition to their immediate impact in correcting wrongdoing, cautions have a prospective force, for they may be cited in future court proceedings against a business to support the imposition of a more severe penalty. Cautions are not fully exploited in this way because many enforcement officers believe that cautions are excluded by the rules of evidence. In thinking this, enforcement officers fail to distinguish between evidence admissible during a trial or hearing, and the wide range of factors which may be taken into account in imposing punishment once a decision to convict has been made. That such a misconception can have prevailed for so long is testimony to the fact that, in everyday life, individuals unquestioningly accept a wide stock of knowledge, whatever its truth or falsity, as long as it enables them to accomplish their tasks reasonably competently.[2] Believing that cautions are inadmissible, and that the defendant solicitor or the clerk of the court will object to their mention, enforcement officers conducting their own prosecutions resort to various subterfuges to inform the courts of previous cautions. For example, by way of background to the present proceedings, reference will be made to previous occasions when enforcement officers visited the business about a similar matter. The court can then be expected to draw the inference at least that the business was cognisant of the relevant law.

In essence, a caution involves drawing an offence to the attention of a business, requiring its correction and, depending on the circumstances, offering advice on how to avoid similar occurrences in the future. Written cautions tend to be confined to cases where a national business is involved, where a business is outside the area, or where an offence is more serious than usual. Oral cautions have the advantages of immediacy and of minimising record-keeping, but they carry less weight than written cautions, and there is the possibility that they may be directed to someone who is not in a position to prevent a repetition of the offence. To overcome the disadvantages, there are no oral cautions in Metropolitan County, but informal cautions are used which comprise notices of the offence, completed on the spot by the investigating officer, and which a responsible official in the business is expected to sign. By reducing oral cautions to written form, the impact is assumed to be more forceful. Consumer agencies deliberately manipulate the threat inherent in cautions to secure compliance with the law. Particular techniques are designed to heighten the apprehension of a business and hence to effect a greater than usual improvement in its relevant practices. An example was given by an enforcement officer:

> If I really went to town on the manager and the girl assistants, I got the manager out separately, and the girls who stamp the prices and maybe the section head, and I'd make a fuss, make quite a scene at the time. I think that can have a greater effect than merely handing out a caution.

Another technique in cautioning is to manipulate uncertainty. If a business is uncertain whether the consumer agency will prosecute it may prefer to avoid the risk by desisting from its objectionable practices. The approach of some officers is to give the impression that legal proceedings will be instituted, but eventually to caution, on the assumption that that will have a greater deterrent effect. With reputable firms, the technique is said by some enforcement officers to be particularly effective in securing compliance with law. 'When you send a caution when they expect a prosecution, then you get a lot of good will. They try harder for you because you didn't prosecute.'

THE DEVELOPMENT OF DISCRETION

Consumer agencies evolved the practice of exercising discretion in their administration of weights and measures legislation. As early as 1842, an enforcement officer reported that he permitted slight inaccuracies in weights.[3] Justifications for the exercise of discretion were developed by consumer agencies in the following years. 'We want the Act properly enforced, but a good way of doing it is to warn those who are not really fraudulent,' said the president of the professional association of enforcement officers in 1908.[4] In the 1930s, a powerful attack against the policy of advising businesses when offences occurred instead of prosecuting them was vehemently rejected by the overwhelming majority of enforcement officers.[5] Experience was called upon to verify that rarely was there further cause to complain once a business had been advised or warned about an offence.

The imprimatur of central government was given to the exercise of discretion by consumer agencies relatively early. In their evidence to a Royal Commission in 1869, government officials suggested that the correct procedure for weights and measures officers was not to prosecute in cases of trifling offences, since magistrates were not required to convict where the public suffered no injustice.[6] In fact the Royal Commission recommended that agencies should be entrusted with a discretionary power and be directed not to lay informations for trivial deviations, but only in cases of culpable negligence or fraud. Model regulations drafted for consumer agencies in 1890 indicated that businesses should be treated leniently and given time to correct inaccuracies, unless fraud were suspected. The more detailed regulations of 1907, which remained in force for over fifty years, were slightly more explicit and directed that consumer agencies should take into consideration 'the effect of the offence as regards both buyer and seller, and the explanation, if any, offered by the person committing the offence'.[7]

Official support is still regularly expressed for the notion that consumer agencies should hesitate before they commence a prosecution. Government committees commend consumer agencies for acting by advice and negotiation rather than by prosecution.[8] Comments in Parliament are that consumer agencies should look to the reputation of a business before prosecuting; should treat innocent offenders leniently but mete out strict punishment when intentional wrongdoing is involved; and should try to obtain redress for the consumer if a matter is not serious enough to warrant prosecution. As a government Minister put it during the committee stages of what became the Trade Descriptions Act (1968):

We do not want a spate of trivial prosecutions where, when the mistake is drawn to the attention of the department store, or whatever it is, the customer is immediately appeased, the mistake admitted, and the loss to the customer, whatever it may be, corrected.[9]

Judicial decisions have acknowledged that in general enforcement officials should have a wide discretion to enforce the law as long as they do not totally abdicate their responsibility. Specifically, the courts have criticised consumer agencies for prosecuting unnecessarily and for attempting to push the interpretation of consumer legislation to its limit. The strongest judicial support for the idea that consumer agencies should exercise moderation in prosecuting derives from certain observations in the House of Lords in *Smedleys Ltd* v. *Breed*.[10] Approval was given by two other members of the court to remarks by Viscount Dilhorne that it was not a basic principle of the rule of law that a prosecution should be automatic wherever an offence was detected, and that consumer agencies should always have regard to the general interest of consumers when exercising their discretion.

In so far as there is any public view of how consumer law should be enforced, this is generally against widespread prosecution by consumer agencies. Academic commentators mention that the intention of Parliament is to secure compliance with consumer legislation and that this might be achieved just as effectively by using prosecution as a last resort.[11] Obviously, business supports the concept of advice rather than prosecution, and it justifies this on the basis that positive control can be exercised by informal procedures other than prosecution. The usual approach to prosecution in the commercial world is adequately summarised in an editorial in a trade association journal.

It was never intended that the [Trade Descriptions] Act should be used to prosecute over petty infringements. Indeed this was stated in Parliament when the Bill was being debated. If this is being forgotten, more and more of the courts' time will be taken up with matters which could best be settled by a telephone call or a courteous letter. The decision to prosecute should surely depend on firstly whether the infringement was deliberately intended to deceive and secondly whether harm had been or was likely to be done to consumers.[12]

Public opinion when voiced supports the exercise of discretion. During the course of the field work, industrial trouble in English bakeries led to a bread shortage. A few retailers in Metropolitan County obtained supplies from outside England but imposed an extra charge because of the additional transport costs. The prices they charged were consequently in breach of a price-control order imposing maximum prices for bread. When it became known that at least one consumer agency was investigating the matter with a view to a possible prosecution, public opinion – at least as reflected in the mass media – reacted sharply and indicated that no legal action should be taken against the errant retailers.

THE ROLE OF CONSUMER LEGISLATION

Although consumer legislation does not explicitly entrust consumer agencies with discretion, it provides some support for a policy of not prosecuting automatically when an offence is detected. Offences are excused under consumer legislation if they are of a trivial character. An inconsiderable variation in quantity is exempt from prosecution under the weights and measures legislation; a false description of goods is not caught by the Trade Descriptions Act (1968) unless it is false to a material degree; and a deficiency in the expected standard of food must be to the prejudice of the consumer, which according to the courts means that a reasonable person must not consider it trifling.

Enforcement officers also refer to the statutory defences to justify the way they exercise discretion. Consumer legislation creates, in the main, offences of strict liability. A business is culpable as soon as it commits a prohibited act irrespective of whether this is done innocently or intentionally, and a business can be penalised for the actions of its employees even though its higher executives have not approved or do not know. But the harshness of strict liability is mitigated by the statutory defences contained in consumer legislation which exculpate a business from liability if an offence is the result of mistake, the act or default of someone else, or factors beyond its control, and if it can also show that reasonable precautions were taken and all due diligence exercised to avoid the offence. These defences, say consumer officers, show that Parliament realised that every offence did not warrant prosecution and support the idea that only intentional or grossly negligent acts should be penalised. In particular, the introduction of standards of reasonableness and due diligence are used to argue that consumer agencies should temper enforcement in the light of the commercial and technical realities in which business is conducted.

There are a variety of reasons why consumer law should be modified in everyday use from its formal manifestation in legislation and court decisions. Consumer officers do not have a thorough knowledge of consumer law nor are they in a position to devote careful attention to every matter they handle. Legal norms can be misinterpreted; after all, consumer officers are not trained extensively in the law. Several instances were observed in the course of the field work where concepts from the civil law were used in interpreting criminal provisions, with a consequent restrictive effect on the latter. In brief encounters with businessmen, consumer officers may not remember the relevant law and even if they know the text of a certain rule there could still be problems of interpretation, which can only be solved by reference to the case law. Furthermore, in particular cases rules combine with the various other factors examined below and are therefore modified in order to attain other objectives, which in some cases replace the original goals envisaged by Parliament or the courts. With these non-legal factors present, law may simply have a justificatory function and be used to account for a course of conduct pursued by an agency.

If legal rules are modified to fit particular situations and if they entwine with non-legal factors, this does not occur in a way which causes difficulties for consumer officers in their routine work. Any bureaucracy translates complex information and transmits it in usable form to points in the organisation.[13] Consumer protection work, like other bureaucratic activity, is routinised to facilitate its performance, particularly by experienced consumer officers. Routinisation is also necessary because of the constraint on resources; it enables consumer officers to handle a substantial volume of matters without strain. Legal rules and other organisational goals are thus transformed to provide practical guidelines for consumer officers as they go about their everyday activity. Legislation and judicial decisions are incorporated in the practices of consumer agencies and their implications for most matters encountered become well-established. Consumer officers can therefore manage problems in a constant, repetitive and normal manner.[14] An obvious danger of this is that although simple matters can be handled relatively effectively, complex matters may be resolved less expertly. The nature of these practical guidelines becomes evident in the sections that follow.

II DISCRETIONARY JUSTICE: CONSUMER AGENCIES AND THEIR CONTEXT

The exercise of discretion by consumer agencies implies criteria which enable them to make decisions on how offences are to be treated. Consumer officers sometimes assert that they can assess whether a business deserves to be punished, but it is impossible to reduce discretion to any all-embracing concept such as 'moral fault' on the part of a business, for this glosses over a number of crucial factors.[15] While the presence of moral fault may be a good reason for proceeding further with a case, its absence is never a sufficient reason for not prosecuting an offence.[16]

Consumer agencies have long accepted that legal proceedings must be instituted in cases of intentional wrongdoing or serious carelessness. A representative example of this view is the official prosecution policy of London Borough as set out in an internal memorandum: 'This Department will only prosecute if there is evidence of either dishonesty, fraud, sharp practice, gross negligence or flagrant breaches of the law.' A consumer offence committed intentionally brings it closer to traditional categories of crime. As one chief officer phrased it, intention in consumer matters is 'tantamount to theft'. Gross carelessness is equally culpable, for it suggests a pursuit of profit regardless of lawful requirements. Beyond situations of intention or culpable carelessness, the parameters of discretion exercised by consumer agencies are less easily drawn. Few consumer agencies have enunciated a prosecution policy to spell out the rules which apply in relation to the wrongdoing they detect. Some claim to be unable to formulate a detailed policy because of the multiplicity of situations which can arise. Public statements of policy are of the vaguest character, of which the following – from Annual Reports of consumer agencies – are typical: 'Prosecutions are undertaken with reluctance, as a final sanction in cases of severe infringement.' 'The department does not prosecute unless the errors are on a wholesale scale and suitable warnings have previously been given.'

Despite this public modesty, consumer agencies regularly structure their discretionary decisions in accordance with definite criteria, although these are largely unwritten, sometimes unstated, and occasionally not recognised officially. In discussion that follows the analysis is not intended to be causal. Although one factor may have been especially salient in a particular case, individual decisions are generally the outcome of an amalgamation of factors. To handle cases on a day-to-day basis in the light of legal and non-legal criteria, consumer agencies have had to develop benchmarks of decision-making. For example, decision-making is greatly assisted where offences can be translated into numerical terms. Thus the seriousness of a mispricing offence can be readily evaluated from the magnitude of the overcharge – a prosecution is justified if it consists of a single substantial overcharge or cumulated smaller discrepancies.

THE SETTING OF CONSUMER AGENCIES

The setting of consumer agencies structures the way they operate and in particular how they exercise their discretion.[17] The legal setting of consumer agencies affects the decisions they can make. Where Parliament has set quite specific standards, for instance, consumer agencies play very much the handmaiden role, and their task is simply to sample a range of products and then to submit them to an expert for an opinion about whether they comply. The social setting of consumer agencies affects the demands placed on them; for example, there are proportionately more complaints from consumers in urban areas. The political complexion of a local authority affects the division between enforcement and advice work, with local authorities controlled by the Labour Party favouring advice. Because there is a greater emphasis in some consumer agencies on consumer advice, there are fewer resources available for enforcement (although this is not conclusive about how discretion is exercised). In the discussion that follows, three elements of the milieu of a consumer agency are highlighted: the resources available to it, its relation to the courts, and its position in the organisation of government.

Resources are an overriding limitation on the activity of consumer agencies. Breaches of consumer law which escape public attention can only be detected by consumer agencies on their own initiative if they have the resources. The magnitude of the substantive law and the volume of unlawful activity make it virtually impossible for consumer agencies with limited manpower and finance to enforce the whole range of legislation.[18] The limitations inherent in the lack of resources cannot be overcome by the dedication of enforcement officers or the efficiency of consumer agencies. Prosecution, for example, involves preparing a report, collecting witness statments, drafting an information, and perhaps appearing in court to give evidence. Even prosecution-minded enforcement officers confess that they could not cope with the labour involved in prosecuting every offence they detect. The preventive work of inspecting business premises and of advising businesses about how to comply with consumer law is thus justified in terms of its cost-effectiveness when compared with prosecution. Where remedial action by a business can be achieved by advice or persuasion, the indiscriminate bringing of proceedings is said to be wasteful and unnecessary.

The attitude which consumer agencies have to the courts (as bodies which are remote from the problems of protecting consumers) influences whether they initiate legal proceedings. Once a prosecution is commenced, a consumer agency forfeits controls over the matter to a court, and therefore it is reluctant to take action if it is uncertain about the outcome.[19] Judicial decisions are a factor in considering whether court action is worth while. When these make it difficult to comply with, or enforce, an aspect of consumer law, a consumer agency can either ignore an offence, or it can threaten legal proceedings although there is no intention or possibility of proceeding further. However, the reaction of the courts is not a major factor in the routine decision-making of consumer agencies. Once a legal precedent affects the enforcement of consumer law, consumer agencies incorporate that knowledge into their enforcement practices. The broader problem of deterring business wrongdoing, and the effect of a legal decision on this, are remote from the mundane activity of enforcement officers. Similarly, the belief that judicial punishment is sometimes too lenient has little relevance for the routine aspects of law enforcement. If an offence is sufficiently serious, enforcement officers begin without a great deal of thought as to the level of the probable sanction because their foremost concern is to obtain a conviction.

Consumer agencies come within the ambit of local government and are responsible to local authority committees comprising elected represen-tatives. Considerable power is delegated by the committes and they interfere only exceptionally with the exercise of routine discretion by consumer agencies. For example, in Metropolitan County prosecutions must be authorised by the chairman of the relevant committee and he receives a summary of the facts of proposed prosecutions, although without mention of the name of the business involved. Approval has proved to be a formality, however, and no suggested prosecutions have been rejected.

In a few authorities, consumer agencies conduct their own prosecutions in magistrates courts. The argument is that they have the specialist knowledge to enable them to convey crucial points to the bench but in plain English and without legal terminology. Where consumer agencies do not conduct cases, a shackle on their discretion may be the attitude of the local authority legal department, which will handle any prosecutions. Consumer protection ranks low in the priorities of these legal departments, and in the sphere of litigation it is subordinate to other matters such as planning or land resumption. Lawyers assigned to consumer protection cases are usually of junior status with little litigation experience, and in some cases have an aversion to litigation, preferring the advisory aspects of legal work. Just as the courts are detached from the context of enforcement, legal departments lack the commitment which consumer agencies have to particular cases. What the latter regard as reprehensible malpractices may appear to a legal department as legitimate, if somewhat sharp, business dealing, whose adverse consequences consumers should be able to avoid. While legal departments usually confine themselves to vetting potential prosecutions for deficiencies in the evidence or the legal argument, a few intrude deeper into the decision to prosecute. For example, in London Borough the town clerk, the chief legal officer of the local authority, has limited the circumstances in which he will permit a prosecution for a consumer offence. The only categories of cases in which he considers prosecution appropriate (as set out in a memorandum) are deliberate offences and offences where public safety is endangered; where the offender has a previous record; or where a caution is inadequate. Moreover, there must be a 'strong possibility' of the case succeeding, and the overriding guideline (to quote the memorandum) is 'to enforce the legislation in a reasonable and intelligent way rather than to secure the maximum number of convictions'. The attitude of the town clerk, together with the fact that the present chief officer favours consumer advice, dissuades enforcement officers in London Borough from submitting prosecution reports except in cases of blatant wrongdoing.

THE ATTITUDE OF ENFORCEMENT OFFICERS

Variations between consumer agencies in the enforcement of identical consumer laws are partially explained by the interests and attitudes of the higher officials setting agency policy.[20] If they adopt a particular policy (be it committed to advising businesses or be it more disposed to prosecuting wrongdoing) enforcement officers tend to adjust the way they exercise discretion. Newly appointed enforcement officers are socialised into the prevailing policy of a consumer agency as they discuss consumer offences with colleagues or supervisors, and they soon acquire a fair knowledge of whether an offence will be approved for prosecution. The remark of an enforcement officer reflects this: 'If you want to get on in life you fit in with the department. You have to adapt to the department you work in.' There is no more painful experience for an enforcement officer than to have a prosecution report rejected. Not only will considerable time and effort have been wasted in its preparation, but an unfavourable reaction reflects on an officer's judgement. A decision not to proceed when an enforcement officer has submitted a report recommending prosecution can have a devastating effect on morale. A number of enforcement officers described how they resolved not to submit further cases for prosecution when reports which they thought justified legal proceedings were allowed to lapse. For example: 'When I arrived I was ever so keen. But I'd put up reports and they'd reject them. Gradually they wore me down so that I just accepted the routine and plodded along.'

The policy of a consumer agency regarding prosecution is not automatically reflected in the action of its enforcement officers. Broadly, it is possible to identify three different situations. First, in consumer agencies with a policy unfavourable to prosecution, enforcement officers are discouraged from recommending legal proceedings except in the most serious cases. At the other extreme are prosecution-minded consumer agencies where the performance of enforcement officers is evaluated almost wholly in terms of the number of prosecutions they conduct. Since in the words of one chief officer 'prosecution shows work', pressures are exerted on enforcement officers to submit prosecution reports. In the case of both categories of consumer agency, the prosecution rate is effectively regulated. However, although enforcement officers are limited by the prevailing policy on prosecution, they still retain a substantial discretion on other matters. Provided they submit the requisite number of prosecution reports, if any, and recommend proceedings in cases in line with the general policy, their everyday exercise of discretion is largely unmonitored. The third group of consumer agencies – by far the largest – neither encourages nor discourages prosecution, and as long as a reasonable number occur enforcement is left to the discretion of field officers. Prosecution is only one feature in judging the competence of enforcement officers, and any variation between them in the number of legal proceedings initiated is not significant in their advancement.

The extent to which the policy of a consumer agency on prosecution may not be fully implemented by enforcement officers is best illustrated by an example. The official policy of the Metropolitan County consumer agency disapproves of prosecution to control the unlawful behaviour of businesses. Intentional wrongdoing by businesses is assumed to be abnormal and the bulk of consumer offences are regarded as the product of carelessness by employees. The policy of the agency is to achieve compliance with consumer law by advising businesses on their trade practices. Prosecution is seen as counter-productive, for it jeopardises a working relationship with commerce and industry. Although this orientation is shared by those in the upper echelons of the agency, its influence is muted at the lower levels. Because of administrative burdens, and because prosecution is a low priority for the agency, higher officials do not examine prosecution reports to vet them for consistency with the official policy. Instead, they gauge its implementation in numerical terms: the situation is satisfactory if the absolute number of prosecutions is neither too small nor too large. Since the overall number of prosecutions gives the impression that agency policy is being followed through, enforcement staff in the area offices can largely formulate their own approach, which in some cases is inconsistent with agency policy, being either too antipathetical or too favourable to prosecution.

Because enforcement officers exercise some discretion – whatever the prosecution policy of a consumer agency – their personal characteristics intrude to a varying extent on decision-making. Temperament, personal ideology, social background and commitment to the job can be important. Also relevant are experience; the prominence given to law and to agency policy; the belief that particular action will be supported by, or please, supervisors; and the guidance provided by colleagues.[21] If enforcement officers recognise organisational objectives and give them effect in the exercise of discretion, their personal values obviously play a less important part in their decisions.

Enforcement officers vary enormously in the number of prosecutions they conduct: some undertake only one or two prosecutions a year; others an average of twenty. As the remark of one officer in a prosecution-minded consumer agency indicates, some enforcement officers find prosecution distasteful.

> I don't like doing people. It's my job, but I don't like it. Now I take down what everyone says and send it off to HQ and let them decide. I'm afraid I identify more with the trader than the consumer. [Why?] I'm from a business background.

Cautiousness is one explanation for the lack of enthusiasm. Enforcement officers fear failure and will only recommend legal proceedings in the clearest of cases. Every consumer agency has those who desire 'a quiet life' or who 'don't want to know'. These officers are readily identified by their colleagues and supervisors, for, although their action in particular cases may be unmonitored, their overall approach is well known. Some enforcement officers are more interested in the routine side of the job, particularly the weights and measures aspects, than in prosecution. By contrast, enforcement officers who find prosecution the highlight of law enforcement resent the routine inspection of business premises, for it uncovers little wrongdoing. In part, they find prosecution satisfying because a heavy responsibility rests on their shoulders in undertaking an investigation, and there is also the enjoyment of solving legal problems or of appearing in court. It was said of one prosecution-minded chief officer that he missed his vocation, which was to be a barrister. Age also has a role, and in several agencies the appointment of a number of young and recently qualified enforcement officers produced an upsurge in prosecutions, disproportionate to the increase in manpower. To prosecution-minded officers, there is also the satisfaction of punishing businesses responsible for malpractice. It is worth quoting one enforcement officer:

> One does not enjoy prosecuting someone, but if the circumstances dictate, you do it to protect the public. When you nail someone who has set out to deliberately deceive the public then the job becomes really satisfying.

THE STATUTORY DEFENCES

A particular example of the role of law in the discretion of consumer agencies is the operation of the statutory defences contained in consumer legislation. These enable businesses to avoid liability in certain circumstances even if they have committed an act which is prohibited. Since consumer agencies are solicitous of their success, they always carefully assess the possible defences that a business might raise if prosecuted. The relationship between the exercise of discretion and the statutory defences is complex and the contours are by no means fixed by the statutory language.[22] Historically, discretion antedates the statutory defences, which were not incorporated in consumer legislation until the Sale of Food (Weights and Measures) Act (1926) – well after the exercise of discretion was an accepted practice in consumer agencies.

The larger goals of consumer agencies bear on the manner in which the statutory defences are applied in routine situations. Prosecution is regarded as being purely punitive if measures cannot be suggested to prevent the recurrence of offences, and businesses are not expected to adopt procedures which are so burdensome that they would be virtually forced to close down. If the procedures of a business were geared to making all items equivalent to the requisite standards, for example, by having everything checked emanating from a factory, the cost would be increased unreasonably. As long as businesses are efficient, employ modern technology, and keep deviant products to the minimum feasible, consumer agencies treat them as taking the reasonable precautions required by the statutory defences.

The courts are another factor in the operation of the statutory defences. The view which consumer agencies have of the precautions taken by businesses does not always coincide with that of the courts. Consumer agencies are generally of the opinion that the courts accept too readily that businesses exercise due diligence and take reasonable precautions. It appears to consumer agencies none too difficult for businesses to impress courts with a paper scheme of supervision and control, despite warnings by some judges that businesses must be able to show a satisfactory operation in practice.

The application of the statutory defences draws heavily on notions current in everyday life. Take the defence of mistake. Experience informs enforcement officers that mistakes regularly occur in all forms of social activity, including the commercial world. Said an assistant chief officer: 'In these big companies we know how mistakes occur. After all, mistakes occur in this office. It would be pompous of me sitting here to say that an offence has occurred and to prosecute people for mistakes.' Consumer agencies regularly take the view that those punished for mistakes are bound to feel resentful even if their reputations suffer no harm. Instead of deterring wrongdoing, the result may be to dissipate any motivation a business has to obey the law. Thus, consumer agencies are alive to the consideration that they may make criminals out of honest businessmen by prosecuting them unfairly.

Not every business is to be believed, however, when it claims that a mistake has occurred. The views of a consumer agency will be coloured by its typification of a business, the less reputable being less successful in claiming that its wrongdoing is the result of a mistake. In identifying the 'genuine' or 'honest' mistake, enforcement officers derive assistance from experience, and accounts make good sense if they are compatible with what is known or expected. In the absence of other factors, a reasonable inference of mistake can be drawn if an incident is isolated. Other clues to the authenticity of a mistake are whether the offender has been prosecuted previously; the lapse of time between the offence and its discovery; the steps taken once it was detected; and whether its perpetrator benefited. If consumers consistently suffer as a result of a practice, a claim of mistake is less likely to be accepted. The following extract from an Annual Report appeals to common sense in discounting mistake as the explanation for supermarket mispricing:

> The defence of mistake has been offered in many instances of overcharging, but it is interesting to report that in 250 test purchases made at supermarkets in not one single instance was there evidence of undercharging, whilst a considerable number were overcharged.

In determining the applicability of the statutory defences, enforcement officers also rely – although to a lesser extent – on expert knowledge. Expert knowledge features prominently, for example, in deciding whether a manufacturer of prepacked food is safe from prosecution because it has taken reasonable precautions. Relevant in this context are a knowledge of food technology and of quality-control techniques. Deciding whether the best available technology is being used requires an expertise in production-line equipment, and sampling techniques must be utilised to determine whether the chosen method of production minimises the probability that offending items will occur.

Expert knowledge is not overriding, however, in such situations. The most impressive edifice of control cannot be accepted at face-value and its efficacy may be disproved by simple enquiry. A not uncommon theme of prosecution reports is that the control systems businesses supposedly have are clearly not working; indeed, are a sham. A business may not be able to produce written records of its operation, and even if it can these may not be an accurate portrayal of actual events. Elaborate control machinery may be installed but insufficient care taken to ensure its correct functioning. The recollection of a senior enforcement officer of his investigation into the presence of a nail in a loaf of bread illustrates how elementary tests can destroy the defences invoked by businesses: 'I went to the bakery. They said it couldn't happen. "We have metal detectors," they said. I threw three nails through. Nothing happened.'

Part of the task in considering the statutory defences is choosing whether to prosecute a business or its employees. A business can excuse itself if it establishes that an offence was due to the act of an employee and that it took reasonable precautions and exercised due diligence. While consumer agencies accept that businesses should be able to transfer liability to manufacturers and suppliers, they have misgivings about attempts to attribute responsibility to employees. Underlying their attitude on this point are notions about the cause of commercial wrongdoing. On the other hand, consumer agencies are attuned to the barriers facing businesses in achieving perfection and realise that in many situations further preventive action cannot be taken. Sympathetic consideration is extended to businesses in areas of commerce where the economic realities, and the nature of the work, produce recurrent problems with staff: no matter how adequate the training or how strict the supervision, the carelessness of employees cannot be eliminated completely. On the other hand, there is a countervailing tendency for consumer agencies to expand the responsibility of businesses and to postulate a causal link between the policies of high-level executives and the lapses of junior employees. The argument is that by adopting certain marketing techniques some businesses create situations which can easily lead to consumer offences. Employees are regarded as the victims of promotional practices, which impose on them an impossible burden of preventing inaccuracies. When errors occur, employees in these businesses often have no choice but to accept the blame if they want to retain their jobs and prospects. The indignation of consumer agencies at this situation is enhanced because the illicit profits from such wrongdoing accrue to the business and not to the employees.

THE NEED FOR CERTAINTY AND SUCCESS

Consumer agencies much prefer straightforward, successful prosecutions, a fact reflected in the high conviction rate for the prosecutions they bring. In the *Prosecution Survey* 90 per cent of the 791 defendants were convicted, and there was an 89 per cent conviction rate for the 8489 cases conducted under the Trade Descriptions Act (1968) from its inception to 1975.[23] Straightforward cases are beneficial in conserving scarce resources which can be utilised in a variety of other ways to protect consumers. Successful cases maintain the prestige of consumer agencies and their officers and minimise the costs of controlling business wrongdoing. A series of unsuccessful prosecutions may encourage a greater number of businessmen to defend proceedings instead of pleading guilty, thus requiring an increase in the resources devoted to each prosecution. Consumer agencies which regard prosecution as an index of protecting the consumer find straightforward and certain cases especially attractive because a substantial number can be quickly and satisfactorily completed. In the main, consumer agencies regard moral fault alone as an insufficient basis for prosecuting businesses and are reluctant to stigmatise them by association with the legal process unless their guilt is clearly capable of being proved in a court of law. In the words of an assistant chief officer:

> You shouldn't take cases against people unless you are certain that they are guilty. I have heard it said that you should prosecute if you think a person is wrong. If you are prosecuted personally on something and plead not guilty, and the case is dismissed, there is a certain smell to it. Police cars come to your door.

There is little recognition among consumer agencies that merely to institute legal proceedings may have a deterrent effect, whatever the outcome. Exceptionally, the chief officer of a consumer agency with a reputation for being prosecution-minded said:

> If there is a public interest or scandal, I will try to make the law fit, win or lose. And if I lose, there is a public value because of the publicity. There is a big sign: 'Beware'.

Only one of the prosecution files in the *Prosecution Survey* recommended legal proceedings irrespective of the result, but then only after the legal department of the local authority had expressed misgivings about prosecuting because the magistrates would probably dismiss the case. In reply, the chief officer of the consumer agency insisted on a prosecution and the need to test an important principle even at the risk of acquittal. 'This is a common form of sales promotion and I feel we must resist any suggestion that it can be placed outside the law.'

Policy prosecutions are not unknown, however, where consumer agencies institute legal proceedings to bring home to a particular business or an area of commerce that certain practices are unacceptable. For example, if enforcement officers are assigned to an area where few prosecutions have been undertaken and where the standard of trading practices is low, they may begin a policy of widespread prosecution in the hope that this will have a deterrent effect on businesses. Occasionally it is said by consumer agencies that prosecution is necessary to reveal anomalies and weaknesses in consumer law. A few of the bolder consumer agencies engage in a policy attempting to modify the law by taking court cases to procure the benefits of easier enforcement and to regulate commercial activity more effectively. This attitude is not widespread, however, and consumer agencies take an unadventurous view of novel legal claims. Law is surrounded with a mystique and is assumed to be largely unchallengeable and immutable. Most consumer agencies avoid the test case to overturn existing case law or to extend the meaning of the statutory language in consumer legislation. Only 10 of the 699 prosecutions in the *Prosecution Survey* were test cases, of which only 1 was taken on appeal on a point of law. The prevalent attitude to test cases is brought home by the reaction to an unsuccessful prosecution in Metropolitan County, which was designed to establish the principle that retailers should not advertise products which are likely to be unavailable for sale for a considerable period. Instead of appealing against the decision, the Metropolitan County consumer agency accepted it as establishing a narrow interpretation of the legislation and as relieving it from having to take any action when consumers complained about the practice. Reasons advanced by consumer agencies for their reluctance to take appeals to the High Court are the legal difficulties in overturning a dismissal; the attendant burden on resources; and the desire not to alienate local magistrates who hear consumer cases on a regular basis.

The interest which consumer agencies have in straightforward, certain cases derives in part from their view of courts as remote from, and unsympathetic to, the practicalities of enforcing consumer law.[24] There is no guarantee for consumer agencies that magistrates will take as serious a view of a prosecution as they do; the level of fines, which is regarded as too low, is taken as evidence of this. Consequently consumer agencies ignore or caution less important offences because they think trifling fines will be imposed, and the more serious cases are not prosecuted unless a conviction is almost certain. The attitude of the higher courts to consumer prosecution is not viewed any more favourably than that of magistrates courts. To some extent this is because consumer agencies interpret court decisions too circumspectly or occasionally misinterpret them. There is no better example than the widespread condemnation by consumer agencies of the decision in *Beckett* v. *Cohen*,[25] which established that a business can not be convicted for making a false statement about services to be provided in the future unless it can be disproved at the time it was made. The case has resulted in the folklore amongst enforcement officers that *no* false statements about future services can be prosecuted.

Preoccupied with winning cases, consumer agencies give close attention to the evidence necessary to prove a consumer offence. The elements of the offence must be established and its commission attributed to a business. This is relatively simple with a continuing offence or with one where there is evidence in addition to that provided by a complainant. It may be possible for an enforcement officer to solicit a repetition of an offence, or a series of complaints about a practice may establish whether an allegation by a consumer is justified. Prosecutions are facilitated if legislation requires transactions to be documented. Car log books are useful because they contain details of previous owners. Where a car mileometer is altered, they may provide information for establishing which person was responsible, and they certainly serve as evidence that a car dealer could quite easily have checked its validity with previous owners before sale.

The task of proving consumer offences is simplified because most consumer legislation creates offences of strict liability, which obviates the need to introduce any evidence about the state of mind of an offender. An exception is where services are falsely described, for intentional or reckless behaviour must be proved. The difficulty of establishing this means that under this head prosecutions are undertaken cautiously and consumer agencies usually confine themselves to obtaining redress for complainants. Whereas 55 per cent of the prosecutions in the *Prosecution Survey* were for misdescribed goods or for mispricing, as few as 5 per cent were for making false statements about services – yet there is no evidence that this offence is any less prevalent than the other two.

In the absence of an admission of wrongdoing on behalf of a business, consumer agencies are reluctant to institute proceedings on the basis of the unsupported oral evidence of a complainant. Consumer agencies receive some support for this approach from consumer legislation, as proceedings must be brought within six months when an oral misdescription is involved, as compared with a year for a written misdescription. The following account of an investigation for a misdescription offence, contained in a pungent note by the enforcement officer, is illustrative.

> Complainant bought dress. Told by assistant: 'The only one of its kind'. Took to mean an original dress. Visited shop. Manageress says statement was: 'The only one of its kind in the shop'. Conflicting statements and meanings attached. Evidence not clear. No further action.

Where a case depends on the oral evidence of a complainant, the tendency of consumer agencies is not to proceed with the criminal aspects of the matter but to attempt to obtain redress for the consumer. An exception is where the offence is serious and the complainant is a forceful and credible witness.

Corroboration of oral evidence requires careful scrutiny for inconsistencies and disagreements before a prosecution can be undertaken. Experience informs an enforcement officer that a complainant and his witnesses can be unshakable in their evidence until the time arrives for the court hearing. Of paramount importance is the honesty of a complainant and his witnesses, but truthfulness alone is insufficient. Although a consumer agency may be certain that an offence had been committed, there is always the difficulty of producing sufficient evidence to satisfy the court. A consumer agency will be dissuaded from prosecution if a complainant's personality means that his or her credibility is capable of being undermined. For example, consumer agencies are alive to the possibility that the aged or inarticulate can be confused by defence lawyers, although it is precisely these people who are likely to be the victims of consumer fraud.

Delay can weaken the evidence of an alleged offence. For example, the lapse of time before a consumer complains about a faulty product reduces the chances of proving that the fault existed when it was sold, for a plausible argument may be that it developed through subsequent use. Delay is compounded in such cases by the initial reaction of consumers to try to repair the fault or to return the product to the retailer or manufacturer to give it the opportunity to do so. Consequently, it may be impossible to make any convincing statement about the condition of the product at the time of the transaction. Another type of delay is that resulting from the dilatoriness of consumer agencies. With the passage of time witnesses become less sure of their evidence or perhaps unavailable through illness, migration or death. Table 5.3 is derived from the

Table 5.3. Delay in handling and prosecuting offences, *Prosecution Survey*

Offence	Average Time in Days	
	Average overall delay (N = 755)	Average delay due to the agency (N = 591)
Misdescribed goods	223	64
Mispricing	128	48
Misdescribed services, etc.	231	66
Incorrect quantity	100	30
Other weights and measures offences	82	23
Substandard food	108	42
Other offences	167	–
All offences	156	47

Prosecution Survey and summarises the average delay in the prosecution of different offences. The first set of figures shows the time between the date of the offence and the date of hearing, while the second calculation attempts to measure the extent to which delay was attributable to the agency by using as the reference points the date when it became aware of the offence and the date when it formally completed its investigation. Mispricing and incorrect quantity offences are more quickly dealt with than offences involving the misdescription of goods or services. One explanation is that consumer agencies are more likely to have independent evidence of the first type of offence instead of having to rely on the oral statements of complainants, and another factor is that these offences are generally more straightforward and certain.

III BUSINESSES AND THEIR OFFENCES

The nature of the businesses prosecuted by consumer agencies and the offences involved can be described in objective terms. Table 5.4, for example, is drawn from the *Prosecution Survey* and shows that the largest number of prosecutions in the three consumer agencies studied were of car dealers for misdescribing the cars which they sold and of supermarkets for mispricing offences. The present concern is how this pattern of prosecutions is produced.

Table 5.4. Businesses and offences prosecuted, *Prosecution Survey*

	Offence							
	Misdescribed Goods	Mispricing	Misdescribed services, etc.	Incorrect quantity	Other weights & measures offences	Substandard food	Other offences	Total
FIRMS								
Car dealers	135	9	1	–	–	–	1	146
Supermarkets	2	54	1	15	1	2	1	76
Manufacturers	18	–	2	23	–	9	–	52
Importers, wholesalers, packers, etc.	11	1	–	15	–	1	6	34
Grocer shops	1	13	–	10	2	1	1	28
Service stations	12	6	1	1	6	–	–	26
Coal merchants	1	–	–	19	1	–	–	21
Bakers; dairies	–	–	–	17	–	4	–	21
Fruit shops	4	–	–	8	8	–	–	20

Table 5.4. (*Continued*)

	Misdescribed Goods	Mispricing	Misdescribed services, etc.	Incorrect quantity	Other weights & measures offences	Substandard food	Other offences	Total
Butcher shops	2	1	–	15	1	–	–	19
Sand & ballast, construction demolition, etc.	2	–	–	12	4	–	–	18
Domestic & electrical appliance stores	8	3	3	–	2	–	–	16
Pubs and wine shops	1	12	–	2	–	–	–	15
Travel firms	–	–	14	–	–	–	–	14
Departmental/variety stores	–	12	1	1	–	–	–	14
Co-operative stores	1	3	–	3	–	3	–	10
Building & home maintenance firms	2	–	7	–	–	–	–	9
Repair firms – cars & electrical goods	1	–	7	–	–	–	–	8
Furnishing stores	3	3	–	1	–	–	–	7
Hardware stores	3	2	–	–	–	–	–	5
Jewellers, toy & sports stores	3	2	–	–	–	–	–	5
Mail-order firms	4	–	1	–	–	–	–	5
Discount houses	–	1	2	1	–	–	–	4
Entertainment businesses	–	1	3	–	–	–	–	4
Clothing stores and dry cleaners	2	1	–	–	–	–	–	3
Mass media	2	–	–	–	–	–	–	2
Others	10	10	3	5	4	–	–	32
INDIVIDUALS								
Coalmen	–	–	–	44	1	–	–	45
Branch managers	11	23	–	7	–	–	1	42
Market traders, hawkers, one-day salesmen, etc.	17	–	–	16	5	–	–	38
Shop assistants, salesmen, etc.	7	3	–	21	2	–	2	35
Company directors	5	2	–	2	–	–	–	9
Door-to-door salesmen	3	–	–	–	–	–	–	3
Others	2	–	1	–	1	1	–	5
Total	273	162	47	237	39	21	12	791

The discretion of consumer agencies is distinguished by the individualised treatment of business wrongdoing. This is not unique to consumer agencies, but characterises the whole range of law enforcement: for example, in sentencing, the law examines the record of a person. In the decision whether to prosecute a business, its attributes, including its record and attitude, have particular salience for the master strategy adopted by consumer agencies of using persuasion, rather than force, to achieve compliance with consumer law. The business with a record of conscientious obedience to law, when it undertakes to prevent future offences, is not likely to be prosecuted if it commits an offence. On the other hand, prosecution is almost certain if a business has a history of deliberately flouting the law, and rejects overtures by a consumer agency designed to induce lawful behaviour.

THE NATURE OF BUSINESSES

The approach of consumer agencies to law enforcement draws on their typifications of businesses.[26] Enforcement officers are quickly made aware of the link between the typification of a business and the appropriate response to its wrongdoing. The following statement appears in lectures notes used by trainee enforcement officers:

> The aim is to obtain compliance with the law by advice and encouragement rather than prosecution. Of course the ultimate weapon of prosecution must be retained and there should be no hesitation to use it if necessary, but the policy requires a state of mind on the part of the enforcement authority to the effect that almost all traders are honest people, who, like the rest of us, are careless and negligent from time to time.

The assumption is that by their nature reputable businesses do not intend to commit offences and will take steps to prevent the recurrence of any which are the outcome of ignorance or mistake. Since they comply with the law if informed of their obligations or of defects in their trade practices, an effective alternative to the criminal sanction in most cases is advice or a caution. The additional assumption is that it is undesirable to prosecute those attempting to comply with the law for this can create resentment and perhaps a fall in standards. As the course notes for the Diploma in Consumer Affairs remark: 'If an honest man is prosecuted for a temporary lapse of good management, he will resent it and future co-operation with him will be more difficult.'

For unscrupulous businesses there is no assumption that advice or a caution has an equivalent effect to a prosecution. By definition, unscrupulous businesses are inclined to evade the law and will only comply when the costs – those associated with being prosecuted and fined – affect their profits. If an unscrupulous business is responsible for an offence the chances of its being prosecuted are relatively high, whereas a reputable business in similar circumstances would avoid prosecution. Offences of unscrupulous businesses are assumed to be committed intentionally and thus to deserve the application of formal sanctions. The essence of the following comments was repeated on many occasions by enforcement officers with respect to secondhand-car dealers: 'I could caution secondhand-car dealers until I am blue in the face. It's just so ludicrous to contemplate.' 'Even where I hadn't known of a car dealer before, I would prosecute, because it's possibly a symptom of something that's been going on for a long time.'

A consumer agency feels less apprehensive about prosecuting an offence if a business has already been cautioned or prosecuted. Notions of fairness underlie this attitude because the business has been informed of its obligations but has done nothing. Similarly, consumer agencies will not prosecute when the relevant legislation is recent or where an inspection has not been made for a considerable period, on the grounds that businesses must be given reasonable notice of a law or of its continued enforcement.

The prior cautions or convictions of a business are also valued for their instrumental role in the exercise of discretion.[27] Previous cautions or prosecutions highlight whether a consumer agency can achieve obedience to consumer law without recourse to court proceedings. Prosecution is not the automatic response to every violation but is used for its perceived efficacy in producing results. Less serious responses than prosecution having failed, resort to prosecution is almost inevitable. 'Nothing short of proceedings will affect an improvement' – the comment in one prosecution file – is a common theme when cautioning has been unsuccessful in preventing repetition of an offence. In this way the risk of future offences being committed is a factor in the exercise of discretion. If a business has already been advised or warned about an offence, the chances that it may be repeated or that a more serious offence may be committed are too great simply to caution. Where a business has been advised or warned about an offence it is possible to conclude that it has been negligent, that it has not taken reasonable precautions, or that intentional wrongdoing is involved. Complaints from consumers can serve a similar function.

Although important in the exercise of discretion by consumer agencies, the previous record of a business is by no means crucial to the institution of a prosecution. Previous cautions were referred to in the reports recommending prosecution in only 10 per cent of the 791 offences in the *Prosecution Survey*. Prior convictions were cited slightly more frequently than cautions (just under 11 per cent) and in 6 cases – all of which could be categorised as consumer fraud – the convictions mentioned were for non-consumer offences. These figures underestimate slightly the importance of a previous record in that the prosecution reports did not always mention when a business had been cautioned or prosecuted. On occasions, an enforcement officer obviously considered that an offence was sufficiently serious to justify prosecution and thought it unnecessary to include a reference to the record of the business. A comparison of the caution and prosecution records in Metropolitan City over a five-year period shows that of the 316 offenders prosecuted 14 per cent had been previously cautioned or prosecuted. The figure would be slightly higher in a less prosecution-minded agency but still quite small in relation to the total number of prosecutions.

In a direct sense, then, previous cautions or convictions are important but not crucial. Nevertheless, they have an indirect bearing on discretion, for they are an influence in the typification of businesses. With local or provincial businesses, a consumer agency has direct knowledge of previous cautions and prosecutions, for it will have been responsible for the bulk of them. The Office of Fair Trading provides lists of recent convictions to consumer agencies contemplating a prosecution. Knowledge of whether national businesses have been cautioned is acquired more circuitously; for example, through the confidential bulletins circulated by the professional association of enforcement officers. Despite the importance of previous cautions or convictions, the growth of consumer advice work means that businesses without any record are now depicted as unscrupulous if they fail to resolve justified consumer complaints.

Generally, enforcement officers are not consciously influenced by their personal knowledge of, or friendship with, particular businessmen. Although a number of enforcement officers recounted odd incidents of how particular prosecutions were aborted by superiors because of their association with the businessmen involved, the only cases approaching this which I encountered directly in the course of the field work were where enforcement officers, who had known businessmen for a number of years on a professional basis, decided to caution them for consumer offences because they regarded them as incompetent but not as dishonest. Incidents of this nature seem to be more likely to arise if consumer agencies lack a prosecution-minded approach to law enforcement; where the turnover of staff in both an agency and business is low; and in rural areas, where enforcement officers are more influenced by the norms of the community.[28]

Personal factors associated with an offender enter the prosecution calculus in another way. An illustration is provided by an incident in one of the most prosecution-minded consumer agencies in the country. A test purchase of spirits in a pub by an enforcement officer, posing as an ordinary person, was of sufficient short measure to justify legal proceedings against the licensee, irrespective of other factors such as his record. On investigation it was found that the barmaid directly responsible for the offence had been told of her husband's attempted suicide an hour previously. The agency exercised its discretion and cautioned both the licensee and the barmaid. As this example suggests, offenders may be exonerated if they demonstrate that an offence is unintended, because in those circumstances a prosecution would be ineffectual. Such incidents are generally of a fortuitous character although enforcement officers have formulated some ideas about their occurrence. Thus they maintain that only the malevolent among them would prosecute an elderly grocer managing a small corner store because offences committed by these traders are a product of dithering and forgetfulness and not of intentional wrongdoing. Certainly supermarket managers receive less sympathy in similar circumstances, no matter how newly arrived to their employment, or how hard-pressed they are by staff shortages.

A faint undercurrent among some consumer agencies is to prosecute large businesses when small businesses in similar circumstances would be cautioned. Cautions, so the belief runs, have a greater effect on small traders because the impact on the moving forces behind them is more immediate, as compared with that on the remote officials of large businesses. Moreover, local traders are anxious to avoid the unfavourable publicity attendant on a prosecution because their trade is very dependent on their reputation. An argument in favour of prosecuting large businesses is that offences committed by them are likely to have adverse repercussions for a substantial number of consumers. A chief officer told me: 'The bigger, the better, because they are the people who are doing the business.' And a senior officer said: 'In a big shop you have to go to court because you don't know how many people have been defrauded.' Further, large businesses are said to determine the standards of a considerable part of the commercial world, so that if they are induced to improve their practices small businesses will emulate them.

The attitude in favour of prosecuting large businesses was observed in this study in only one area office of a consumer agency. Proceedings were instituted almost exclusively against national and multinational corporations as a matter of policy. Only one-tenth of the offenders prosecuted were local or provincial firms, whereas the comparable figure for the *Prosecution Survey* as a whole was 55 per cent. Elsewhere it seemed that the policy of prosecuting large businesses was an expression of opinion rather than a guideline for enforcement activity. In the many prosecution reports I read the only reference to the scale of businesses was in terms of maintaining even-handedness between large and small firms. A few prosecutions were justified on the basis that a difference in approach to businesses of different sizes was inequitable or that the agency had tended to concentrate on businesses of a certain size in the past, which had encouraged laxness in the practices of others.

The clear implication of several other prosecution files, however, was that legal proceedings had been abandoned in what would have been cases normally justifying prosecution, simply because large organisations were prepared to call the bluff of the agency by making plain that they would strenuously contest the charge. A few enforcement officers confirmed this.

For example, one recalled the approach in the previous agency in which he worked:

> There was a policy of using cautions where it was a bit dodgy. Not only where the evidence was poor but, say, where the company would bring along a QC. We failed in a prosecution against [a national business] where a QC was employed. After that we never prosecuted them although we found things wrong.

Conversely, consumer agencies sometimes take advantage of the ignorance of small businesses about consumer law. One example observed was of a consumer agency which regularly obtained convictions against secondhand-car dealers although, according to judicial interpretation of the legislation, no criminal offence was involved. The agency was secure in the knowledge that these car dealers, who mainly operated part-time from private premises, would plead guilty and would not defend a case by relying on the case law that no criminal offence was committed.

Size also has an indirect bearing on discretion in consumer agencies in the application of the statutory defences. All businesses are expected to exercise a certain amount of care and skill, but in assessing whether reasonable precautions have been taken consumer agencies expect larger businesses to adhere to more onerous standards. Their resources are regarded as such that they should be knowledgeable about consumer law and have the necessary expertise to incorporate its provisions into their business practices.

THE ATTITUDE OF A BUSINESS

Features of a business, such as the nature of the trade, provide a general indication of where it falls within the range from reputable to unscrupulous, but to locate it specifically requires more precise information. Attitude is one parameter shaping the typification of a business. It is particularly relevant for small organisations because in national businesses it may be that obstreperousness, say, can be dismissed as the idiosyncrasy of a single branch manager. The way enforcement officers use the manner of their reception by a business to typify it is illustrated by what one told me:

> The way a chap answers your questions, you can come out and think: 'He's a crook. I can't have him this time, but in future.' Or you might come out thinking that he's an honest man, trying to make a living, and has made a mistake.

The diligence with which a business answers written enquiries may also be influential, for it characterises a business as being either concerned with, or indifferent to, legal provisions. Attitude is more significant for enforcement officers in the course of their field duties. If a business adopts a defiant attitude, an enforcement officer has an incentive to investigate further to detect any offences. Businesses regularly avoid prosecution when they correct defects and take precautions to prevent their recurrence, particularly when remedial action is taken before the matter comes to the attention of a consumer agency. Thus businesses offering reassurances that their manufacturing or marketing methods will be varied, withdrawing items or advertisements from circulation, or offering redress to dissatisfied customers, may escape prosecution. Of course such action will not automatically exculpate offenders if the remedial steps are regarded as insufficient, or if other factors are overriding, such as disregard of previous warnings.

Guilt is almost conclusively presumed when an enforcement officer is obstructed by a businessman who gives false information, refuses to divulge details of the matter or of the business, or in the extreme case uses physical threats. It was along these lines that an enforcement officer drew negative inferences in a report about the proprietor of a mail-order business, who failed to clarify his explanation of an offence, although given a suitable opportunity:

> The very fact that he has not, as he puts it, found time to gather his facts together, would tend to go against him, in that a person who has a genuine explanation would, usually, make a written statement straight away so as to clarify the position and, possibly, go someway to helping him should proceedings be instituted against him.

An unhelpful attitude towards a complaint may have similar implications for it may have drawn attention to an offence which the business should have rectified without hesitation. Attitude is a useful predictor of the future behaviour of a business and is a guide to whether prosecution is required to achieve reform. An unco-operative attitude – a refusal to remedy an infraction immediately or to provide redress for a justified complaint – indicates that the objectionable behaviour may recur or continue.

The attitude of a business does not exist in isolation from other factors. A business will escape prosecution, whatever its attitude towards a consumer agency, if this is not symptomatic of wrongdoing; even the most defiant business cannot be prosecuted if evidence of wrongdoing is either insubstantial or non-existent. On the other hand, a business which displays co-operation and a willingness to adopt remedial action is not immune from prosecution. The attitude may be spurious, as with the fraudulent business which attempts to conceal its unlawful endeavours behind a screen of apparent co-operation. National businesses commonly adopt a respectful approach in their dealings with consumer agencies but are hardly exempt from legal action.

To some extent, the response of enforcement officers to a businessman whose demeanour is defiant derives from the need to maintain their authority.[29] The following comment by an enforcement officer shows such a concern with exacting respect from a particular businessman:

> I'm not vindictive, but the other day I went into a shop and said there was an overcharge of one p[ence] and he said there wasn't. Now if he had admitted it and explained the circumstances I would have left it there. But he's the sort of person who gets prosecuted.

The relationship between attitude and authority is sometimes apparent with enforcement officers who see their main task as obtaining redress for consumers. These officers overlook consumer offences if redress is obtained but will prosecute if a businessman fails to comply with their suggestion about how the matter should be settled. Enforcement officers are not normally preoccupied with a desire to see their authority accepted. The incidence of disrespect by businessmen is low. An inkling of its magnitude is available in the number of prosecutions conducted under sections of consumer-protection legislation which prohibit the obstruction of enforcement officers acting in the course of their duties. In the *Prosecution Survey* there were only eight prosecutions of this nature – 1 per cent of the total.

The quest for authority intrudes in another way, for a business cannot be continually warned about a consumer offence without making a mockery of a consumer agency. At some point the agency must support its threats with more serious measures or see its authority diminish, and perhaps be faced with an escalation of wrongdoing. As an enforcement officer succinctly put it: 'At some time you've either got to put up or shut up. You can't go on cautioning them for years.' Over five years, Metropolitan City issued 733 cautions of which 194 were directed to businesses which committed similar offences on more than one occasion. Table 5.5 sets out the extent to which the same businesses were warned about similar offences.[30] At first glance there seems to be a not inconsiderable degree of defiance of cautions issued by the agency. In examining the figures, however, two points should be noted. First, many of the offences

Table 5.5. Businesses repeatedly cautioned for similar offences, Metropolitan City, five-year period

Number of times cautioned	*Number of businesses*
Once	539
Twice	44
Three times	10
Four times	5
Five times	5
Over five times	4

cautioned are trivial in nature and their repetition hardly compounds their significance. Second, it may be incorrect to group together the cautions given to different branches of national businesses, for the immediate cause of some of these offences may have been the local staff. The fact remains, however, that businesses are treated with considerable leniency.

THE NATURE OF THE OFFENCE

Another contingency in the exercise of discretion is the nature of the offence. Generally it is not possible to categorise an offence merely on the basis of its magnitude or seriousness. The same offence committed under different circumstances may be treated as warranting prosecution or as suitable to be dealt with informally. A constant practice of consumer agencies, however, has been to identify technical or trivial offences and to refuse to prosecute these unless the circumstances are exceptional. An argument supporting this approach has been that courts will not be impressed if an agency prosecutes trivial offences, if only for the practical reason that they will be over-burdened. The tendency to treat trivial offences lightly is illustrated by a comparison of the proportion of different offences which were cautioned and prosecuted in Metropolitan City over a five-year period. Table 5.6 shows that weights and measures offences other than incorrect quantity comprised three-fifths of the cautions, but less than one-tenth of the prosecutions. These offences are usually of a minor nature involving slight inaccuracies in weighing and measuring equipment.

Consumer agencies have evolved different guidelines to assist them in evaluating the seriousness of an offence. An enforcement officer explained the policy of his agency: 'If it's only a question of a couple of items that are half a p[ence] overcharged we simply bring them to the attention of the

Table 5.6. Offences cautioned and prosecuted in Metropolitan City, five-year period

	Cautioned %	Prosecuted %
Misdescribed goods	7 (50)*	27 (86)
Mispricing	12 (85)	25 (79)
Misdescribed services, etc.	4 (27)	8 (24)
Incorrect quantity	17 (127)	30 (96)
Other weights and measures offences	57 (425)	9 (27)
Other offences	1 (6)	1 (3)
Miscellaneous	2 (13)	– (–)
Total	100 (733)	100 (315)

*Figures in brackets show the number cautioned or prosecuted.

shop manager. But if it is several items which are two pence or three pence overcharged it is a different matter.' There are similar guidelines for quantity offences which involve fixing a figure for a permissible percentage deficiency in terms of the total product. This is then considered, together with the equivalent monetary value, and modified according to whether the deficiencies are spread over a number of items. The effect of these indices is modified, of course, by the context of an offence. Small offences are not for that reason insignificant but may be symptomatic of a deeper malaise – a breakdown in supervisory proceedings, gross carelessness, or sharp practice. Previous history may magnify their culpability, as where cautions about their occurrence are consistently ignored. Retribution loomed large in the explanation of one enforcement officer as to why trivial cases could be the subject of legal proceedings: 'You may see some trivial prosecutions because, in the past, he [an officer] has had a good prosecution go down; he has been cheated out of conviction by a technicality.' Another justification for prosecuting minor offences is to deter a business which has engendered numerous consumer complaints which it refuses to resolve satisfactorily, but which has committed few criminal offences. Since the agency cannot take direct action for breaches of the civil law, the only sanction it can impose as an incentive for these businesses to reform themselves is to prosecute the few, and perhaps insignificant, offences which they commit.

The question whether profits have accrued to a business from an offence can fix its gravity for consumer agencies. It is within this framework that a multiplicity of trivial deficiencies over a period is viewed when these are not compensated for by excess quantities of the same order. Consumers are perhaps not sufficiently affected to complain about individual deficiencies and thus their losses will remain uncompensated. The stark reminder of unlawful behaviour is the increment in business profits – however unintended these may be. Profits can also unmask a disregard for, or evasion of, legal requirements. For example, a business which commits offences in stepping up output to make available a product which is in short supply will receive little sympathy if the disproportionate profits reaped point to the exploitation of the consumer rather than to the performance of a service. A profit from an offence may sometimes lead to the inference that dishonesty is involved; conversely, an absence of profit may indicate that an offence has occurred innocently. A neat illustration is provided in a report recommending that a service-station proprietor be cautioned and not prosecuted for displaying a sign indicating that the station gave trading stamps, whereas it had ceased doing so. The investigating officer, who had a reputation for being prosecution-minded, wrote: 'I am personally quite satisfied that there is no intent upon [the proprietor's] part. The garage is situated in a residential district and does not attract any "passing trade" so that any gain to the business would have been offset by loss of good will.'

Harm to the consumer, and whether it can be remedied, are other indices of the seriousness of an offence. This accords with the notion of strict liability – that it is irrelevant whether a business is at fault, for the aim is to prevent harm to the public. A prosecution-minded chief officer expressed the sentiment succinctly: 'If the consumer is injured, we prosecute. The consumer is not really interested in whether it is a matter of fraud or accident.' If an offence arises from complaint, concrete evidence of harm is available. Otherwise, the matter must be framed in hypothetical terms: would prospective consumers be misled and suffer a loss as a result of the offence? In this regard, the comment in one prosecution report – that 'the original complainant was misled, and so would the average person' – illustrates the process of practical reasoning employed by enforcement officers. Consumer awareness of potential harm is irrelevant in this calculation.

Harm is a prominent yardstick in the implementation of the section of the food and drugs legislation which penalises deficiences in the expected standard of food. Almost all offences under this section arise from complaint. Referring specifically to the presence of foreign bodies in food, the annual report of a consumer agency justifies the prosecution of apparently insignificant offences because consumers *do* regard them as significant: 'What is factual, however, is that all the complainants were prepared to give evidence in court to substantiate their distaste when the foreign matter was found.' Harm in the case of an offence under the food and drugs legislation is rarely financial, for the monetary loss will be insubstantial if the incident is isolated. Neither is it always physical harm although a foreign body, for example, may be dangerous if accidentally ingested. The test commonly used is whether the feelings of the consumer are affronted – whether the offence is obnoxious to public sensibilities.

The probability of a prosecution being brought is greater if an offence is detected by a consumer. To some extent a complaint is significant because consumer agencies tend to feel obliged to prosecute if they think that the public demands it.[31] They attempt to reflect community preferences and to respond to most offences with independence and flexibility. Individual complainants have little comprehension of the distinction between civil and criminal law and their main motivation for complaining is to obtain redress. A common reaction is for consumers to be reluctant to involve themselves in prosecutions, particularly if they have been reimbursed for their loss. An agency may interpret this as an indication that an offence is not serious enough for prosecution and, in any event, must assess its threat to the success of a case. On the other hand, an agency may undertake legal proceedings, whatever the desire of a complainant, if it has invested considerable resources in an investigation and has independent evidence of an offence. One example is where an agency resolves to prevent a business from reaping considerable profits as a result of unlawful behaviour.

Complaints entwine with the exercise of discretion in other, less direct, ways. A disproportionate number of justified complaints about a business, even if they involve the civil law, is symptomatic of an objectionable trade practice: 'One [complaint] is a breach of contract, but ten is a criminal offence, because you have malice aforethought,' was the reasoning of one enforcement officer, which was shared by others. A single complaint can amplify the gravity of an offence and move the balance in favour of prosecution, if a business fails to remedy the wrongdoing of which it is now aware. A justified complaint is thus invested with the properties of a caution by a consumer agency, for both notify a business of behaviour which should be rectified.

The official position of consumer agencies is that arrangements between a consumer and a business in settlement of a complaint have some, but not a crucial, influence on law enforcement. The benefit to the community from a prosecution, runs this argument, will usually transcend that which will be obtained if the individual consumer is compensated for his loss. And particularly when only some of the consumers adversely affected by a practice identify themselves by complaining. Thus a supermarket was prosecuted in Northbridge (Blankshire) for a mispricing offence. Its offer to sell the mispriced items at a discount equivalent to the overcharge for a comparable period was rejected, because there was no guarantee that those who had paid an excessive amount would obtain the benefit. In addition, an overemphasis on securing redress for consumers is said to place consumer agencies in the invidious position of appearing to abuse their power by exerting pressure on businesses. Agencies also find it distasteful that the acceptance of compensation in settlement of a complaint could be portrayed as the corruption of the enforcement process. Thus consumer agencies emphasise that any recompense offered to consumers following their investigations is never at their behest, and that not the slightest pressure is exerted on businesses in this regard.

In practice, a business offering redress to a complainant can frequently avoid prosecution. The redress-minded enforcement officers treat compensation as the resolution of a complaint and in effect as an alternative to prosecution. From the moment a complaint is received, attention is concentrated on obtaining satisfaction for the consumer, and prosecution ranks as a secondary consideration. At times, the prosecution-minded also refrain from initiating legal proceedings if a consumer is satisfied with the recompense offered by an offending business, although ostensibly they take the enforcement of law as their prime duty. Furthermore, many enforcement officers suggest to businessmen that compensation will be accepted in settlement of an offence despite standing instructions, such as those in Metropolitan County, that 'there must be no suggestion, however vague, to a trader that a prosecution might be avoided if he were to make amends or reparations to the complainant'. In contacts with businessmen, some enforcement officers subtly hint that redress will settle a matter. Alternatively, some define the choice quite starkly – to compensate the consumer or be prosecuted. An instructive example comes from my notes of a lengthy interview between an enforcement officer and the two partners of a secondhand-car firm. The officer had investigated five complaints against the partnership – which had no previous record – and uncovered a number of consumer offences. Although prosecution-minded, he decided to caution if the business settled on his terms:

> I give everyone one chance. The outcome is up to yourselves. I am going to take all these offences together in a package deal. If you put these things right you'll be cautioned. But if you come again, then you'll be put down for prosecution. You know what's going to happen if I take these to court. It will cost you compensation as well . . . I'm giving you the opportunity to put these matters right. I'd like you to go away and give these people satisfaction and learn what you've heard this morning. Tell your salesmen, and if you get complaints in future, deal with them so they don't come to us.

An argument advanced by consumer agencies is that, with limited resources, consumer agencies must concentrate their preventive programme on the greatest abuses. If the consumer is satisfied with the result, the time-consuming process of prosecuting an offence is unwarranted. The payment of compensation indicates the desire of a business to remedy the offence and suggests an intention to prevent its recurrence. If a consumer agency ensures that an offence is rectified, and that the consumer is compensated, prosecution is superfluous. Redress is a particularly satisfactory solution if the outcome of a prosecution is uncertain. The one exception is fraud, where the exaction of compensation will not have the deterrent effect of a prosecution. Consumer agencies realise that fraudulent operators have no objection to paying out occasional small amounts in settlement if they are free to continue their deceptive practices. Indeed, fraudulent businesses actually take the initiative to compensate consumers, to dissuade them from pressing their complaints.

6 The Impact of Consumer Law and its Enforcement on Businesses

Businesses are affected by consumer law in different ways. Some aspects they largely ignore because both the government and consumer agencies do not regard them as being of crucial significance. The impact of consumer law on a business is minimal if its trade practices already coincide with or are in advance of the provisions of the law. Businesses which readily offer an exchange or a refund when a consumer complains about goods or services are rarely involved with consumer agencies or legal claims. Well-managed firms, which tightly control their promotional practices and adequately train their staff, are unlikely to breach consumer law.

Any study of the impact of consumer law faces certain difficulties. Consumer law is one among a number of instruments of social control, and it is impossible to isolate its effects on trade practices from those produced in other ways. A business may comply with the terms of consumer law because of factors such as inertia or the failure to realise that there are viable alternatives. In the context of consumer protection, the change in the general climate of opinion in favour of consumers, the pressure exerted by the organised consumer movement, and the growing awareness by consumers of their rights, are particular influences to be taken into account. In assessing the impact of a particular aspect of consumer law, an important variable is the attitude of businessmen towards it. This depends in part upon their evaluation of its attributes, but businessmen vehemently opposed to a law may follow it to the letter because of their belief that in general laws should be obeyed. The mere fact that Parliament makes certain behaviour unlawful influences their opinion about it and determines their action.[1] This does not mean that they will never be in breach of a law since this can happen accidentally.

Another difficulty is identifying the changes in business behaviour when consumer legislation is enacted by Parliament or enforced by consumer agencies. One means of ascertaining this is to obtain access to the decision-making processes of businesses to determine whether there are any changes in their policy. An alternative approach is to observe the external behaviour of businesses following the introduction of new law or its enforcement, for any variation can be attributed to the legal changes in the absence of other obvious causes. Sometimes the impact of consumer law on businesses can be related to changes in other social factors. Criticism of the enforcement of the Consumer Protection Act (1961), for example, focuses on the fact that there has been little change in the number of persons suffering physical injury from products supposedly made safer by regulations under it.

This chapter is an exploratory study of the impact of consumer law and its enforcement. It is based on statistical data, information from consumer agencies, a survey of trade magazines, and interviews with a number of businesses. Contact was made with thirty-two firms and six trade associations. In all, forty-eight persons were involved – in the businesses, four company solicitors, four sales assistants, five proprietors (all small businesses), ten branch or section managers, and the remainder head office executives. The firms were by no means representative, although they formed a range of those most relevant for consumers – three manufacturers, two national supermarkets, five variety or department stores (all but one national), six other national firms, a nationalised industry, ten businesses in trades from clothing to electrical equipment, a solid-fuel distributor, two used-car dealers and three market traders. Of those contacted, eighteen were interviewed when I was negotiating with them as an advice officer in London Borough. In these cases, I did not identify myself as a researcher, but the course of conversation made it possible to discuss in broad terms the impact of consumer law. While most of these conversations did not extend beyond fifteen minutes, the other interviews lasted on average between forty-five minutes and an hour.

I THE GENERAL DIMENSIONS OF BUSINESS COMPLIANCE

It seems clear that consumer law and its enforcement produce changes in the practices of businesses. Detailed regulations, such as those on the labelling of food, have produced an observable transformation in the contents of particular labels. Descriptions which would have appeared regularly in advertisements before the Trade Descriptions Act (1968) have disappeared or appear in a modified form. For example, double-pricing has been curtailed in a number of areas of commercial activity, and in advertisements either only one price is listed or prices are completely omitted. In one small survey of the effect of enforcement, the consumer agency in London Borough recorded the amount of non-compliance with two statutes – the Trading Stamps Act (1964) and the Advertisements (Hire Purchase) Act (1967) – on two occasions: when it first assumed responsibility for their enforcement and then a year later. Both statutes had been in force for a considerable time, but no one in the area had been specifically charged with their implementation and any compliance was

Table 6.1. Effect of enforcement of two statutes in London Borough

	Trading Stamps Act (1964)		Advertisements (Hire Purchase) Act (1967)	
	Year 1	Year 2	Year 1	Year 2
Premises visited	334	243	309	165
Premises infringing legislation	124	26	226	9
Incorrect advertisments	Not applicable		507	5

because businesses had taken the initiative. The amount of non-compliance and the improvement after a year of enforcement is set out in Table 6.1.

The fear that the government will introduce new consumer law has sometimes induced businesses voluntarily to amend trade practices in an effort to forestall this possibility.[2] In recent times codes of practice for different trades have been stimulated by the combination of government pressure and business self-interest. The most notable example is the tightening of the voluntary controls over advertising following government intimations that legislation would be introduced if they were not improved. In the result, the Advertising Code was strengthened, extra staff were employed by the Advertising Standards Authority to monitor misleading advertising, and the code was publicised to make the public more aware of where complaints could be made in the event of dissatisfaction.

Businesses concede that they have tightened their procedures as a result of consumer law. Following the introduction of the Trade Descriptions Act (1968) and the successive amendments to the Advertising Code of Practice, businesses have devoted a greater effort to monitoring advertising to eliminate exaggerations and statements which cannot be justified. A company solicitor explained how the marketing and promotional ideas of his business were vetted more stringently than previously: 'We look at things more closely, whereas ten years ago, if someone had a bright idea for marketing, they would go ahead. Now if someone has an idea they drop me a note.'

Similarly, businessmen recognise that a prosecution can have a reformative effect. The partner in a small secondhand-car firm in London Borough told me of legal proceedings taken against him under the Trade Descriptions Act (1968): 'A couple of years ago I was caught out when I misdescribed a car and now I am very careful what I say.' The prosecution of a large business, because of the lapse of one of its employees, can have a salutary effect throughout the organisation. Members of the staff in a supervisory position will take action to prevent the occurrence of a similar offence within their area of responsibility. Prosecution can improve the marketing techniques of a business. For example, the style of pricing in supermarkets has been modified because of a series of prosecutions under the Trade Descriptions Act (1968). A particular illustration I encountered was a national supermarket which was fined £1000 and £2000 in quick succession for mispricing offences. As a result, the business instituted a new system whereby, in addition to the occasional random checks, branch managers were required to carry out regular full comparison of display prices and those marked on individual items against the price catalogues issued by head office.

Although consumer law and its enforcement can effect changes in business practices, these do not occur as a matter of course. Fundamental changes are less likely to occur than those requiring a slight alteration to the existing ways of conducting business.[3] As a generalisation it can be said that consumer law has produced modifications in the point-of-sale conditions upon which products are supplied, but that it has had little impact on general marketing methods or on the design and construction of products. For example, the Trade Descriptions Act (1968) has changed the way prices are advertised, but it has not resulted in the dropping of basic promotional practices, such as the use of manufacturers' recommended prices, although these indirectly give rise to mispricing offences. Moreover, it seems that businesses rarely respond in a planned and co-ordinated manner to consumer law or its enforcement, but that their reaction is characteristically *ad hoc*, coping with particular problems as they arise.[4] Certainly this is not the universal reaction, and I shall refer below to a minority of businesses which have adopted basic trading philosophies which determine their whole approach to consumer protection matters.

The limited effect of consumer law and its enforcement is evident in the fact that some businesses are repeatedly prosecuted for similar offences. Table 6.2 summarises data about local and provincial businesses located in Metropolitan City which were prosecuted under consumer legislation at least twice over a five-year period. Table 6.3 then follows with national figures on the frequency with which certain national businesses were prosecuted for consumer offences over an overlapping six-year period. Information contained in both tables demonstrates that the degree of recidivism of businesses for consumer offences is high.[5] This is particularly evident in Table 6.3, for there is no pattern over the six years to suggest that the enforcement of consumer law had a deterrent effect. Similarly, there is no pattern when the data is broken down for individual offences. An exception is Business 6, but the reason for the downward trend in prosecutions after 1970 is that it began defending prosecutions by using the statutory defences to transfer blame to its employees.

An explanation by the commercial world for the repetition of similar offences is that a minimum amount of wrongdoing is inevitable whatever

Table 6.2. Persistent offenders: local and provincial businesses based in Metropolitan City, five-year period

Number of times prosecuted	Number of firms	Type of firm
Twice	27	Manufacturer, dairy, contractors, sewing-machine retailer, supermarket (2), grocer (2) market trader (2), butcher (2) car dealer (7), coalman (9).
Three times	1	Car dealer
Four times	1	Market trader
Eight times	1	Co-operative society

Table 6.3. National prosecutions for consumer offences for certain national businesses, six-year period

	Year 1	Year 2	Year 3	Year 4	Year 5	Year 6	Total
Business 1	–	1	5	2	4	5	17
Business 2	1	5	–	4	6	4	20
Business 3	4	4	4	3	4	2	21
Business 4	4	6	4	5	2	1	22
Business 5	1	1	5	5	11	7	30
Business 6	43	18	14	12	11	15	113
Business 7	18	31	14	24	15	14	116
Business 8	19	24	25	19	32	29	148

precautions businesses take. Errors will always occur, which give rise to consumer offences, simply because employees are fallible and make mistakes. There are good reasons for refuting this argument, which I consider below, but at this point it is sufficient to refer to the fact that some of the businesses mentioned in Table 6.3, which are comparable to one another, have widely differing prosecution rates (see Table 6.4).

There is little support for the argument that the larger and more profitable a business the more reputable it is. The argument is that large businesses are prone to comply with the law because they are more visible and thus more susceptible to action by enforcement agencies.[6] The flexibility of large businesses to evade regulation by varying their procedures is lessened because once a decision has been made to follow lawful requirements, the needs of bureaucracy demand that the policy be applied consistently. As for profitable firms, they are said to have the financial resources and the research facilities to familiarise themselves with

Table 6.4. National prosecutions, size and profitability for certain national businesses

		Size of turnover* £m	Net profit before interest and tax* £m	Prosecutions over six-year period
Supermarkets	A	65	3	20
	B	223	5	22
	C	326	14	30
	D	359	22	113
Department/ variety stores	A	120	16	5
	B	190	15	6
	C	427	45	116
	D	592	80	4
Electrical stores	A	25	5	2
	B	40	5	6
	C	43	2	6

* These are the latest figures available and are to nearest million.

their legal obligations and to introduce the requisite changes in their practices. By contrast, where profit margins are small, the temptation of a business is to ignore the law if this will improve its financial position. Some slight evidence to support this is that consumer agencies find that certain businesses which operate on a high turnover but a low proft-margin are reluctant to satisfy consumers who have justified complaints against them. But national data available on the prosecution of certain national businesses suggests that size and profitability are not especially important in business wrongdoing. Table 6.4 lists the number of times that certain national firms were prosecuted throughout the country over a six-year period and also contains an indication of their size and profitability towards the end of that period. On the assumption that because each business is in the same sphere of commercial activity there is a similar propensity to commit consumer offences, it is apparent that size and profitability have no clear relationship to the amount of wrongdoing detected and prosecuted by consumer agencies (on the further assumption that they exercise their discretion uniformly with all businesses).

The present research suggests that the basic trading policy of a business is the most plausible explanation for the extent to which it complies with consumer law. Some businesses adopt a deliberate policy of ensuring that their practices conform with – indeed are in advance of – legal requirements. This may derive from self-interest or it may be that a sense of social responsibility acts as a brake on economically determined interests. The executives controlling several national businesses make it quite clear within their organisations that any policies adopted must scrupulously observe the provisions of consumer law. These businesses are prosecuted relatively infrequently and their trading practices incorporate features which the consumer movement has argued should be adopted universally. Contrast other businesses where a commitment to commercial success takes precedence over obeying the law. These businesses find it worth while to continue with trade practices which cause offences, and treat a degree of wrongdoing as incidental to continuing with their marketing and promotional practices. A secondhand-car dealer explained to me that his advertisements were exaggerated and occasionally over the borderline drawn by the Trade Descriptions Act (1968) because he thought that this was necessary if he was to survive in business. A solicitor to a national business recalled that the advertising of one of its newly established subsidiaries had initially neglected legal safeguards because the commercial judgement of key executives had overridden any concern with legal provisions. Other businesses conceded in interviews that the pressure of competition forced them to engage in practices which sometimes gave rise to breaches of consumer law. National supermarkets for example, expressed a distaste for flash offers – promotions in which an advertised price is claimed to be less than the manufacturer's recommended price – because they led to mispricing offences, but they felt that if they abandoned them they would lose trade to their competitors.

II THE IMPACT OF LEGISLATIVE SANCTIONS

Because businesses are rational and goal-oriented, it seems a reasonable hypothesis that their behaviour can be controlled by law to a greater extent than that of individuals or other entities who are committed to illegality as a way of life.[7] But because businesses are prone to calculate the utility of a course of action, they may be slow to change unlawful behaviour unless the tangible and symbolic gains of doing so outweigh the losses. As Max Weber noted, business practices can be insensitive to legal influences when they are estimated to be economically advantageous.[8]

As I have indicated, the cost-benefit calculation is not important for some businesses which adhere to legal requirements from a sense of social responsibility. Consumer law is effective for other businesses, however, only if the economic disincentives attaching to a course of action are sufficiently undesirable – if its sanctions bite into business profits. For this reason, the civil law is a weak instrument to ensure that businesses provide products and services of a reasonable standard. Businesses which know that few consumers take matters as far as civil proceedings and that not all of these succeed lack the incentive to satisfy consumers' complaints. As an example, a national retailer with a reputation in central government and consumer agencies for a harsh policy on consumer complaints was sued on fifty-two occasions by dissatisfied consumers over a six-year period. The outcome of these cases was as follows:

Consumer successful	10
Consumer unsuccessful	5
Settled	21
Pending	16

Conversations with executives of the business revealed that consumer success in civil proceedings, such as it was, would not change its trading policy. They remained adamant that they resolved complaints generously and that dissatisfied consumers had unjustified claims.

Similarly, the main sanctions of the criminal consumer law – fines and publicity – are of limited effectiveness.

THE FINE

The growth of 'practical morality' is said to have weakened the stigma associated with the imposition of a fine.[9] An enforcement officer commented: 'We've got a change in moral attitudes. Prosecutions are not important because of the moral code. Things previously criminal are regarded as social misfortune.' The violation of consumer law is often hidden from the public, and the reputation of errant businesses is therefore unaffected. Furthermore, it is worthwhile of businesses to commit consumer offences if the fine and other costs associated with being prosecuted are less than the economic gains accruing from continuing their existing practices.[10]

The maximum fine in consumer legislation is £400 if the prosecution is brought in a magistrates court – which compares with a figure for companies of approximately £31,250 in recent Australian legislation. Government committees, Parliamentarians and consumer organisations have all pointed out that the fines fixed by consumer law are too low to provide an adequate deterrent. Combined with the fact that magistrates rarely impose the maximum, this contributes to a situation where fines can be treated as equivalent to a licence fee to infringe the law. Moreover, courts often ignore the fact that the expense of fines imposed on business executives is mainly undertaken by their employers. The deterrent effect of fines is further weakened because businesses can often shift the burden on to the public. Monopolies or oligopolies can recoup the cost of a fine by increasing prices, although in theory businesses are less able to do this in a competitive market if demand is elastic and there are close substitutes for their products.

The total value of fines imposed during six years operation of the Trade

Table 6.5. Average fine per prosecution and average fine per charge, *Prosecution Survey*

	Misdescription of products	Mispricing	Misdescription of services, etc.	Incorrect quantity	Sub-standard food	All offences
	£	£	£	£	£	£
Average fine (N = 710)	84*	105*	94*	40	25	69
Average fine per charge (N = 700)	50	32	63	14	30	33

* The figures compare with national averages of £84, £52, and £92 respectively.

Descriptions Act (1968) was only £567,036 – an average of £76 per offence – although an additional £39,901 was awarded against businesses in the form of compensation for consumers.[11] Table 6.5 is drawn from the *Prosecution Survey* and shows the average fine for prosecutions for various consumer offences and, where these involved more than one charge, the average fine for each. Misdescription offences attract higher penalties than those under the Weights and Measures Act (1963) or the Food and Drugs Act (1955). The highest average fine is quite low: £105 for mispricing offences. Table 6.6 follows with a cross tabulation of the average fine per prosecution for national, provincial and local businesses. Since there is no significant relationship between these factors it must be that the courts do not impose heavier fines on the larger businesses.

Because fines can be treated as an expense to be passed on to the public, some commentators argue that prejudicial business practices will only be

Table 6.6. Average fine per prosecution for businesses of different sizes, *Prosecution Survey**

Size of business	Misdescription of products	Mispricing	Misdescription of services, etc.	Incorrect quantity	Substandard food	All offences
	£	£	£	£	£	£
National	84	133	129	38	20	99
Provincial	79	105	50	55	23	71
Local	90	57	78	34	10	67
Others	67	57	163	38	31	48

* A further breakdown for average fine per charge produces similar results.

eliminated if businessmen are forced to serve jail sentences.[12] Various arguments are advanced as to why businessmen are more susceptible to the threat of even short periods of imprisonment than are ordinary offenders. First, they are less likely to have been incarcerated previously; second, they are acting in an area of instrumental behaviour and are less committed to transgression of the law as a way of life; and third, imprisonment has a high *in terrorem* value because their reputations will suffer greatly from the stigma.[13]

Imprisonment under consumer legislation is possible if a case is taken on indictment to the Crown Court. In the *Prosecution Survey*, proceedings in only two of the 699 cases were on indictment, in both cases because of the very practical reason that the time limit for summary proceedings had expired. Neither case resulted in imprisonment being imposed. In the first six years of the Trade Descriptions Act (1968) only seven defendants were given prison sentences and six of these were suspended sentences.[14] In fact the courts have adopted the practice of not imprisoning offenders under consumer law unless the offence is accompanied by dishonesty.[15] In addition, businessmen are unlikely to receive immediate prison sentences, for even if dishonesty is involved they will rarely have a criminal record. However, there is still a dearth of consumer cases taken on indictment and the major reason is the apprehensiveness of enforcement officers about the Crown Court. They are familiar with the magistrates courts and believe that it is easier to obtain convictions there. Most enforcement officers justify their position by claiming that the circumstances in which indictment proceedings are appropriate are limited to serious fraud. However, a small minority refute this and point out that the police proceed against relatively minor offences in the Crown Court. They report that when they have presented cases on indictment, the judges have been impressed with the gravity of the consumer cases involved.

PUBLICITY

Publicity of prejudicial business practices may act to protect consumers. Businesses may expect a consumer law to be vigorously enforced, particularly when newly enacted, if it receives considerable publicity. The perceived as opposed to the actual consequences of non-compliance may induce businesses to modify their behaviour until they have become aware of the true pattern of enforcement.[16] Publicity is also useful to inform consumers of adverse trade practices on the assumption that they can then take steps to protect themselves. The American federal consumer agency, the Federal Trade Commission, uses publicity to mobilise public opinion against commercial methods or against particular businesses. In Britain, government officials occasionally criticise trade practices prejudicial to consumers, and the Office of Fair Trading now details in press releases the names of businesses from which it has obtained undertakings because of their persistent breaches of criminal or civil law.

Another aspect of publicity is when the conviction of a business for a consumer offence is publicised. In theory, this increases the deterrent value of a prosecution because it inflicts monetary loss on a business through a down-turn in sales.[17] Amongst consumer officers, the effect is thought to be particularly strong in the case of a prosecution of a local business in a small community. A business which receives adverse publicity is likely to incur further loss if it is unable to secure capable managerial talent and a willing labour force. The assumption is that managers are not motivated exclusively by the desire to increase their salaries, but are also influenced by whether they are associated with a prestigious organisation. The best evidence supporting a connection between publicity and deterrence is that businesses attempt to influence their public image through advertising. If efforts to enhance their reputation have a positive effect on sales, the latter must also be susceptible to adverse publicity.

All this assumes that a business receives unfavourable publicity when it is prosecuted. In fact, prosecutions under consumer law attract little attention. At one time consumer legislation such as the Adulteration of Food Act (1860) provided that a court could order publication of a conviction – the name and place of business of an offender, the offence, and the penalty imposed. One such provision was in force until 1963, but it was rarely used, and then nothing more was involved than affixing the details of the offence outside the court.[18] Nowadays it is solely a question for the press whether a conviction is reported. Newspaper reporting is haphazard and by no means all consumer cases are mentioned in local newspapers, let alone in the national press. Some consumer officers claim that the coverage a business receives in a newspaper when it is involved in legal proceedings varies inversely with the advertising revenue it provides. Yet consumer agencies share the blame for the lack of publicity, for they do not use the press in a positive manner. Very few contact the press about an impending prosecution but leave it to chance whether there will be a reporter at the hearing. Even publicity in Metropolitan County, where the consumer agency has two persons engaged in public relations work, is at the initiative of the press.

Moreover, adverse publicity does not always have an effect, for its impact is diffuse.[19] The public may not perceive the main issues of a case, even assuming they have been correctly reported. As the executive of a national business commented cynically:

Whether we win or not it is still publicity if there is a reporter in court. I'm not too worried about publicity because we have never been a roguish firm like turning speedos back. People read a thing in the newspaper one day and forget it the next. They only remember seeing the name in the newspapers. We work on the principle that any publicity is good publicity, as long as they spell the name right.

The publicity of a single prosecution can hardly dent a favourable image fostered by advertising. An official in the consumer movement commented: 'Publicity as a means of galvanising things into action hasn't really worked. Manufacturers regard it as a nine-day wonder, and in the PR field industry can wrap us around their little finger.' Public opinion may not regard the behaviour of a business as opprobrious or as sufficiently serious to warrant a boycott of its products. Reputation is not all-important for a business in a monopoly position, although it may be more highly valued by competing firms engaged in product differentiation. A company solicitor remarked that his firm was not really concerned with whether its convictions were publicised, because its prices were competitive and that was the major factor influencing consumers. When serious fraud is involved, it is doubtful whether any publicity a business receives has an influence and the deterrent is more likely to be the executives' fear of personal discovery leading to punishment and disgrace.[20]

Publicity is a two-edged sword for consumer agencies, for there is an argument that it may encourage greater violation. For example, publicity of a conviction may reveal that penalties for flagrant breaches of consumer legislation are trivial or that only the most serious transgressors are prosecuted.[21] It may actually disseminate knowledge in the business community about how a legal provision can be successfully avoided. Publicity may show a consumer agency in an unfavourable light and undermine its public image of effectiveness. For example, it may become obvious that an agency has not prosecuted offences under consumer law in the past, that it prosecutes trivial cases, or that on this occasion it has been tardy in taking action.

Although some businesses recognise that they have little to fear from the publicity surrounding a prosecution, others are worried about the effect on their reputation. This, rather than the fine imposed, is their main concern. A report about a recent prosecution, prepared for internal use in one national company, specifically mentioned that there was no newspaper reporter at the court hearing. The memorandum of a national supermarket which I also saw noted that recent prosecutions cost 'a great deal more than the fines imposed, £1000 and £2000, for the publicity received was of the very worst possible kind.' Two national firms informed me that they adopt the general rule of not appealing against the decisions of magistrates courts when they are prosecuted because any success would be more than counteracted by the further publicity they would attract.

THE POINT OF IMPACT OF CONSUMER LAW

Another aspect of the effectiveness of consumer law which relates to, but in many ways cuts across, the discussion of fines and publicity is the point in a business at which legal sanctions have their impact. *A priori* sanctions would seem to be most effective if they involve both the business and the executives directly responsible for the unlawful activity. The imposition of sanctions on the business may deprive a business of any illegal profits and also attacks the source of loyalty for employees. In a large business, where decision-making is diffuse and policies can result from the accretion of many individual decisions, it may be that only the business can be prosecuted because it is impossible to locate any person responsible for the particular consumer offence.[22]

If these are good reasons for punishing the business, there is still the problem that a basis must be found for imputing to it acts performed by individuals. The law provides that a business is liable for acts performed by high-level executives. In addition, the courts have held that the intention of consumer legislation is to extend liability to the actions of employees, however junior, when they are committed in the course of their employment. A justification for such extensive liability is that substantial authority is delegated to the lower echelons of modern business organisations. Lower officials can endanger the public and profit a business by unlawful acts to the same extent as management.[23] Another reason is that high-level executives would have a greater incentive to supervise closely the activities of lower officials. As has already been mentioned, however, consumer legislation contains certain defences which enable a business to avoid conviction for an offence if it can establish that an employee lower down in the hierarchy was responsible, provided it has taken reasonable precautions and exercised due diligence to avoid such an occurrence. Therefore a business cannot always be held liable for the acts of its employees at the lower levels. The result is that a business may still be able to use promotional practices which cause junior employees to commit infringements without exposing itself to legal sanctions.

Should the officials of a business as well as the business itself be punished when an offence occurs? If they are not, a fraudulent businessman could escape personal punishment and also wind up his business to avoid any loss to its assets. With a larger, well-established business, there is the separate difficulty that if only the firm is prosecuted the deterrent effect on individuals is indirect. Assuming the stigma of conviction attaches to a business, it is highly unlikely to filter through to the employees. Similarly, when a business is fined, this will rarely affect the employees financially. In both cases the law would be relying on internal disciplinary action being taken by the business against the relevant individuals.[24] On the other hand, although there is a good case for the punishment of individuals at higher levels in a company who devise marketing schemes which give rise to offences, there is a strong argument that it is socially undesirable for other employees to be punished for offences which they commit not for their benefit, but in the course of their employment. Why should they be blamed when they are locked into a system where they have to carry out the marketing schemes of a business and – in the case of junior employees – for low wages in an uncreative environment?

Consumer law in general provides that employees as well as a business can be prosecuted if they are directly responsible for an offence. Consumer agencies, however, usually only proceed against either a business or its employees, not both. In the *Prosecution Survey*, just under 11 per cent of the cases brought to court involved a charge against both a business and its employees. Table 6.7 is drawn from the *Prosecution Survey* and breaks down the charges instituted into those against businesses and those against individuals. It can be seen that few directors or other high executives who are in a position to control the policy of businesses are prosecuted, and that the individuals punished are most likely to be minor functionaries such as branch managers, or junior employees such as salesmen and sales assistants.

Table 6.7. Prosecutions against businesses and individuals, *Prosecution Survey*

		%	%
Businesses			83·2 (658)
Individuals:	Coalmen	5·7 (45)*	
	Branch and sectional managers	5·3 (42)	
	Shop assistants, salesmen etc.	4·4 (35)	16·8 (133)
	Directors and other executives	1·1 (9)	
	Others	0·36 (2)	
Total			100 (791)

* The figures in brackets show the number of prosecutions.

If the higher executives in a business are immune from direct sanction, there is evidence that sometimes they are chastened by the internal repercussions when the business is prosecuted. An internal memorandum in a business can have a salutary effect if it identifies the action of a particular executive as the reason for a prosecution. Businesses are not monolithic and there is a strong incentive for certain executives to prevent offences. An executive responsible for legal matters within a national company commented: 'If anything goes wrong then someone gets it in the neck – probably me.' Executives in similar positions act as a brake on those on the marketing side who are less concerned that the company's advertising and promotion comply with the statutory requirements. These executives can use the threat that the business will be prosecuted to convince their colleagues in the organisation that dubious practices should be avoided. This is not always successful, as a company solicitor indicated: 'Obviously they will take a commercial judgement; i.e., the commercial advantage is greater than the legal risk. Well, that's a commercial judgement, but my position is on file.'

III THE PERSPECTIVE OF CONSUMER AGENCIES

Consumer agencies give the impression that the interests of consumers are being effectively championed and protected. Even if it is unintentional this serves the function of justifying the continued existence of consumer agencies, together with the fact that prejudicial trade practices are never fully eradicated. Consumer agencies are observed to prosecute businesses and to resolve a substantial volume of consumer complaints. Concealed from public view is the full extent of business wrongdoing and any inefficiencies in the operation of the agencies.[25] For example, central government officials have few criticisms of the way in which consumer agencies perform their tasks and take the view that consumer law is being implemented satisfactorily. As one commented:

> I don't get the impression that there's a great groundswell of complaint about the enforcement of consumer protection legislation. We don't get a great flood of complaints coming back saying that the [consumer protection] departments are no good. I should have thought that the public image of [consumer protection departments] is pretty good. This reflects when MPs deal with complaints. If the departments were no good MPs would quickly say so.[26]

A similar view prevails amongst many small businessmen, who have the impression of an efficacious network of consumer agencies which quickly contact them about criminal offences or consumer complaints. Larger businesses are more sceptical and complain about the variation in enforcement policies between consumer agencies, but realise that overall this places businesses at an advantage. If a consumer agency draws their attention to a minor breach of consumer law, they will not always correct it in their other branches if it is uneconomical to do so, or if the matter is unlikely to be raised by other consumer agencies. National firms also recognise that investigations are often closed without legal proceedings if they respond positively to the suggestions of consumer agencies. Although national businesses perceive the deficiencies of consumer agencies, they still regard them as hostile and claim that the agencies are unduly harsh and lack any understanding of commerce – particularly the role of profit and of how errors occur in commercial organisations. Problems, they contend, could often be resolved if consumer agencies contacted them, but instead an overzealousness and desire to catch out reputable businesses lead to the prosecution of technical and relatively harmless offences.

Consumer agencies themselves are not greatly concerned with the impact of consumer law or with the wider issues of the effectiveness of their activity. In the main the obtaining of convictions is perceived as the fulfilment of their obligation to enforce legislation. The prevailing assumption is that, generally speaking, a prosecution or a caution will have the desired effect both for the business prosecuted and for the commercial world as a whole. One reason for this unquestioning attitude to deterrence is that the pressure of new work makes it difficult for consumer officers to return to businesses which have been cautioned or prosecuted to assess whether they have desisted from their objectionable behaviour. Several times consumer officers remarked to me that a business had reformed, without being aware that their colleagues were still handling complaints about it. Besides, consumer officers know of numerous instances where businesses have altered their trade practices following a caution or a prosecution. Supermarkets, for example, can be observed to have improved their mode of operation as a direct outcome of a spate of convictions for mispricing. Similarly, consumer officers see that tour operators have amended the format of their brochures to avoid future prosecutions for misdescription.

Consumer officers concede that a succession of prosecutions is necessary to transform the trade practices of some businesses, but claim that eventually they do change. The isolated prosecution is not sufficient to penetrate to the higher executives of these businesses, and a number of prosecutions is necessary before someone at that level institutes a re-examination of policies and procedures. A chief officer offered his experience of one business:

> They were prosecuted about nine times. They said: 'Oh, he'll get tired of it before we do.' But I didn't, and finally it was admitted in court that the trouble was because the factory had three times the production it should have had. As a result of the prosecution, it agreed to cut back on production.

With some businesses, however, consumer officers admit that their efforts are not fruitful. Prosecution has a superficial effect but beneath the veneer of reform the objectionable practices continue. Less detectable means of committing offences are adopted. For example, consumer officers say that secondhand-car dealers no longer misdescribe their merchandise in the press or alter odometers to the same extent as they did before the Trade Descriptions Act (1968), but that they still misdescribe cars orally and sell them in breach of the standards of quality required by the civil law. Consumer agencies regard the change, however inadequate, as an achievement because consumers are not misled as much as previously. Written descriptions are an inducement to purchase and to the extent that they are accurate the consumer is better, although not completely, protected.

Consumer officers recognise that prosecutions have least effect on unscrupulous businesses. Examples are referred to where businessmen avoided fines imposed on their companies by winding them up and then forming new companies with the same assets. Provisions in consumer legislation permit a consumer agency to prosecute the principals of a business as well as the business itself, but this does not alleviate the problem unless the courts impose penalties on the former rather than the latter. Consumer officers realise that since unscrupulous businessmen have few compunctions about breaking the law, the only fact influencing their behaviour is whether the profit accruing from the illegal activity outweighs the cost of a possible fine. An enforcement officer related that a car dealer told him in the course of an enquiry: 'I shan't bother to go to court. I'll plead guilty; if they fine me £100, so what?' The same officer was informed by another car dealer after a record £2000 fine was imposed: 'Tough luck, I still made a profit on the deal.' But even with unscrupulous businesses fines may eventually inflict their toll. Consumer officers recall instances of how secondhand-car dealers were forced out of business by persistent prosecution. The cause is not always clear, however, and officers admit that secondhand-car dealers are marginal businesses and may have intended from the beginning to carry on trade for only a short period so as to reap quick, if illicit, profits. Again, a business may simply have moved to another part of the country to continue its undesirable practices there, which from the point of view of individual agencies is effective but is hardly so on a national scale. In an effort to counter these movements, consumer agencies exchange information on unscrupulous businesses, but it is done in a rather incomplete and unsystematic way.

IV THE PERSPECTIVE OF BUSINESS

BUSINESS PERCEPTIONS AND CONSUMER LAW

The official business view divides the commercial world into the majority of honest and law-abiding traders on the one hand, and the small minority of disreputable and shady operators on the other. Very rarely will businessmen admit that they infringe consumer law deliberately and, if they do, their rationalisation is that their competitors are behaving similarly. A secondhand-car dealer, convicted of altering the odometers of cars which he had sold, commented: 'Everyone in the trade does it. No one had borne any grudge against me, but I suppose I had better stop it now.'[27] The pursuit of profit is said to be the main reason for the minority acting as they do. 'They want to make a fortune without doing any work,' said one executive. Boom industries are said to attract marginal men who have no real commitment to a line of business but who bend the law for their own enrichment. Because they are interested in making quick profits they are not concerned with their reputation. Pressure for sales from the management of such organisations forces employees to violate consumer law and codes of practice.[28] The official business view takes dramatic shape in the activities of the Retail Trading Standards Association (RTSA), which includes amongst its members department stores, textile manufacturers and advertising agents. The Association is pledged to act against 'rogues' and other businessmen who set out to mislead the public in their advertising announcements or in their selling methods.[29] Since 1950, it has instituted some fifty private prosecutions against businesses applying false descriptions to their products.

National businesses in particular are prone to claim that their approach is highly ethical. A common assertion is that their operations are so reputable that they are already in advance of the law and are the pattern to follow.[30] I was told in interviews: 'Without sounding pompous, when law comes out it conforms with what has already been carried out.' 'I think that in many ways our trading practices were in advance of the Trade Descriptions Act because we are that type of company.' National businesses concede that their behaviour is to some extent in their long-term interests because they cannot mistreat the public and hope to survive. Undesirable practices are laid at the door of a minority. As two executives told me: 'Much of this legislation is aimed at what you might call the side man – the marginal trader.' 'This legislation is out to catch the sharp-dealer. You're talking to the wrong people.' In this view the minority should be controlled because their behaviour results in the commercial world as a whole being stigmatised:

> Recent and forthcoming legislation will not just benefit the shopper: it will restore confidence between the shopper and the shopkeeper by making it increasingly difficult for the rogues and tricksters to indulge in their petty frauds and discreditable advertisements.[31]

Of course, the competitive advantages of established businesses are assisted by any curbs on the activities of the minority. Established businesses admit their commercial self-interest – the minority undercut them with their trading practices.

The actual conduct of businesses which profess a high standard sometimes approximate to their assessments of others.[32] Their record in the consumer protection field is often in flat contradiction to their pretentions. 'We have a company policy of fair dealing which is old-fashioned – a reputation which is very jealously guarded,' remarked the lawyer employed by one national firm; yet it had been prosecuted for twenty-one consumer offences in the previous six years. The national supermarket with the poorest reputation among consumer agencies had similar aspirations:

'Our rules are stricter than the law because we are, as I say, a firm with a reputation.' However erroneous they may be, these assertions enable businesses to argue that statutory controls are unnecessary. Consumers are already protected since most businesses are honest and there is no need for legal regulation.

To some extent businesses are inhibited from outright opposition to consumer law because it might suggest that their trade practices are not up to standard. Despite this they still have a wide scope to argue against consumer legislation. It can be objected that it is not a practical way of dealing with a problem or that it is politically motivated. It can be said that the government has not demonstrated that it is necessary or that the present law is inadequate. Another argument is that consumer legislation brands honest businesses as criminals, for they can be prosecuted for a technicality or the mistake of an employee. The officer of a trade association explained its preference for voluntary controls and its opposition to legislation as follows: 'With legislation you only have to make one mistake, a few ounces short, and you're branded a criminal.' Similar sentiments were expressed by the managing director of a firm following its conviction under the Trade Descriptions Act (1968): 'Acts of negligence have now become a crime . . . This act was meant for spivs, but it has got us all worried.'

Resistance to consumer law can also concentrate on its attendant costs. A national supermarket with some 200 own-brand labels claimed to have had three design staff working over a year on bringing its labels into line with new food-labelling regulations. Businesses also point out that new consumer law can lead to a reduction in the range and variety of products and services available. A point emphasised in recent years is that new consumer law actually threatens the collapse of many businesses in an economy where they already operate on narrow margins because of price control. Often unstated, however, is that the cost of compliance with consumer law can frequently be transferred to consumers.[33]

Perhaps the central argument that businesses have against consumer legislation rests on the notion of consumer sovereignty. Consumers are said to determine the success or failure of any product or service by their purchasing decisions. Each business has an interest in satisfying consumers for otherwise it will lose trade to its competitors. The standard of products and services is therefore determined by consumers rather than the legal system, particularly where subjective qualities are involved such as design and experience.

The division of the commercial world into the honest majority and the dishonest minority enables businesses to regard consumer offences as essentially non-criminal. Whereas the violations of the minority may be fraudulent, those of the majority constitute either technical error or the mistakes of employees.[34] A consequence of this attitude is that a prosecution is not the occasion for a fundamental reappraisal in the trade practices of a business. Responsibility can be completely transferred to employees or, alternatively, minor adjustments may be made to marketing techniques. Another result is that well-established businesses can stake a claim to be consulted by government about the drafting of consumer law. They can argue that their trade practices are in the interests of consumers and therefore any new legislation must be drafted with a knowledge of those practices. Government for its part relies on established businesses for information about what is feasible and it is also reluctant to create hostility by enacting standards which require radical changes in the behaviour of businesses. For these reasons consumer legislation is mostly a codification of the practices already adopted by certain businesses.

BUSINESS EXPLANATIONS OF BREACHES OF CONSUMER LAW

Businesses emphasise that in the context of the total trading situation there is a modicum of breaches of consumer law. Prosecutions in isolation appear quite serious, but they pale into insignificance when compared with the number of lawful transactions. A company solicitor emphasised: 'I receive the journal of the Institute of Trading Standards. You see cases [prosecutions] there and they look quite bad. But when you think – it is only occasionally in all the hundreds of thousands of sales that they occur.' Businesses maintain that criminal offences rarely occur because of an intention to deceive consumers. When they do the fault is rarely with the executives of a business but rather with employees well down the hierarchy. The argument runs that employees are sometimes 'over-enthusiastic', or alternatively that they are a cross-section of the population and understandably contain a few who are dishonest.

There is a well-developed collection of justifications used by businesses when breaches of consumer law occur. The sampling below is taken from press and magazine reports about the prosecution of particular businesses:[35]

The offence was committed in good faith and unconsciously by the business.

The legal position was complex and muddled and the offender was hardly culpable.

There was no intention to deceive, and the offence was a 'succession of unfortunate occurrences which could not have been foreseen'.

An employee made a mistake but it could not be prevented. There was an understandable although perhaps unfortunate breakdown in the quality-control machinery.

The offence was entirely out of character. The business had tried to put the matter right with any consumers affected and 'had been quick to plead guilty as soon as they realised their mistake'.

There may have been a certain laxity in administration but it would be tightened without delay.

The following discussion examines three of the explanations used by business to rationalise the occurrence of breaches of consumer law.

(a) The Role of Consumers

In view of the business, the cause of many consumer problems lies with consumers themselves. Of course this notion contradicts that of consumer sovereignty where consumers occupy a more exalted position. Consumer dishonesty is sometimes posited as the cause of complaints and another argument is that complaints result because consumers misuse products or have unreasonable expectations. Problems are also said to arise because consumers choose to pay less than they could but then expect the same quality as with more expensive items.[36] Then it is said that sometimes they do not properly appreciate the information available or they fail to adhere to the instructions. Businesses believe that the amicable resolution of genuine complaints is not assisted by the general suspicion with which they are viewed. Consumers also adopt adamant but erroneous stances about their legal rights. Together with the generally critical approach that most people have, these factors are said to lead consumers to make unreasonable and unjustified demands: 'What's happened in this country overnight has been an over-reaction. Everyone has become a lawyer and they go out and buy the Sale of Goods Act and then complain.' Businesses regard it as tantamount to blackmail when consumers threaten to take a matter to a consumer agency unless it is settled to their satisfaction.

In mitigation of breaches of consumer law, businesses frequently emphasise that little if any harm is caused to consumers. The aim of consumer law, they say, is not to punish every lapse committed but to prevent the public being harmed. They add that it should be remembered that practices which occasionally prejudice the consumer almost always involve associated benefits. In the exceptional cases where consumers are harmed, businesses attribute the cause to a deviant product or to the personal characteristics of the particular consumers. A multinational cosmetic firm, which was convicted for falsely advertising that one of its products had been fully screened for possible irritants, asserted in a press release:

> Our products have been fully tested by qualified dermatologists involving thousands of human patch tests before being marketed. Millions of units of the product in the Swedish formula range have been sold successfully and safely throughout the world. Any ingredient may cause sensitivity in particular individuals and circumstances.

A variation of the argument is that few complaints are received from consumers even about trade practices which lead to official proceedings. When complaints are made the automatic reaction is to resolve them to the satisfaction of consumers. Businesses also point out that consumers continue to patronise them although they may commit breaches of consumer law. Commenting on the prosecution of a firm, its managing director was quoted in the press as saying:

> I do not believe that a retail store can thrive for very long by following a policy of deception, and whilst technically our company has been found guilty in law, the best judgment will be whether the public continue to patronize [it] . . . Since the case, trade has been better than last year.

There are good reasons for resisting the suggestion that complaints are always, or nearly always, the fault of the consumers themselves. Consumer agencies accept that many of the complaints they receive are justified – the London Borough consumer agency quotes a rate of 82 per cent – because they see too many poor-quality products and services to blame consumers. Moreover, consumers are harmed by breaches of consumer law. A financial loss will almost always be involved, which for individuals can vary from the insignificant on the one hand to the substantial, if not crippling, loss which low-income consumers may face because of their entanglement with fradulent trade practices. A rough estimate by the London Borough consumer agency of the amount at stake in consumer complaints received by them over a nine-month period was £29,328. American consumer advocates have documented the legacy of physical harm caused by the marketing of unsafe products, and, although quantitatively such cases are small, they again refute the suggestion by businesses that harm is either non-existent or the fault of consumers themselves.[37]

(b) Ignorance

As Aubert noted, an important variable in measuring the influence of a law is the level of information among those to whom it is directed.[38] A not uncommon assertion in the commercial world is that consumer offences occur through ignorance. If true it would throw in doubt the efficiency of the advisory policy of consumer agencies. An example of this approach was the insistence of one trade association official that many secondhand-car dealers commit offences under the Trade Descriptions Act (1968) because they are still ignorant of their obligations years after its enactment. A variation on the theme is that businesses cannot understand the practical implications of consumer law because of its obscurity, its constant amendment, and the disagreement between courts and between consumer agencies.

Although the interviews conducted by me were limited in scope, they suggest that while businesses are generally aware of their obligations under criminal law there is some doubt about what is expected of them under the civil law. Particular mysteries are the responsibilities of retailers *vis-à-vis* manufacturers for faulty products, and more generally the division between the criminal and civil law. An illustration is provided by a family business with three shoe shops in Metropolitan County, which was under the misapprehension that a consumer agency could actually *force* it to refund the purchase price to consumers who complained about faulty shoes, whereas in fact only the civil law is relevant, which involves at most individual consumers suing. The confusion about criminal and civil law obligations arose after the business had been successfully sued twice under the small claims procedure in the County Court. On the two occasions it had not defended the action because it had expected to be burdened with heavy costs.

Such basic ignorance should be distinguished from that which arises because businessmen are not aware of the many nuances of consumer law. During the research I attended a training session for an arbitration scheme for consumers run by an association of local traders. Although there was a general understanding of legal obligations, it was clear from the discussion among the businessmen on the panel that they were not always accurate in applying the law. For example, they awarded damages for only the immediate and not for any consequential losses, and they took into account irrelevant factors such as the length of time before the consumer complained.

These comments are not meant to suggest that ignorance is confined to smaller businessmen. In interviews several branch managers of national businesses showed that they were unaware of important aspects of consumer law, although this is of little consequence because the trade practices of the businesses tend to be in accordance with consumer law. Legal requirements are incorporated into their trade practices and become just a part of the muted background to trading. In larger businesses, law is contained in manuals which set out its requirements in procedural rather than legal terms. New legislation is translated into an understandable form and is distributed by supplementary memoranda. An example of how law works in larger businesses is provided by national supermarkets. To comply with the pricing provisions of the Trade Descriptions Act (1968), branch supermarkets are instructed as to the procedure they should adopt when pricing products individually, attaching display tickets, undertaking special promotions, and instituting any checks.

The crucial issue therefore is not whether the staff of businesses know the provisions of consumer law, but whether they are acquainted with and adopt as a matter of routine the practices designed to implement it. A key variable is the amount of resources allocated to staff training. Generally speaking, employees in national firms receive at least some in-store training, although the emphasis is on supervisory and managerial staff. The position is somewhat different with smaller businesses, which are without the experts to advise on legal problems or the facilities to train staff. However smaller businesses can obtain assistance from trade associations, which notify their members of their legal obligations and in some cases even make available the materials with which to carry them out. An example is that trade associations may provide standard forms, which are drafted in accordance with legal provisions, to be used in consumer transactions. Small businesses can then incorporate the law into their routine practices.

(c) Mistakes

Mistakes are another explanation advanced by businesses for breaches of the civil and criminal law. Mistakes are considered by courts when fixing the fines for consumer offences and, as we saw, consumer agencies take their occurrence into account in deciding whether to prosecute. The argument of businesses is that errors are inevitable, however extensive the preventive measures may be. Machinery breaks down, and suppliers, on whose reputation businesses must rely, commit mistakes, or lead businesses to do so, by changing their systems without warning. The mistakes most frequently referred to are those of employees who were said to be bound to commit mistakes because of human fallibility.[39] The lawyer for a national firm explained the occurrence of breaches of consumer law in its stores:

> It's almost exclusively human error. It is seldom that you get caught on a problem that is a result of managerial error. In other words, our trade practices are not suspect because we have the know-how. There is no doubt that you come unstuck because you've got 8000 employees throughout the country.

According to the prevailing view, employee mistake has several aspects. Often it is the fortuitous combination of factors, e.g. there may be a temporary staff shortage because of illness or holidays. Particular tasks lend themselves to error; for example, the tedious job of pricing products in a supermarket. Circumstances beyond the control of a business compound the problem; for example, inflation increases the possibility of mispricing because price changes must be made more frequently.

Businesses have different approaches to invoking the statutory defences in consumer law to transfer blame to their staff. Those who use the defences in this way justify it as the course intended by Parliament and argue that a business is hardly culpable if it employs an efficient system of management and institutes a training programme for employees. According to one company solicitor: 'The law could not mean that a company should be penalised because one forty-seventhousandth of its staff should make a mistake in one minute.' It is also said that employees know the policy beforehand and therefore it acts as a deterrent to their carelessness. The same solicitor continued: 'Frankly, it would be dishonest if I accepted the can and the staff would go along carelessly.' As shown below, another national business has had a mixed experience in using the statutory defences against branch managers on six of the eleven occasions it has been prosecuted under the Trade Descriptions Act 1968:

Manager accepted blame and convicted	2
Manager resigned and convicted	1
Court rejected the defence and company convicted	2
Consumer agency did not proceed against manager	1

The majority of businesses refuse to involve their employees when prosecuted for consumer offences. Their rationale is that everyone makes mistakes, and in any event as far as the public is concerned the company is to blame. A more immediate concern of these businesses is that a policy of blaming individual employees could lead to staff dissatisfaction.

Despite the heavy emphasis which business places on the mistakes of their employees, it has considerable control over their incidence. In so far as inefficiency is the cause of employees committing offences, the responsibility clearly lies with management. Businesses can reduce the scope for employee error if they exercise tight control over their operations. National businesses in which branch managers have wide discretion to conduct special promotions to reduce prices and to advertise tend to be those with a poor record for consumer protection. By contrast errors are less common and then more quickly detected in those organisations in which promotions, pricing and advertising operate uniformly throughout the country.[40]

Businesses complain about the quality of their staff, and certainly in retailing the standard tends to be below average. Part-time employees comprise an important percentage of the work-force and there is a substantial turnover of staff, particularly in the larger urban areas where alternative employment is available.[41] But this is not the whole story. Remuneration in retailing lags behind that in other industries and it should not be surprising that it attracts school-leavers with lower educational standards. However, some retailers use the resources at their disposal to better advantage than others. One national store, which is highly regarded in consumer protection circles, has introduced specific programmes to attract and retain efficient staff. Conditions encouraging high standards of work and staff loyalty include subsidized meals, a non-contributory pension scheme and medical and dental care. Employees are encouraged to place their views before management and to identify themselves with the business by undertaking additional responsibilities. When the Trade Descriptions Act (1968) was first introduced, shop assistants were awarded prizes for uncovering infringements. By comparison another national firm, with a poor record in prosecutions and consumer matters generally, appears to treat its junior employees with little consideration. Executives at its head office freely attribute the blame for offences to the foolishness of branch managers or to the laziness of shop-assistants. The business has few compunctions about using the statutory defences to blame employees when it is prosecuted. The firm even believes that some of the offences for which it is prosecuted arise because of sabotage by resentful employees. In the interests of competitive prices the business admits that it keeps wages and fringe benefits as low as possible.

When one moves to servicing, the same line of argument is used. Businesses admit that the situation is unsatisfactory, with bad workmanship leading to breaches of both civil and criminal law. The problem is said to be that of recruiting and retaining competent staff. By itself, however, the explanation is unsatisfactory. Businesses have not taken the lead to establish certificates of competence for those engaged in servicing. Moreover, the economics of servicing is often the reason that consumer problems arise. For example, servicing is the least important component in the profitability of businesses associated with the motor trade when compared with the sale of vehicles or of petrol and oil. Naturally this dictates the low priority of servicing and of training motor mechanics.[42] Even with new cars there is no incentive to provide repair facilities beyond the minimum specified in franchising agreements with manufacturers. The position is similar with repairs to household appliances where the profit is in the initial sale and not in after-sales service. Consequently semi-skilled persons are employed to replace whole components although only minor repairs may be necessary. The principal of a small repair organisation criticised the standard of servicing by two national electrical manufacturers: 'I could name the local representatives of two of the largest concerns in the country, one of whom was until recently delivering bread for the Co-op, and whose crash course taught them little other than how to replace faulty units.'

V BUSINESSES AND CONSUMER COMPLAINTS

This final section directs attention to the way in which businesses settle consumer complaints. Much of the discussion concentrates on faulty products although what is said also relates to services. As would be expected from the previous discussion, a wide range of relevant factors other than consumer law must be considered.[43] The expectations of the consumer, for example, often have a crucial bearing. If a consumer simply requires that a faulty product be repaired, there is a temptation for the retailer not to raise the question of an exchange or a refund. The discussion that follows is oriented around three factors which appear from my research to be particularly salient in the policies which businesses adopt for complaints. It then concludes with how businesses actually implement their complaints policies.

THE NATURE OF A BUSINESS

The role of good will ranks high in forming the policies of many businesses regarding complaints. Certainly transient firms, or those which rely on passing trade, can afford to be unsympathetic, since any impairment of their reputation is unlikely to effect the general level of sales. Similarly, many businesses with unscrupulous methods continue unhindered, for a bad reputation seldom catches up with them and they can generally elude any action by consumers or consumer agencies.[44] Reputation is important for many businesses, however, and this inclines them to be generous when faced with discontented consumers. For example, the larger mail-order companies have a liberal policy because they realise that the initiative for purchasing rests largely with consumers. To build up a regular clientèle and because consumers cannot examine the merchandise before purchase, mail-order companies send items on approval and normally accept them back at their expense if consumers are not satisfied. Another example is that many established retailers take a long-term view of complaints on the basis that they are in business for the forseeable future.[45] Satisfied customers are likely to return, and therefore there are benefits in settling complaints, even if they are unjustified. As an executive in a national business put it: 'It's a matter of customer good will. If a woman comes back, we'll make money out of her for the next fifty years.' Moreover, satisfied customers are active propagandists for a business among their acquaintances. A small independent retailer observed: 'In the small percentage of cases where something goes wrong, then I put the matter right without quibble. This attitude has paid off handsomely by virtue of the recommendations which I receive.'

Some businesses have marketing policies which lead to a disproportionate amount of consumer discontent. A business selling a product may not keep in stock an adequate number of spare parts or devote enough effort to after-sales service. Methods of reimbursing employees can encourage a denial of consumers' legal rights. For example, paying bonuses to staff to encourage sales, if calculated on the turnover of a store, can be a disincentive for them to refund consumers who receive faulty products.[46] Instead of giving a refund, the staff will prefer to have the defect repaired, or to offer an exchange or a credit note, because these courses will minimise the loss of profit on the sale. Another illustration is the repair of new cars by dealers under manufacturers' warranties. Manufacturers recommend lengths of time for particular repairs and dealers are reimbursed on this basis. There is an obvious incentive to do superficial repairs because the full amount is payable, even if a job is completed in a shorter period.

This is a convenient point at which to mention that the type of merchandise being sold is important. If a consumer returns a faulty product which can be easily resold, businesses are more inclined to be generous, at least to the extent of giving an exchange. In doing this they may go beyond their legal obligations and satisfy consumers who have simply changed their minds about a product. When complaints are received about items which are relatively inexpensive, national department and variety stores tend to have a liberal approach. The good will gained is usually assumed to outweigh the cost of satisfying the consumer, even if the item complained about cannot be resold, and no claim is made against the supplier. By contrast, businesses marketing expensive items tend to be reluctant to give refunds because of loss of profit. For example, retailers of electronic products criticise consumer agencies and government officials for failing to distinguish between their industry and those with a rapid turnover of inexpensive items. The contrast was highlighted by a director of one national business.

> Mothercare and Marks & Spencer have set too high a standard for other people. It is cheap for them to be generous. They can give a refund on a £3 shirt. It's difficult with an item worth £70.

Consumers are said to share part of the blame because they expect too high a standard from more expensive products when compared with the faults which they tolerate on cheaper items, yet these expensive products are precisely those which are so complex that it is impossible to guarantee perfect performance. With expensive items, then, consumers receive short shrift if they want a refund simply because they have changed their minds. In these cases businesses shelter behind their rights under civil law and resist claims which lack any legal foundation. Interestingly, the different approaches with inexpensive and high-priced items are evident in certain businesses which sell both types of products.

THE COST OF COMPLAINTS

Part of the output of any mass-produced product is defective, because it is uneconomic to adopt procedures to ensure that every item is perfect. This is quite apart from the average quality of a product, which may be well below the standard which is technically possible because of the influence of fashion, planned obsolescence, or the allocation of resources to advertising rather than to research or investment. Certain products have a lower incidence of faulty performance, but this is usually reflected in their price. Complaints are not a problem as long as the associated disadvantages – the cost of resolving them and any loss in sales because of the effect on the reputation of a business – are less than those involved in tightening quality control. Of course, businesses rely on consumer inertia and expect that only a fraction of those who receive below-standard products will complain.

There are two main components involved in the cost of resolving complaints. First there is the immediate cost of satisfying the consumer.

Resolving certain complaints is virtually costless because it simply involves a reallocation of priorities. For example, if a consumer complains about delay, it may be purely a matter of giving him preference over others. Mention has already been made of the different approaches with high- and low-priced items. With expensive items, it is economic to repair them rather than to give a refund. Standing instructions in some businesses are that as long as a repair can be effected within a reasonable time, a credit must not be granted. In recent years the cost of repair has increased, and with some moderately priced items a greater number of part-credits are offered.

Second, certain administrative costs are associated with investigating and processing complaints. Ross in his study of insurance adjusters noted that the 'nuisance value' of claims meant that claimants routinely obtain money in return for their good faith and persistence. Even claims of doubtful validity are paid out in an attempt to close files at minimum cost: 'The typical adjuster is not fixated upon the goal of denying claims; his fixation is rather on terminating them, and in most cases the easiest way to do so is to make a payment.'[47] For the same reason, a number of finance companies have given standing instructions to the County Courts that their actions for the recovery of debt are to be discontinued if a defence is entered.[48] It is rational for a business to settle a complaint automatically if this costs less than opposing it or investigating whether it is justified. The principal in a small mail-order firm dealing in relatively inexpensive electronic components told me:

> Most people are honest and sometimes we don't check whether they have returned goods because it takes time and money. We simply give a refund. To look through the list to find them is not worth it. Some firms microfilm the records but that's an extra cost. Complaints are uneconomical. Every time we write a letter it costs £2.50 and we are not going to make a profit. On a time and money view it's not worth the problem. When you sell them by the thousands and the odd one or two go wrong – you just buy off the customer. The company are interested in making a profit.

In addition to minimising the administrative cost, business employees coming into contact with consumers desire to avoid embarrassment and stress. 'To avoid more agro' and 'to get the consumer off my back' were genuine explanations given by businessmen as to why specific complaints were resolved.

If complaints are not resolved, there may be a loss of future sales. At its simplest, shop assistants are tied up with complaints when they could be making sales. Dissatisfied consumers are unlikely to return if they can shop elsewhere, and the reputation of a business suffers if other consumers learn of its harsh policy. A market trader observed that it was simpler to concede victory to a complainant, for any altercation deterred potential consumers. Not to be excluded is the possibility that a complainant will contact a consumer agency. Businessmen are mindful that a liberal complaints policy can avoid an official enquiry and in some cases a prosecution.

RETAILERS, MANUFACTURERS AND OTHERS

The attitude of a retailer when faced with a complaint from a consumer varies. Some retailers seek to create a favourable impression with consumers by promising to act as the conduit to manufacturers, although this is hardly a matter for congratulation, because in most cases the retailer will be avoiding its legal obligations if it conditions redress on the decision of its suppliers. The exception is where the consumer is not the purchaser and hence there is no legal claim against the retailer although there may be a claim in negligence against the manufacturer.

Circumstances arise where a retailer will have no claim against a supplier. An unusual example encountered in the research was where a retailer who was not an authorised dealer obtained his merchandise cheaply in a manner unknown to the manufacturer. The typical case is where a business decides that it is more economic to receive a discount and to forfeit its rights to claim a credit from suppliers for complaints about faulty products.[49] Businesses which work on a narrow profit-margin frequently operate along these lines because they obtain lower prices in return. A practical way of doing business for a retailer importing inexpensive items directly from abroad is to forgo its rights to be reimbursed in return for a discount. A solicitor in a national firm was displeased that its buyers objected to inserting such clauses in their contracts negotiated with suppliers, although they conceded that to omit the clauses would mean increased prices. Another aspect, as he saw it, in the buyers' reluctance was the 'old boy network' between them and their opposite numbers in the suppliers.

Whether a retailer retains a contractual right to claim redress from a supplier, and how that right is exercised in practice, depends largely on the relationship between the two parties.[50] Basically, there are three situations.[51] First, there is the manufacturer–multiple retailer category, in which manufacturers are numerous and relatively small, and where much of the merchandise is sold under the retailer's own brand name. Closely related is the situation in which a number of retailers combine in a voluntary chain to carry on joint merchandising activities. At the other extreme is the small retailer – large manufacturer combination, where the advertising and branding of items are on the whole furnished by the latter. The size of such manufacturers, as well as the multiplicity of retailers, means that the manufacturers are the dominant party. Intermediate between these situations is where the parties are of relatively equal strength.

The implication of this typology is that on the whole a powerful retailer will be in a strong position to claim against a supplier on behalf of consumers. Several national retailers contract with suppliers on the basis that the latter will accept liability if they are the cause of any breach of legal requirements by the retailers. The wide-ranging conditions exacted by one national firm read as follows:

> In consideration of you from time to time placing orders with us for the supply of goods intended for human consumption we hereby warrant, that in addition to any warranties implied by law, all goods supplied by us to you and all labels and descriptive matter thereon will comply in all respects with the requirements of the Food and Drugs Act, the Weights and Measures Act, the Trade Descriptions Act and all other Acts, regulations and by-laws relating to goods of all description ordered and Hereby Indemnify you against all liability of whatever description arising by reason of any such goods not being in conformity with the foregoing warranty.[52]

Consumers benefit if retailers use their bargaining strength to improve the quality control of suppliers. Merchandise may be rejected when the proportion of defective items in any consignment is quite low, but the retailer still considers it unsatisfactory. A few powerful multiple retailers actually obtain their merchandise from chosen suppliers according to detailed specifications. With such contracts for production, the quality control is usually so severe that the number of defective products is below average. Large retailers have also forced manufacturers to expand the scope of the guarantees given to the ultimate consumer. An example encountered through the interviews was where a manufacturer was induced to accept liability for any transport costs incurred by consumers who returned faulty products. In a well-publicised case, the Electricity Board refused to sell the household appliances of one manufacturer until it improved its after-sales service.[53]

On the whole, where retailers lack bargaining power with their suppliers, the difficulty for consumers is greater. This is one reason why some smaller retailers are less sympathetic to complainants who are not part of their established clientèle. Certainly a constant theme of many small retailers is that their suppliers refuse to support them after they have reimbursed consumers who had justified complaints. Manufacturers discriminate against small retailers in this regard for they readily reimburse the multiple retailers. Small retailers also claim that manufacturers do not decide matters expeditiously, but that the retailer is the one who is subject to consumer anger. Furthermore, they argue that, because they are economically weak, they have no choice but to refer complaints to manufacturers and to adopt their views. The result for the consumer is that he finds that his complaint is settled only if the manufacturer is prepared to accept responsibility which, needless to say, conflicts with the legal obligation of retailers. Many small retailers favour legal reform to prevent suppliers excluding themselves from their obligations under civil law to provide products of a merchantable standard, and to impose liability for faulty goods directly on manufacturers.[54]

Manufacturers in some areas of trade, particularly manufacturers of electrical and household appliances, urge consumers to make direct contact with them when they have complaints about newly purchased products.[55] The reason is their system of manufacturers' guarantees, which are advertised as a positive reason for consumers to buy particular brands. Under a manufacturer's guarantee, the manufacturer undertakes to remedy defects which manifest themselves within a stated period after purchase. Consumers either send defective products directly to it or they are forwarded through the retailer. Consumers generally benefit because they are not obliged to prove that any legal standards have been breached. As long as the complaint is made within the period, faults are usually corrected without argument, except for those obviously the result of consumer misuse. However, retailers use manufacturers' guarantees to refer matters to manufacturers, thus avoiding their legal obligations. Normally a consumer is not prejudiced, but there are occasions where manufacturers are slow in taking any action, and the retailer simply washes his hands of the matter. Retailers occasionally reimburse the consumer in such circumstances in the hope of claiming later from the manufacturer.

If a faulty product is provided on credit, even if the finance house is not a party to the contract of supply, it is now liable along with the retailer under the Consumer Credit Act (1974). Unless a refund is involved, finance companies are in no position to handle complaints of this nature. Usually the retailer resolves such complaints and finance companies are not involved, but occasionally they can be where a consumer refuses to pay his instalments because he is not satisfied with a product. If the finance company agrees with the consumer, it will contact the dealer and suggest that the fault be remedied. Theoretically, it can threaten either to reduce the retailer's commission or to deny it further credit facilities. In practice, finance companies are not free to follow these courses because they rely on retailers to introduce business to them. Particularly with secondhand-car dealers, a major criticism has been that finance companies do not care sufficiently about the trade practices of the retailers they support.[56] In many cases when consumers complain finance companies avoid their responsibilities and are not prepared to use their influence with retailers to have them resolved.

Car manufacturers are in a much stronger position in relation to those who retail their products.[57] A franchise for selling new cars is highly valued, and the threat that it will be withdrawn is a powerful incentive for car dealers to abide by the manufacturer's policy on correcting defects. Car dealers effect repairs under the manufacturer's warranty, which tends to supplant the civil law in determining how consumers' complaints will be handled. Consumers are at a disadvantage, because manufacturers press dealers to be sales-oriented, and take the view that warranty repairs are a necessary evil. The manufacturer exerts his control by refusing to reimburse the dealer unless the repair-work is according to his narrow guidelines. Trading-stamp companies are in a similar position; there are few of them but many retailers wishing to use this form of promotion. Therefore trading-stamp companies have the market power to force retailers to resolve complaints such as those arising when the advertised number of stamps are not available.

POLICY, PROCEDURE AND COMPLAINTS

Businesses provide guidelines to their staff about handling complaints. The policy of a business and its legal obligations are simplified and incorporated into routine practices. For businesses with a liberal complaints policy their staff may simply be instructed to satisfy any genuine complaint. Experience informs those handling complaints whether a product is prone to faults, if it was purchased a considerable time earlier or at another retailer, or if the defect was caused by consumer misuse. A business with a less generous policy needs more sophisticated, if unwritten, criteria for distinguishing between complaints. Deciding whether to repair a faulty product or to offer an exchange or a refund, may turn on the extent of the defect. A repair may be considered satisfactory with a minor defect, but the consumer could receive a full refund with one that is substantial. A business may also consider the time-period within which a complaint is made. Many businesses offer consumers some form of satisfaction if a faulty product is returned within a specified period of its purchase, ranging from two weeks to three months. Beyond that the consumer will obtain recompense in only limited circumstances; for example if the defect has become manifest within the period.[58]

Law plays little direct role in the average complaint and negotiation is carried on without reference to it. 'There's nothing in the manual about law; I try to look at it from what I expect as a customer,' was how one customer relations officer expressed it. Even organisations which employ lawyers handle complaints without their intercession, including matters which remain unresolved at a relatively advanced stage. The trade association official in charge of a frequently used conciliation and arbitration service for disputes between consumers and its members, remarked:

We keep away from law and statutes. It's more a matter of conciliation. When a complaint comes here we want to reach a satisfactory conclusion. Success in our view is to maintain and reestablish good customer relations – that they will wish to continue to do business with each other.

In parenthesis, it may be noted that a consumer will not always obtain the same benefit by virtue of a conciliatory approach as he would by taking court proceedings. Conciliation cuts both ways, however, and he may do better if the state of consumer law is unfavourable to consumers but the standard business practice is to maximise consumer satisfaction. Retailers, including whose who normally shelter behind their strict legal obligations, may offer exchanges or refunds, even for items without any defect. For example some shoe stores adopt a liberal policy on complaints by placating consumers who find that shoes which they have purchased are unsatisfactory when fitted again at home.[59] Of course others stand firm and refuse redress on the basis that the consumer had the opportunity to examine the shoes before purchase.

Complaints are usually resolved by employees in relatively low positions in the organisational hierarchy. Businesses with a lenient complaint policy permit junior employees to resolve complaints, and matters are only referred to higher officials if consumers remain dissatisfied. Generally speaking, the more senior the level, the more generous the approach. Staff at the branch level often complain that their head offices are too ready to reverse their assessments and consumers whose complaints are clearly unjustified are said to receive compensation when head offices intervene. The comments of a section head and branch manager are illustrative: 'It's not my money. I'm a housewife too. She thinks she's being swindled but I think she's swindling us.' 'It's criminal, really. Some individual managers have tried to hold the line but when they contact head office they give in.' Some head offices actually log complaints which reach them from their branches, and if their managers appear too harsh instruct them accordingly. The benevolent approach which many head offices adopt is explicable because they appreciate more readily the nuisance value of a complaint.[60] They are also impressed by the good will aspect of a transaction, and prefer a satisfied customer to denying a small claim. Further, they are not subject to the same budgeting controls or general limits on discretion as the branches. Also relevant in the branch-head office context is that a business with a less generous complaints policy will lean towards stricter control of its branches. It will require refunds and exchanges over a certain amount, or after a specified period, to be referred to head office for approval. With refunds, they justify this partly for accounting reasons, because branch officials may favour their acquaintances, or because technical questions are best assessed at head-office level. The fact that a branch manager lacks discretion rebounds on the reputation of these businesses because delay increases consumer dissatisfaction. However, it should be mentioned that some businesses deliberately use delay to discourage consumers from continuing to press their complaints.[61]

7 Conclusion

The structure of legal rules – the law in the books – shapes the way in which consumer agencies operate. The nature of legislation determines in part how consumer agencies become aware of breaches of consumer law and how they respond to those breaches. The major conclusion of the present study, however, is the importance of other factors. The prominent role which consumers play in the operation of consumer agencies is one. Consumer agencies are not endowed with massive manpower and resources and it is impossible for them to detect every violation of consumer law, especially the less serious. They rely on the public to bring to their attention instances of wrongdoing so that they can take remedial action, including the initiation of criminal proceedings. The extent to which consumers involve consumer agencies in their problems varies with whether they realise that they have a problem; whether they know about their legal rights or about the existence of consumer agencies; and whether they have the motivation and confidence to pursue a grievance. Government fostering of Consumer Advice Centres is designed to enlighten a broader spectrum of the public about their legal rights as consumers, and to provide access to a source of assistance for complainants who are unable to obtain satisfaction on their own.

A danger arising from the concentration of the resources of consumer agencies on consumer advice is that it can be at the expense of law enforcement. Many consumer agencies are tempted to favour the negotiated settlement of consumer complaints without investigating them further for possible criminal offences or to see whether they fall into a pattern of wrongdoing by the businesses involved. While negotiated settlement may solve individual complaints, it need not have a preventive effect on commercial practices. It can be more profitable for businesses to agree to settlements to satisfy consumers than to remedy their trade practices. To deter wrongdoing the number of settlements would have to be at such a level that businesses would find it more economic to mend their ways than to have consumer agencies constantly intervening on behalf of dissatisfied consumers. A heavy reliance on complaint is also dangerous because certain deceptive business practices will only be discovered if consumer agencies take the initiative and themselves engage in monitoring efforts.

Negotiated settlements, however, have obvious advantages: they can be carried out by consumer officers with relatively little training; they involve fewer resources per case than law enforcement; and a significant number of successful settlements can be achieved in a comparatively short period.[1] Most consumers prefer settlement because it obtains satisfaction for them without involving them in legal proceedings. No doubt the consumer preference for settlement is an important consideration in the public policy of favouring consumer advice over law enforcement. Of course it goes without saying that most businesses prefer the settlement of consumer complaints if these are relatively few, because it is more economic for businesses to deal with complaints in this way than to be subject to the law-enforcement process.

The decision of consumer agencies to enforce the criminal law is influenced by their perception of the 'seriousness' of an offence, which takes concrete form in factors such as the magnitude of wrongdoing, the harm caused to consumers and the extent to which the business has been cautioned or prosecuted previously for consumer offences. Underpinning the prosecution policy of consumer agencies is the view, to which all adhere to varying degrees, that compliance with consumer law can be achieved more efficiently by advice and persuasuion than by threats and court proceedings. Consumer agencies justify their approach by claiming that they are charged with implementing consumer law and not with prosecuting every breach of it. It is said that prosecution in many cases would be nothing more than a punitive response to wrongdoing, because businesses are basically law-abiding and simply need to be informed or reminded of their legal obligations. Since the use of prosecution is downgraded by consumer agencies, little thought is given to how existing remedies could be used more effectively.

Possible explanations for consumer agencies eschewing prosecution are that although they purport to be neutral they have absorbed the values of the business community and their policies are influenced, albeit indirectly, by businessmen. No direct evidence is forthcoming from the present study to support either proposition, but they are possible inferences from the findings.

The focus of the study was on the more directly observable factors in explaining the number of prosecutions implemented by consumer agencies. The limitation on their resources is one, although it cannot be denied that it reflects a political judgement by those making such decisions about the relative importance of curbing commercial practices which are prejudicial to consumers. Historical factors cannot be ignored: there is the dissatisfaction of consumer agencies with the courts, leading to the attempt to by-pass judicial processes by advising and cautioning businesses, and there is the organisation of consumer agencies on a local authority basis, with the ramifications of this for their willingness and ability to undertake prosecutions. Consumers, when they complain about matters to consumer agencies, are interested in securing personal redress rather than in having the business subjected to criminal sanctions. In so far as there is any public opinion about the enforcement of consumer law, it therefore supports consumer agencies in their policy of using persuasion rather than compulsion to achieve compliance with its provisions.

Are consumer agencies correct in asserting that advice and persuasion are more effective instruments in enforcing consumer law than legal proceedings? Certainly it is wasteful of resources and brings the administration of justice into disrepute if prosecutions involve trivial matters, or if they are undertaken when there is little chance of success. The use of criminal sanctions for every technical violation of law would be self-defeating, even if it were administratively possible. Of course, what has been said is subject to the qualification that a prosecution is sometimes justified where a defendant is morally guilty although the legal point is arguable.[2] The real difficulty with the approach of consumer agencies is that there is no evidence that advice and persuasion are more efficient than prosecution in reforming prejudicial business behaviour. In other words, it cannot be said that to prosecute consumer offences on a larger scale would not lead to a decrease in their incidence. A specious point made by consumer agencies with a low rate of prosecution is that the policy of prosecution-minded consumer agencies has not led to a decline in consumer offences in their areas. Quite apart from the absence of empirical evidence on which such a conclusion could be based, it neglects the fact that prosecution-minded consumer agencies normally engage in more detection work and discover a greater number of consumer offences than does the average consumer agency. The evidence which I discussed in the last chapter suggests that many businesses adopt marketing practices which avoid consumer offences from a sense of social responsibility, yet others decline to take similar action. And there are rational reasons for the latter to continue their indifferent attitude because at the present level of prosecution it remains profitable to do so. For this reason I tend to agree with the assessment of an experienced prosecution-minded consumer officer who told me:

> After 40 years of experience I am sure that, when it comes to a national company, one little prosecution saves a lot of hard work. In a lot of firms there is a lack of communication between the sales side and the production side. You can write letters to big companies from morning to night and it won't have any effect. But one prosecution will make all the difference.

The present prosecution policy of consumer agencies may appear quite arbitrary to outsiders. Although enforcement officers structure their discretion according to a variety of guidelines, these are by no means explicit, constantly applied or uniformly accepted. There is the occasional informal discussion among enforcement officers about what type of prosecution policy they should adopt, but very little has been formalised.

Public discussion has been very limited and mainly concerned with the need to publicise the criteria used in decisions to prosecute. Since the criteria for prosecution are not subject to debate it is difficult to relate discretion to legislative intention or social policy.[3] Discussion in future must focus on the system of priorities to be adopted in prosecution policy. A possible outline is suggested in the Nader Study of the Federal Trade Commission:

> Ideally, priorities must be carefully set to help those who need help most. Deceptions and other practices that endanger health and physical safety must come first. Practices affecting the poor must be given high priority because the poor can afford to lose less. The number of persons affected must also be weighed. For that reason, unconscionable practices by large corporations that sell products across the country must get urgent attention.[4]

The routinisation of activity within consumer agencies, whether in resolving consumer complaints or handling consumer offences, has the danger that larger problems are overlooked. There is a preoccupation with the processes of applying established rules of practice rather than with considering the larger purposes of consumer protection. There are no effective procedures in consumer agencies for monitoring individual matters and terminating those where the possible benefits do not justify the resources being invested. Many consumer agencies evaluate their achieve-ment in terms of the number of retail premises inspected, the number of consumer complaints dealt with, or worse, still, the amount of monetary redress obtained for consumers. The question of whether these figures have any relevance to the general goal of protecting consumers is ignored. Routinisation in law enforcement means that the prosecutions undertaken are largely straightforward and predictable. Most consumer agencies avoid the complex and less certain prosecutions, even where the business practices involved are clearly prejudicial to consumers or are sophisticated frauds with far-reaching effects.

An examination of the regulatory process of consumer agencies raises the question of whether it is successful. Do we conclude that consumer protection is a myth; that consumer law is modified in its implementation in favour of those being regulated; that consumer agencies and businesses have evolved an accommodation which harms neither; and that the occasional prosecution for a breach of consumer law is ritual with little practical significance? Is consumer protection actually favourable to the business community because it falsely deludes the public into believing that something is being achieved, and permits businesses to continue their traditional practices while surrounded with an aura of social responsibility?[5]

In assessing the effectiveness of consumer law and consumer agencies a factor which cannot be underestimated is that businesses which commit consumer offences neither conceive of themselves, nor are commonly thought of, as criminals. The businessman's conception of himself does not change following a conviction for a consumer offence, and neither is there any loss of status among his commercial associates. Businessmen do not think of consumer offences as morally wrong, for they are regarded as the outcome of employee carelessness or the inevitable consequence of conducting a business. A clear expression of the prevailing attitude was when the official of a motor-trade association explained why when its members committed a series of consumer offences it did not always expel them:

> You can infringe the TDA [Trade Descriptions Act] innocently. But if they have fiddled around with the clocks we would throw them out. But if they advertise the car as in 'very good condition' and it's only in good condition, we wouldn't boot them out. Well, we're all in business.

Consumer officers are characteristically not morally outraged at unlawful business behaviour, and their strongest expression of opinion tends to be cynicism at the motives of businessmen. Similarly, there is an absence of any groundswell of public opinion condemning businesses which engage in practices prejudicial to consumers. In one American study, a sample of consumers was interviewed to ascertain how they would punish businesses which had violated the Food and Drugs Act. The responses, which did not vary with demographic features or with whether consumers had purchased adulterated or misbranded foods, were then compared with the actual decisions in the cases. The majority of consumers would have imposed more severe penalties than the actual court decisions, but their choice of punishment was within the limits prescribed by law and was less severe than the maximum of one year's imprisonment. 'In effect,' concludes the author, 'respondents viewed food adulteration as more comparable to serious traffic violations than to burglary.'[6]

One reason that trade practices prejudicial to consumers are not condemned by society is because there is no agreed body of values to be protected as in the case of ordinary crime. The traditional notion of *caveat emptor*, that consumers must protect themselves, still has a strong hold, although it is opposed to the principles underlying much of modern consumer law. Consumers do not appreciate the anti-social character of many consumer offences, not least the substantial economic detriment which they cause to consumers, nor do they realise that consumer offences undermine the basis of trust in society through their adverse effects on commercial morality. The repercussions of consumer offences are shielded from public view when there is no physical evidence; when they are complex and extend for a long period; and when the victims are unorganised and spread over a wide area.[7] Furthermore, the public is conscious that the production of many goods and services and their increased standard of living is associated with the dominant position of businesses in society. Therefore it should not be surprising that prejudicial behaviour is sometimes overlooked because of the overall benefits that businesses achieve for the population.

The success of consumer law and its enforcement can be gauged along a number of lines. It can be measured in terms of the achievement of legislative goals, and reference was made to the underlying assumptions of consumer law at various stages in the study. This approach was underplayed, however, both because of the difficulties of divining legislative goals and because it still raises the question of whether legislative goals, if fully implemented, would protect consumers. Success can also be looked at in terms of whether public expectations are satisfied. An indication that this is the case is that many consumer complaints are being resolved. Another way of appraising success is through an examination of the workings of consumer agencies. A substantial part of the present study was directed towards a critical assessment of the assumptions of consumer agencies and of their activities. For example, the fact that consumer agencies assume the role of adviser to industry was highlighted, and the implication of this for enforcement policy was viewed sceptically. The impact of consumer law and its enforcement on businesses is yet another strand. One of the drawbacks in precisely documenting this is that many of the variables are unknown, in particular the unlawful behaviour which has *not* occurred because consumer law is on the statute book. A thoroughgoing study of the impact of consumer law and its enforcement requires research at the level of individual businesses. However, on the evidence available, a conclusion of the previous chapter was that businesses which change their trade practices do so more because of a sense of social responsibility than because of the existence of consumer law or its enforcement. On the other hand, some businesses adjust to a particular level of enforcement of consumer law. They adopt certain marketing and promotional practices and are prepared to accept the criminal penalty which they thereby incur, because the advantages outweigh the costs.

The regulatory process of consumer agencies controlling business activity is therefore dialectical: businesses change to meet the objections to their behaviour, but at the same time Parliament and consumer agencies adjust their approach in the light of business demands.[8] If I had to characterise briefly the effectiveness of consumer agencies, I would adopt the views expressed to me by one particularly sophisticated enforcement officer in the Metropolitan County consumer agency.

Can we regard it as a public relations exercise to pacify the plebs? Have you read any of Lewis Mumford's works? All through history you get rising expectations and a few crumbs are thrown to the plebs. You get an army of administrators. You get more and more complaints. You go on the media. You get people going to university and you get people doing theses on it. You get more expectations. Now, its totally impossible to help all the mugs of this world. Therefore the assumption that it is a public relations exercise seems to be right. But if you get a good conviction against one spiv, you create a ripple in the pond. Other people get to know about it and they will slow up. You can't prevent it all, you can only slow some of them up.

In other words, government and consumer agencies create the impression, sometimes by a conscious public-relations effort, that the consumer interest is being actively and aggressively championed. While this is not totally false, it conceals the inadequacies, inefficiencies and failures. For example, many breaches of consumer law pass undetected, and even when detected often continue because sufficiently vigorous action is not taken. At the same time consumer law and consumer agencies do have an impact on commercial practices. A large number of consumers who contact consumer agencies obtain redress only because matters are taken up on their behalf. Businesses can change their behaviour with the introduction of new consumer law or its more vigorous enforcement. In a society where the voice of consumers is much less powerful than that of commerce and industry, it should not be surprising that consumer law and consumer agencies are only partially successful. There is a positive need for a greater consumer input in the formulation of consumer law and in the process of its enforcement.

Notes

1 INTRODUCTION

1 Elliot Currie, 'Sociology of Law: The Unasked Question', *Yale Law Journal*, 81 (1971), 134, 139.

2 Richard Hofstadter, 'What Happened to the Antitrust Movement?', in Joseph R. Gusfield (ed.), *Protest, Reform, and Revolt* (New York: Wiley, 1970) p. 558.

3 Marver H. Bernstein, *Regulating Business by Independent Commission*, (Princeton: Princeton University Press, 1955) pp. 88–9.

4 Edward F. Cox *et al.*, *The Nader Report on the Federal Trade Commission* (New York: Baron, 1969) p. 124.

5 Simon Lazarus, 'Regulation and Corporate Power', in Ralph Nader and Mark J. Green (eds), *Corporate Power in America* (New York: Grossman, 1973) p. 216.

6 Thurman W. Arnold, *The Folklore of Capitalism* (New Haven: Yale University Press, 1937) p. 207.

7 Karl Marx, *Capital* (London: Lawrence & Wishart, 1957), vol. 1, p. 464.

8 Louis L. Jaffe, 'The Effective Limits of The Administrative Process: A Reevaluation', *Harvard Law Review*, 67 (1954), pp. 1105, 1110.

9 Gabriel Kolko, *The Triumph of Conservatism* (Chicago: Quadrangle, 1967).

10 W. G. Carson, 'Symbolic and Instrumental Dimensions of Early Factory Legislation', in Roger Hood (ed.), *Crime, Criminology and Public Policy* (London: Heinemann, 1974).

11 Robert C. Fellmeth, 'The Regulatory-Industrial Complex', in Bruce Wasserstein and Mark J. Green, *With Justice for Some* (Boston: Beacon Press, 1972).

12 Bernard Schwartz and H. W. R. Wade, *Legal Control of Government* (Oxford: Clarendon, 1972) p. 32.

13 Louis M. Kohlmeier, *The Regulators* (New York: Harper & Row, 1969) p. 73.

14 William J. Chambliss and Robert B. Seidman, *Law and Order and Power* (Reading: Addison-Wesley, 1971) pp. 329–30.

15 Lon Fuller, *Anatomy of Law* (Harmondsworth: Penguin, 1968) p. 17.

16 Due to local government reorganisation in the three areas, some 5 per cent of the files were missing.

17 E.g. Margaret Stacey, *Methods of Social Research* (Oxford: Pergamon Press, 1969) pp. 550–68; Norman K. Denzin, *The Research Act in Sociology* (London: Butterworth, 1970) pp. 185–204.

2 LAW ENFORCERS AND LAW ENFORCEMENT

1 Department of Prices and Consumer Protection, *National Consumers' Agency* Cmnd 5726 (1974); no pagination.

2 Pericles, 'The Enforcement of Consumer Protection', (1961) 125 Justice of the Peace, pp. 583, 585.

3 *Weights and Measures*, House of Commons Paper no. 619 (1975) p. 20.
4 Editorial, 'Old Attitudes Threaten!' *Monthly Review*, 83 (1975), p. 45.
5 *Report of the Committee on Consumer Credit*, Cmnd 4596 (HMSO, 1971) pp. 338–9.
6 Cf. Robert A. Scott, 'The Selection of Clients by Social Welfare Agencies: The Case of the Blind', *Social Problems*, 14 (1967) 248, 253.
7 Ministry of Housing and Local Government, *Report of the Committee on the Staffing of Local Government* (HMSO, 1967) pp. 58–9.
8 *Final Report of the Committee on Consumer Protection*, Cmnd 1781 (HMSO, 1962) p. 162.
9 John Martin and G. W. Smith, *The Consumer Interest* (London: Pall Mall, 1968) pp. 220–4.
10 Consumers' Association, *The Need for Consumer Advice Centres*, 2nd ed., (February 1975); Department of Trade and Industry, *Consumer Advice Centres; A Revised Discussion Document* (November 1973).
11 Cf. W. Richard Scott, 'Professional Employees in a Bureaucratic Structure: Social Work', in Amitai Etzioni (ed.), *The Semi Professions and their Organization* (New York: Free Press, 1969) p. 124.
12 Quotations here and in the paragraphs that follow are from internal memoranda and one published article.
13 A. Strauss (ed.) *Psychiatric Ideologies and Institutions*, (New York: Free Press, 1964) pp. 360–1.
14 G. L. Davis, 'Discussion', *Monthly Review*, 81 (1973), 148.
15 W. Roger Breed, *The Weights and Measures Act 1963* (London: Knight, 1964) p. 19.
16 Editorial, 'Say Thank You to the Inspector', *Grocer* (7 December, 1968) p. 21.
17 Harrison Wellford, 'The FTC's New Look: A Case Study of Regulatory Revival', in Samuel S. Epstein and Richard D. Grundy (eds), *The Legislation of Product Safety* (Cambridge; Masachusetts: MIT Press, 1974) pp. 329, 331.
18 *Hansard*, vol. 905 (9 February 1976) p. 68.
19 Marver H. Bernstein, *Regulating Business by Independent Commission* (Princeton: Princeton University Press, 1955).
20 Cf. David Sudnow, 'Normal Crimes: Sociological Features of the Penal Code in a Public Defender Office,' *Social Problems* 12 (1965), 255, 259.
21 Aaron V. Circourel, *The Social Organization of Juvenile Justice* (New York: Wiley, 1968) p. 192.
22 *Hansard* vol. 848 (13 December 1972) p. 457.
23 Ralph Nader, 'The Great American Gyp', in David A. Aaker and George S. Day, *Consumerism* (New York: Free Press, 1971) p. 44.
24 Cf. Elaine Cumming *et al.*, 'Policeman as Philosopher, Guide and Friend', *Social Problems*, 13 (1965), 276.
25 Harold L. Wilensky and Charles N. Lebeaux, *Industrial Society and Social Welfare* (New York: Free Press, 1965) pp. 299–300.
26 Cf. P. S. Kemeny and G. Popplestone, 'Client Discrimination in Social Welfare Organization', *Social Work*, 27 (1970), 7, 12.
27 Cf. Gilbert Smith and Robert Harris, 'Ideologies of Need and the Organization of Social Work Departments', *British Journal of Social Work*, 2(1972), 27, 34–5.
28 Cf. Stanton Wheeler, 'Agencies of Delinquency Control: A Comparative Analysis', in Stanton Wheeler (ed.), *Controlling Delinquents* (New York: Wiley, 1968) pp. 48–9.

29 James Q. Wilson, *Varieties of Police Behaviour* (Cambridge: Harvard University Press, 1968) p. 52.

30 I detected only one criticism of the competence of judges of the higher courts. It was contained in a memorandum to the chief officer of London Borough from another chief officer about a recent appeal that the latter had conducted: 'It therefore seems incredible to me that a High Court judge should omit crucial words and then base his judgement on their absence. Indeed, I feel that this matter is somewhat reprehensible, for if advocates misquoted statements in judgements in this way, judges would be the first to rebuke them.'

3 CONSUMER COMPLAINTS, AGENCY INITIATIVE AND THE ENFORCEMENT PROCESS

1 Howard S. Becker, *Outsiders: Studies in the Sociology of Deviance*, (New York: Free Press, 1963) p. 122.

2 Donald J. Black, 'The Mobilisation of Law' *Journal of Legal Studies*, 2 (1973), 125; Albert J. Reiss, *The Police and the Public* (New Haven: Yale University Press, 1971) p. 84.

3 M. W. Shipley, 'The Trade Description Act in Practice', [1971] *Criminal Law Rev* [1971], 637, 639.

4 Arthur Stinchcombe, 'Institutions of Privacy in the Determination of Police Administrative Practice', *American Journal of Sociology*, 69 (1963) 150.

5 This finding reflects the limited national evidence available, that on average three-quarters of the prosecutions under the Trade Descriptions Act (1968) and some nine-tenths of those under the Food and Drugs Act (1955) arise from complaint.

6 Leon H. Mayhew, *Law and Equal Opportunity* (Cambridge: Harvard University Press, 1968) pp. 29, 168–9.

7 Cf. American Bar Association, *The Federal Trade Commission* (New York: American Bar Association, 1969) p. 2.

8 Pauline Morris, 'A Sociological Approach to Research in Legal Services', in Pauline Morris *et al.*, *Social Needs and Legal Action* (London: Martin Robertson, 1973) p. 50.

9 Eugen Ehrlich, *Fundamental Principles of the Sociology of Law* (Cambridge: Harvard University Press, 1936) p. 368.

10 Phillipe Nonet, 'Legal Action and Civic Competence', in *Proceedings of a Seminar: Problems and Prospects of Socio-Legal Research* (Nuffield College: Oxford, 1972), p. 54: Robert A. Dahl *et al.*, *Social Science Research on Business: Product and Potential* (New York: Columbia University Press, 1959) p. 118 n.

11 Christine Y. Lilleker, *A Study of Consumer Complaints*, M. Sc. thesis (University of Keele, 1970) p. 110; J. Phillips, 'Cambridge Trade Descriptions: A Study in Enforcement', *Criminal Law Rev*. [1974] 25.

12 Takeyoshi Kawashima, 'Dispute Resolution in Contemporary Japan', in Arthur T. von Mehren (ed.), *Law in Japan: The Legal Order in a Changing Society* (Cambridge: Harvard University Press, 1964) p. 50.

13 Albert J. Reiss and David J. Bordua, 'Environmental Organisation: A Perspective on the Police', in David J. Bordua (ed.), *The Police: Six Sociological Essays* (New York: Wiley, 1967) p. 42.

14 B. G. Nelson, 'Prosecutions and Civil Redress', *Municipal Journal*, 78 (1970), 16.
15 'Consumerism', *Political Social Economic Review* no. 2 (July 1975) p. 9.
16 Cf. Eric H. Steele, 'Fraud, Dispute and the Consumer: Responding to Consumer Complaints', *Pennsylvania Law Review*, 123 (1975) 1107.
17 Eric Schnapper, 'Consumer Legislation and the Poor', *Yale Law Journal*, 76 (1967) 745, 757–8.
18 J. E. Carlin & J. Howard, 'Legal Representation and Class Justice', *U.C.L.A. Law Rev.* 12 (1965) 381, 424; David Caplovitz, *The Poor Pay More*, 2nd ed., (New York: Free Press (1967), pp. 171–2, 175–6.
19 Cf. Eliot Freidson, 'Client Control and Medical Practice', *American Journal of Sociology*, 65 (1960) 374, 376–7; John B. McKinlay, 'Social Networks, Lay Consultation and Help-Seeking Behaviour', *Social Forces*, 51 (1973) 275.
20 John E. Mayer and Noel Timms, *The Client Speaks* (London, Routledge & Kegan Paul, 1970) pp. 10–12; Emanuel Tropp, 'Expectation, Performance and Accountability', *Social Work* 19 (1974) 139.
21 William J. Goode, 'Community within a Community: The Professions', *American Sociological Review*, 22 (1957) 194, 198; Terence J. Johnson, *Professions and Power*, (London: MacMillan, 1972) pp. 43–6.
22 Saad Z. Nagi. 'Gate-Keeping Decisions in Service Organisations: When Validity Fails', *Human Organization*, 33 (1974), 47, 48.
23 Wilbert E. Moore, *The Professions: Roles and Rules* (New York: Russell Sage, 1970) p. 101; Clive Grace and Phillip Wilkinson, 'Reforms as Revolutions', *Sociology*, 9 (1975) 397, 412–13.
24 In the discussion, it is assumed that consumers recalled their expectations accurately. Since consumers were interviewed after their initial contact with the agencies, the way their enquiry was handled to that point could have influenced their responses.
25 Douglas E. Rosenthal, *Lawyer and Client: Who's in Charge?* (New York: Russell Sage, 1974) p. 144.
26 A. M. Rees, 'Access to Personal Health and Welfare Services', *Social and Economic Administration*, 6 (1972) 34, 36.
27 Mark Lefton & William R. Rosengren, 'Organisations and Clients: Lateral and Longitudinal Dimensions', *American Sociological Review*, 31 (1966), 802, 805–6.
28 Cf. Thomas J. Sheff, 'Negotiating Reality', *Journal of Social Problems*, 16 (1968) 3, 13.
29 Richard A. Posner, 'The Federal Trade Commission', *University of Chicago Law Review*, 37 (1969) 47, 71.
30 Stewart Macaulay, 'Non-Contractual Relations in Business: A Preliminary Study', *American Sociological Review*, 28 (1963), 55.
31 Pamela A. Roby, 'Politics and Criminal Law', *Social Problems*, 17 (1969), 83.
32 Gary S. Becker and George J. Stigler, 'Law Enforcement, Malfeasance, and Compensation of Enforcers', *Journal of Legal Studies*, 3 (1974), 1, 3.
33 Lawrence M. Friedman and Steward Macaulay, *Law and the Behavioural Sciences* (Indianapolis: Bobbs-Merrill, 1969) pp. 297–8, 420.
34 J. A. Gardiner, *Traffic and the Police* (Cambridge: Harvard University Press, (1969) pp. 111, 153.
35 D. J. Black and A. J. Reiss, 'Patterns of Behaviour in Police and Citizen Transactions', in *President's Commission on Law Enforcement and Administration of*

Justice, Field Studies: Studies in Crime and Law Enforcement in Major Metropolitan Areas, (Washington: US Government Printing Office, 1967) vol. 2, pp. 7–8.
36 D. J. Bordua and A. J. Reiss. 'Command, Control and Charisma: Reflections on Police Bureaucracy', *American Journal of Sociology*, 72 (1966), 68, 70; James R. Hudson, 'Police–Citizen Encounters that Lead to Citizen Complaints' *Social Problems*, 18 (1971), 179, 186.
37 Donald J. Black, 'Production of Crime Rates' *American Sociological Review*, 35 (1970), 732, 735.

4 ASSISTING THE PUBLIC: ADVICE AND NEGOTIATION WITH BUSINESSES

1 R. Parnas, 'Police Discretion and Diversion of Incidents of Intra-Family Violence' *Law and Contemporary Problems*, 36 (1971), 539, 545.
2 Saad Z. Nagi, 'Gate-Keeping Decisions in Service Organizations When Validity Fails', *Human Organization* 33 (1974), 47, 54.
3 Harold Wilensky and C. Lebeaux, *Industrial Society and Social Welfare* (New York: Russell Sage, 1958) pp. 298–303.
4 Don H. Zimmerman, 'Fact as Practical Accomplishment', in Roy Turner (ed.), *Ethnomethodology* (Harmondsworth: Penguin, 1974) p. 129.
5 Cf. T. L. Eovaldi and J. E. Gestrin, 'Justice for Consumers: The Mechanics of Redress', *Northeastern University Law Review*, 26 (1971), 281, 300.
6 Cf. Peter M. Blau, *The Dynamics of Bureaucracy* (Chicago: University of Chicago Press, 1963) p. 170.
7 Note, 'The Role of the Michigan Attorney-General in Consumer and Environmental Protection', *Michigan Law Review*, 72 (1974), 1030, 1056; Laura Nader, 'Styles of Court Procedure: To Make The Balance', in Laura Nader (ed.), *Law in Culture and Society* (Chicago: Aldine, 1969) pp. 85–6.
8 Cf. Max Gluckman, *The Judicial Process among the Barotse of Northern Rhodesia*, 2nd. ed., (Manchester: Manchester University Press, 1955) p. 21.
9 Cf. H. Laurence Ross, *Settled out of Court* (Chicago: Aldine, 1970) p. 158.
10 Cf. Vilhelm Aubert, 'Competition and Dissensus: Two Types of Conflict and of Conflict Resolution', *Journal of Conflict Resolutions*, 7 (1963), 26, 35–6.
11 Cf. Torstein Eckhoff, 'The Mediator, the Judge and the Administrator in Conflict-Resolution' *Acta Sociologica* 10 (1967) 148, 159; P. H. Gulliver, 'Case Studies of Law in Non-Western Societies', in Laura Nader, *op. cit.*, p. 18.
12 Hilary Rose, 'Who Can De-Label the Claimant?', *Social Work Today*, 4 (1973), 409, 412.
13 Irving Goffman, *The Presentation of Self in Everyday Life* (Harmondsworth: Penguin, 1971) p. 148.
14 R. Parnas, 'The Police Response to the Domestic Disturbance' *Wisconsin Law Review* [1967], 914, 923.

5 ENFORCING THE CRIMINAL LAW

1 A. A. Painter, 'Why Prosecute?', *British Food Journal*, 76 (1974), 38, 38.
2 Peter L. Berger and Thomas Luckman, *The Social Construction of Reality* (Harmondsworth: Penguin, 1971) p. 58.

3 *Report of the Commissioners* [on] *Restoration of the Standards of Weight and Measure*, Parliamentary Paper, xxv, No. 263 (1842), p. 80.
4 'Presidential Address', *Monthly Review*, 16 (1907), 178.
5 A. N. Schofield, 'Legal Proceedings in Quasi Criminal Cases', *Monthly Review*, 45 (1937), 107.
6 *Fourth Report of the Commissioners appointed to Inquire into the Condition of the Exchequer* [*Now Board of Trade*] *Standards*, Parliamentary Paper Cmnd. 147, xxvii, No. 249, (1870). pp. 260, 262.
7 *Weights and Measures Regulations*, Schedule, 'Instructions to Inspectors', (1907) r. 25
8 E.g. Food Standards Committee, *Report on Claims and Misleading Descriptions* (HMSO, 1966) p. 8.
9 *Hansard*, Standing Committee A, Trade Descriptions (No. 2) Bill, Session 1967/68, vol. 2, p. 302.
10 [1974] AC, p. 839.
11 R. M. Goode, *Introduction to the Consumer Credit Act 1974* (London: Butterworth, 1974) p. 42.
12 Leader, 'Petty Prosecution', *Hardware Trade Journal* (3 April 1970) p. 15.
13 H. A. Simon, *Administrative Behaviour*, 2nd. ed. (New York: Macmillan, 1957) p. 167.
14 Cf. Peter K. Manning, 'Taking and Becoming: A View of Organizational Sociology', in Jack Douglas (ed.), *Understanding Everyday Life* (London: Routledge & Regan Paul, 1973) p. 244.
15 Cf. W. G. Carson, 'Some Sociological Aspects of Strict Liability and the Enforcement of Factory Legislation', *Modern Law Review*, 33 (1970) 396; The Law Commission, *Strict Liability and the Enforcement of the Factories Act 1961*, Working Paper no. 30, p. 27.
16 Cf. Patrick Fitzgerald, 'Misleading Advertising: Prevention or Punish?', *Dalhousie Law Journal*, 1 (1973), 246, 255; Miles Smith and Anthony Pearson, 'The Value of Strict Liability', *Criminal Law Review* [1969], 5, 9.
17 Cf. Richard Quinney, *The Social Reality of Crime* (Boston: Little Brown, 1970) p. 113.
18 Cf. Malcolm M. Feeley, 'Two Models of the Criminal Justice System: An Organizational Perspective', *Law and Society Review*, 7 (1973), 407, 420.
19 Cf. Wayne R. La Fave, *Arrest: The Decision to Take a Suspect into Custody* (Boston: Little Brown, 1965) p. 103.
20 Cf. John A. Gardiner, *Traffic and the Police* (Cambridge: Harvard University Press, 1969) p. 12.
21 Cf. Nathan Goldman, 'The Differential Selection of Juvenile Offenders for Court Appearance', in William J. Chambliss, *Crime and the Legal Process* (New York: McGraw-Hill, 1969) pp. 287, 289.
22 Cf. Egon Bittner, 'Police Discretion in Emergency Apprehension of Mentally Ill Persons', *Social Problems*, 14 (1967), 278, 291.
23 Office of Fair Trading, *Review of the Trade Descriptions Act 1968* (1975), p. 109. Included in the *Prosecution Survey* figures are cases of absolute and conditional discharges (1.6 per cent).
24 Cf. Jerome H. Skolnick, *Justice Without Trial* (New York: Wiley, 1966) pp. 196–7.
25 [1972] 1. W. L. R. 1593; [1973] 1 All E. R. 120.

26 Cf. C. Wertham and I. Piliavin, 'Gang Members and the Police', in D. Bordua, *op. cit.*, p. 72.
27 W. G. Carson, 'White-Collar Crime and the Enforcement of Factory Legislation', *British Journal of Criminology*, 10 (1970), 383, 393.
28 Verner Goldschmidt, 'Primary Sanction Behaviour', *Acta Sociologica*, 10 (1967), 173, 185.
29 Cf. Irving Piliavin and Scott Brair, 'Police Encounters with Juveniles' *American Journal of Sociology*, 70 (1964), 206, 210; William A. Westley, *Violence and the Police* (Cambridge, Massachusetts: MIT Press, 1970) p. 123.
30 Offences are regarded as similar offences if they fall into the categories in Table 5.6.
31 Donald J. Black, 'The Social Organization of Arrest', *Stanford Law Review*, 23 (1971), 1087, 1095.

6 THE IMPACT OF CONSUMER LAW AND ITS ENFORCEMENT ON BUSINESSES

1 Harry V. Ball and Lawrence M. Friedman, 'The Use of Criminal Sanctions in the Enforcement of Economic Legislation: A Sociological View', *Stanford Law Review*, 17 (1965), 197, 217.
2 Russell B. Stevenson, 'Corporations and Social Responsibility', *George Washington Law Review*, 42 (1974), 709, 725.
3 William O. Starkweather, *Effects of Federal Truth in Lending Legislation on Sales Finance and Consumer Finance Companies*, DBA thesis (Kent State University, 1973) p. 109.
4 Frederick E. Webster, 'Does Business Misunderstand Consumerism', *Harvard Business Review* (September/October 1973) p. 89.
5 Cf. Edwin H. Sutherland, *White Collar Crime*, (New York: Holt, Rinehart, Winston, 1949) p. 14.
6 Philip G. Schrag, *Counsel for the Deceived*, (New York: Pantheon, 1972) pp. 112–13; Robert E. Lane, 'Why Businessmen Violate the Law', *Journal of Criminal Law, Criminology & Police Science*, 44 (1953), 151, 153–4.
7 Cf. William J. Chambliss, 'Types of Deviance and the Effectiveness of Legal Sanctions', *Wisconsin Law Review* [1967] 703, 712; Jerome H. Skolnick, 'Coercion to Virtue: The Enforcement of Morals', *South California Law Review*, 41 (1968), 588, 624–5.
8 Max Rheinstein (ed.), *Max Weber on Law in Economy and Society* (Cambridge, Massachusetts: Harvard University Press, 1954) p. 38.
9 Edwin M. Lemert, *Human Deviance, Social Problems, and Social Controls* (Englewood Cliffs: Prentice-Hall, 1967) pp. 11–12.
10 Comment, 'Increasing Community Control over Corporate Crime – A Problem in the Law of Sanctions', *Yale Law Journal*, 71 (1961), 280, 286–87.
11 Office of Fair Trading, *A Review of the Trade Descriptions Act 1968* (London, 1975) p. 109.
12 President's Commission on Law Enforcement and Administration of Justice, *Task Force Report: Crime and Its Impact – An Assessment*, (Washington: US Government Printing Office, 1967) pp. 105, 112; Gilbert Geis, 'Criminal Penalties for Corporate Criminals', *Criminal Law Bulletin*, 8 (1972), 377, 380.

13 At one of the proceedings I attended, a one-day salesman was anxious about whether he could be imprisoned if found guilty. On being assured that the magistrates could only impose a fine his reaction was: 'It's only money.'

14 Office of Fair Trading, op. cit., p. 109.

15 *R.* v. *Haesler, Criminal Law Review* [1973], 586.

16 H. Laurence Ross, 'Law, Science and Accidents: The British Road Safety Act of 1967', *Journal of Legal Studies*, 2 (1973), 1, 3.

17 W. B. Fisse, 'Use of Publicity as a Criminal Sanction against Business Corporations', Melbourne University Law Rev., 8 (1974), 107, 117.

18 Editorial, 'Publicity and Punishment', *Monthly Review*, 54 (1946), 2.

19 Cf. Sheldon Feldman, 'An Overview of Consumer Legislation', *Business Law*, 27 (1971), 99, 100.

20 *Criminal Liability of Corporations*, Law Commission Working Paper no. 44 (1972), p. 34.

21 Marshall B. Clinard, *The Black Market: A Study of White Collar Crime* (New York: Rinehart, 1952) pp. 79–85.

22 Myron W. Watkins, 'Electric Equipment Antitrust Cases – Their Implications for Government and for Business', *University of Chicago Law Review*, 29 (1961), 97, 107–8; W. B. Fisse, 'Consumer Protection and Corporate Criminal Responsibility', *Adelaide Law Review*, 4 (1971), 113, 116.

23 John Andrews, 'Reform in the Law of Corporate Liability', *Criminal Law Review* [1971], 91, 94.

24 See Bernard M. Dickens, 'Law Making and Enforcement – A Case Study', *Modern Law Review*, 37 (1974), 297, 300.

25 Joseph R. Gusfield, *Symbolic Crusade, Status, Politics and the American Temperance Movement*, (Urbana: University of Illinois, 1962) p. 116; Frank Pearce, 'Crime, Corporation and the American Social Order', in Ian Taylor and L. Taylor, *Politics and Deviance* (Harmondsworth: Penguin, 1973) p. 26.

26 See also *Hansard*, vol. 796 (25 February 1970) col. 1174.

27 *Daily Telegraph* (29 January 1971) p. 3; *See* Donald R. Cressey, *Other Peoples Money* (Wadsworth: Belmont, 1971) p. 110; John C. Spencer, 'White Collar Crime', in Tadeusz Grygier *et al.*, *Criminology in Transition* (London: Tavistock, 1965) p. 260.

28 'Too Many Black Spots Behind the Whitewash', *RTSA Bulletin*, no. 270 (May/June 1972).

29 RTSA, *The Trade Descriptions Acts 1968 and 1972* (London: 1973).

30 Edward Brough, 'Industrial Responsibilities towards the Consumer', *Law Society Gazette*, 69 (1972), 1235, 1236.

31 Leader, 'What's a Fig Worth', *RTSA Bulletin*, no. 278 (November/December 1973).

32 Raymond C. Baumhart, 'How Ethical are Businesses?' *Harvard Business Review*, 39 (July/August 1961), 16–19.

33 Comment, 'Consumer Protection in Michigan: Current Methods and some Proposals for Reform', *Michigan Law Review*, 68 (1970) 926, 940–6; cf. Mark Nadel, 'Economic Power and Public Policy. The Case of Consumer Protection', Politics and Society, 1 (1971), 313, 318, 320.

34 Cf. Vilhelm Aubert, 'White Collar Crime and Social Structure', *American Journal of Sociology*, 58 (1952), 263, 268.

35 On file at the library of the Consumers' Association, to whom I am grateful.

36 *Industry and the Consumer* (London: Confederation of British Industry, 1974) p. 11.

37 E.g. James W. Bishop and Hervy W. Hubbard, 'Danger', in David A. Akker and George S. Day, *Consumerism* (New York: Free Press, 1969).

38 Vilhelm Aubert, 'Some Social Functions of Legislation', *Acta Sociologica*, 10 (1966), 98, 100.

39 Cf. David Boies and Paul L. Verkuil, 'Regulation of Supermarket Advertising Practices', *Georgetown Law Journal*, 60 (1972), 1195, 1210.

40 See R. P. B. Skinner, *An Examination into the Role of the Area Manager of the Multiple Supermarket Company* School of Management thesis (Cranfield Institute of Technology, 1970) p. 19.

41 *See* D. S. G. Redding, *Supermarket Managers and their Staff*, Retail Outlets Research Unit, Report no. 10 (Manchester Business School, 10 December 1974); Christina Fulop, *Competition for Consumers* (London: Allen & Unwin, 1964) pp. 176-8.

42 Prices and Incomes Board, *Costs and Charges in the Motor Repairing and Servicing Industry*, Report no. 37, Cmnd 3368 (HMSO, 1967) pp. 4, 6, 11.

43 Cf. Sten Edlund, 'Negotiation of Disputes in Collective Agreement', *Scandinavian Studies in Law*, 12 (1968), 11.

44 M. G. Jones and B. B. Boyer, 'Improving the Quality of Justice in the Market Place' *George Washington Law Review*, 40 (1972), 357, 361

45 'Mail Order', *Which?* (June, 1972) p. 187.

46 W. B. Fisse, 'Responsibility, Prevention and Corporate Crime', *New Zealand Universities Law Review*, 5 (1973), 250, 268.

47 H. Laurence Ross, *Settled out of Court* (Chicago: Aldine, 1970) p. 61.

48 *Reform of the Law on Consumer Credit*, Cmnd 5427 (HMSO, 1973) p., 302.

49 Cf. Hugh Beale and Tony Dugdale, 'Contracts Between Businessmen: Planning and the Use of Contractual Remedies', *British Journal of Law and Society*, 2 (1975), 45, 56-8; P. J. H. Baily, *Purchasing and Supply Management*, 3rd ed., (London, Chapman & Hill, 1973), p. 157 ff.

50 See Stewart Macaulay, 'Non-Contractual Relations in Business: A Preliminary Study', 27 *American Sociological Review* 27 (1963), 55.

51 Note 'The Marketing Structure and Judicial Protection of the Consumer', *Columbia Law Review*, 37 (1937), 77, 79-81; D. Metcalf, 'Concentration in the British Grocery Trade', in K. A. Tucker and B. S. Yamey (eds), *Economics of Retailing* (Harmondsworth: Penguin, 1973) p. 155.

52 Cf. Food Standards Committee, *Report on Date-Marking of Food* (HMSO, 1972) Appendix IX.

53 *Guardian* (17 September 1974) p. 6.

54 See Law Commission, *Exemption Clauses in Contracts, First Report: Amendments to the Sale of Goods Act 1893* (HMSO, 1971) pp. 36-7.

55 Prices and Incomes Board, *Distributors' Costs and Margins on Furniture, Domestic Electric Appliances and Footwear*, Report no. 97, Cmnd 3858 (HMSO, 1968) p. 29.

56 E.g. Ralph Harris *et al.*, *Hire Purchase in a Free Society*, 3rd ed. (London: Hutchinson, 1961) p. 81.

57 The position is similar to that in the United States: see Stewart Macaulay, *Law and the Balance of Power* (New York: Russel Sage, 1966); William C. Whitford, 'Law and Consumer Transaction: A Case Study of The Automobile War-

ranty', *Wisconsin Law Review* [1968], 1006; William N. Leonard and Marvin Glenn Weber, 'Automakers and Dealers', *Law and Society Review*, 4 (1970), 407.

58 E.g. 'Getting Things Cheap', *Which?* (July 1973) p. 208.

59 'Women's Shoe Shops', *Which?* (August 1974) p. 238.

60 William C. Whitford and Spencer L. Kimball, 'Why Process Consumer Complaints? A Case Study of the Office of the Commissioner of Insurance of Wisconsin', *Wisconsin Law Review*[1974], 639, 675.

61 Alan Milner, 'Settling Disputes: The Changing Face of English Law', *McGill Law Journal*, 20 (1974), 521, 525.

7 CONCLUSION

1 Malinda Berry Orlin, *The Consumer Movement: The Buyer Needs a Thousand Eyes, The Seller only One*, Ph.D thesis, (University of Pittsburg, 1973) pp. 220–5.

2 Glanville Williams, 'Discretion in Prosecuting', *Criminal Law Review* [1956], 222.

3 Cf. Stanford H. Kadish and Mortim Kadish, *Discretion to Disobey* (Stanford: Stanford University PRESS, 1973) P. 79.

4 Edward F. Cox *et al.*, *The Nader Report on the Federal Trade Commission* (New York Baron, 1969), p. 44.

5 Cf. Frank Pearce, *Crimes of the Powerful* (London: Pluto, 1976) p. 90.

6 Donald J. Newman, 'Public Attitudes towards a Form of White Collar Crime', *Social Problems*, vol. 4 (1957) p. 228.

7 Tro, Duster, *The Legislation of Morality* (New York: Free Press, 1970) p. 247.

8 Cf. Donald T. Dickson, 'Bureaucracy and Morality: An Organisational Perspective on a Moral Crusade', *Social Problems*, 16 (1968), 143.

Index

Adulteration of Food Act (1860), 144
Advertisements (Hire Purchase) Act (1967), 135–6
Advertising Code, 136
Advertising Standards Authority, 136
Antitrust laws (USA), 1
Aubert, Wilhelm, 155

Beckett v. *Cohen*, 117–18
Blankshire, 22, 34, 56–7, 59, 80, 82, 101; location of, 9, 25–6
British Standards Institution, 78

Citizens Advice Bureaux, 19, 20; as referrals, 64, 65
Consumer Advice Centres, 21, 23, 27, 44, 61, 64, 66–7, 85; role of, 20–1, 168
Consumer Credit Act (1974), 12, 16, 165
Consumer Surveys, 9, 61–2, 63, 64, 66, 67
Consumers Association, 20, 85
County Court, 90; and small claims, 92, 156
Crown Court, 143
Crowther Committee, 18

'deferred bribe', 31
Diploma of Consumer Affairs, 86, 89, 122; establishment of, 18
Diploma of Trading Standards, 19

Environmental Health Inspectors, Association of, 30

Fair Trading Act (1973), 8, 16, 33; establishment of, 12
Federal Trade Commission (USA), 143
Food and Drugs (1955), 77, 142
Fuller, Lon, 8

Hofstadter, Richard, 2

London Borough, 22, 58, 64, 66–7, 75, 77, 83, 91, 92, 135, 136, 155; location of, 9, 24–5; consumer complaints in, 94–5, 97; prosecution policy of, 107; role of Town Clerk in, 110

Marx, Karl, 3
Metropolitan City, 52; prosecution records in, 124, 128, 129, 137
Metropolitan County, 48, 62, 75, 82, 90, 91, 92, 94, 97, 105, 144, 156, 173; location of, 9, 22–5; prosecutions in, 35–6; consumer advice in, 66–7; attitude to public complaints in, 83–4, 85, 101; and test cases in, 117–18
mispricing, 114–16
Molony Committee, 19
Monthly Review, 15–16

Nader, Ralph, 2, 27; Study of the Federal Trade Commission, 171
National Opinion Polls, 60

Office of Fair Trading, 12, 43, 52, 100, 144; and prejudicial trade practices, 53; and defaulting businesses, 97

Police, 64, 65; as referral agents, 76–7
Press, reporting of consumer cases in, 144–5
Prices and Consumer Protection, Department of, 12, 15
Prosecution Survey, 16, 36, 51, 70, 72, 116, 117, 118 120, 123, 125, 128, 142, 143; definition of, 10; and consumer law, 147

185